D0876701

COEXISTENCE &
RECONCILIATION IN ISRAEL

Studies in
Judaism and Christianity

Exploration of Issues in the Contemporary
Dialogue between Christians and Jews

EDITORS

Michael McGarry, CSP
Mark-David Janus, CSP
Yehezkel Landau
Peter Pettit, PhD
Rabbi Stephen Wylen
Rena Potok

A STIMULUS BOOK

COEXISTENCE

&

RECONCILIATION IN ISRAEL

Voices for
Interreligious Dialogue

RONALD KRONISH, EDITOR
Preface by Rev. Michael McGarry, CSP

A STIMULUS BOOK
PAULIST PRESS ◆ NEW YORK ◆ MAHWAH, NJ

Cover design by Cynthia Dunne, www.bluefarmdesign.com
Book design by Lynn Else

Copyright © 2015 by the Stimulus Foundation, Inc.

All rights reserved. No part of this book may be reproduced or transmitted in any form or by any means, electronic or mechanical, including photocopying, recording, or by any information storage and retrieval system without permission in writing from the Publisher.

Library of Congress Control Number: 2014957836

ISBN 978-0-8091-4900-1 (paperback)
ISBN 978-1-58768-425-8 (e-book)

Published by Paulist Press
997 Macarthur Boulevard
Mahwah, New Jersey 07430

www.paulistpress.com

Printed and bound in the
United States of America

JKM Library
1100 East 55th Street
Chicago, IL 60615

This book is dedicated to leaders and supporters of the work of interreligious dialogue and reconciliation in Israel, whose memory we honor and cherish, with gratitude for their leadership and commitment

Owsley Brown II
Prof. David Cobin
Br. Jack Driscoll
William L. Frost
Judge Mayer Gabay
Nathan Hacker
Ambassador Shmuel Hadas
Abdessallam Najjar
Dr. Mithkal Natour
Dr. Bernard Resnikoff
Daniel Rossing
Archbishop Pietro Sambi
Rabbi Michael A. Signer
Alan B. Slifka
Sr. Rose Thering
Rabbi Prof. Eugene Weiner
Dr. Geoffrey Wigoder

CONTENTS

vii

Contents

Jewish-Muslim Relations in Israel

Trialogue with Jews, Christians, and Muslims

Educating for Peaceful Coexistence: Methodologies and Target Populations

Contents

Reaching Out to the International Community

PREFACE

When leaving Jerusalem in the early 2000s, Notre Dame of Jerusalem Center's German rector Monsignor Richard Mathes is remembered to have said, "When first I came to Jerusalem, my sympathies were with the Israelis and I was angry with the Palestinians. The more I worked in Jerusalem and the more I saw in the land, my sympathies shifted to the Palestinians and I was angry with the Israelis. When I left, my heart wept for both of them."

I would summarize my eleven years of living in Jerusalem as rector of the Tantur Ecumenical Institute (1999–2010) by echoing Monsignor Mathes's remarks. And like Monsignor Mathes's remarks, two things must qualify mine: First, I am an *observer* to the engagement of Israelis and Palestinians and therefore I have less of an existential stake in the dialogue described in the accompanying essays. Second, as a Western Christian, my own history is profoundly stained by the two-thousand-year history of Christian mistreatment of our Jewish brothers and sisters.

At the same time, my eleven years in the Holy Land, on that Tantur hilltop between Jerusalem and Bethlehem, gave me an extraordinary opportunity and vantage point to know the peoples of the land, some of whose voices are gathered in this volume. They were more than observers; they were people, usually Jews and Muslims, although not a few Arab Christians, with profound existential stakes in the engagement who sought ways of dialogue as one means to engage the other.

Straddling the border between Israel and the West Bank, Tantur was privileged to host numerous interreligious and intercultural groups who, even in the darkest days of the Second Intifada (2000–2005), had the courage to engage one another. Such groups, if they resided at Tantur for more than two days, often would follow a certain pattern: For the first day, the Palestinians would loudly recount the many ways the Jews had taken away their rights and how the Occupation made life miserable for them. The Jewish Israelis, in turn, would forcefully recount numerous Palestinian acts of terrorism and their harsh rhetoric about driving the Zionists into the sea. Such often was a classic example of two groups talking past one another. However, if these interlocutors made it to the second day, yelling simmered to include some listening; alternate monologues evolved into dialogues, as "the other" started to melt into a flesh-and-blood person. The stereotype started to have a name and a personal history.

And so true dialogue, including listening, began.

I come from the Roman Catholic tradition where in our theological vocabulary the word *dialogue* is of rather recent vintage. For dialogue implies both that I have something to say—we have always believed that!—and that I have something to learn—we have not always believed that. By the Second Vatican Council (1963–65), we Catholics have entered into a relationship of dialogue with our Jewish brothers and sisters, as well as with our Muslim brothers and sisters. I have come to be so grateful for the gift of dialogue, which some Catholics have said is the Holy Spirit's gift to the church of the twentieth century. The essays in this volume are expressions of that gift that we are all learning, even if awkwardly and by fits and starts. For interreligious dialogue in the land called Holy is neither easy nor frequent.

Over the cultural, religious, social, economic, and political divides, a few people have *faithfully* sought new expressions of understanding through dialogue, listening, seeking to understand. Their testimonies are here.

My privileged position of being an observer of courageous people in dialogue is now *your* gift. And because of the organization he has headed for a few decades, the Interreligious Coordinating Council in Israel, Rabbi Ron Kronish has been an indispensable coordinator of the very interreligious dialogue in which so many of us are seeking to "find our voice." The voices that Kronish has assembled in this volume are now yours to hear, to ponder, to engage. We are so grateful for his work, both in this book and for the decades he has worked in Jerusalem.

Rev. Michael McGarry, CSP
President, the Paulist Fathers
January 2014

ACKNOWLEDGMENTS AND GRATITUDE

I would like to thank all the people who have made this book possible.

First, to all the people whom I listed on the dedication page who are no longer with us, I want to say how much I appreciated their leaders, commitment, and support of my work in this field over many years, especially when this kind of work was marginalized and not well understood.

Second, I want to thank all of the authors who have shared their thoughts and experience in this book. Their wisdom, friendship, and collegiality are greatly appreciated.

Third, I want to express my thanks to the past and current leadership of the Interreligious Coordinating Council in Israel, which I founded in 1991 and have directed for the past twenty-three years, who have guided me and enriched me and many others throughout Israel through their dedication to this cause, the cause of peacebuilding via dialogue and action. I have been blessed by a collegial and cooperative board that has always been supportive of our mission and our vision.

Fourth, I want to thank everyone at Paulist Press for making this happen, and especially Fr. Michael McGarry, CSP, former President of the Paulist Fathers and former rector of the Tantur Ecumenical Institute in Jerusalem, for introducing me to the leadership of the Stimulus Foundation, who agreed to bring this project to fruition through Paulist Press. It is an honor and a privilege for me now to be part of this wonderful family of educational and erudite learning and publishing.

Finally, I want to thank my family for all their love and support for everything I have done in my work in the field of interreligious reconciliation. My father, Rabbi Leon Kronish, of blessed memory, was my teacher and mentor all of his life. My mother, Lillian Kronish, also of blessed memory, read everything that I wrote—every essay, newsletter, magazine article, op-ed, you name it—until she passed away in 2009, and she always offered positive reinforcement and sometimes also constructive criticism. My wonderful children—Sari, Dahlia, and Ariella—have read almost everything that I have written and have always been a source of strength and encouragement. And Amy, my wife of the past forty-five years, has always served as chief friendly critic, stylistic and substantive editor, and strident supporter and fan of my work. No amount of words would be enough to say how blessed I have been to have her as my life partner.

—*Ronald Kronish*
Jerusalem, Israel
January 2015

INTRODUCTION

I am pleased to present this collection of excellent essays by friends and colleagues in the field of interreligious dialogue and education in Israel and Palestine to readers around the world. Putting together this book of reflections from people in my field has been a rewarding professional experience and a labor of love. In many ways, this summarizes much of what I have learned from and together with coworkers in the vineyards of interreligious education over the past two decades or more. It is fitting for me to do this as I approach my retirement and attempt to sum up my career in this field in Israel.

Much of the information in this book is, I believe, virtually unknown and unappreciated in much of the Western world. When I gave a talk about my professional work in dialogue and education for peace a few years ago at an international conference in Europe, one of the participants in the session told me afterward, "I had no idea that anyone in Israel worked for peace through dialogue and education!" With this book, he—and many others like him all over the world—will no longer be able to say this!

The work of educating through dialogue and action in the context of peacemaking and peacebuilding in Israel has been my personal and professional passion for the past twenty years or more. Most of the people who have written essays for this book share this passion and are committed to the cause of reconciliation in Israel. For the past twenty-three years, I have been engaged in interreligious projects and programs with all of the people who have written essays for this book, and many more. It is my hope that these thoughtful articles will shed much light on the thinking and the actions of people involved in the intertwined fields of interreligious dialogue, Arab-Jewish coexistence education, peace education, and more, in Israel, Palestine, and internationally.

As you will see from the table of contents, this book is divided into five sections. The first one brings together voices from some of the leading Christians and Jews in Israel and Palestine who have been involved in the local Jewish-Christian dialogue for many years.

Historically, much of the dialogue in Israel has been between Jews and Christians. During the past two decades, we have attempted to shift the dialogue in Israel away from the all-too-familiar European/American "expatriate" model, which was heavy on theology and intellectual concerns, to the local indigenous Jewish-Christian dialogue, which has brought the dialogue down to earth by focusing on the here and now, with an emphasis on how we can improve relations between local Jews and Christians. Most of the authors who offer reflections in this book on their work in this field represent this new shift in emphasis of the past twenty years.

Second, the realm of Jewish-Muslim relations in Israel is much newer, less well-known in Israel and abroad, with virtually no tradition or culture of how to go about it. Most people in Israel who have engaged in Arab-Jewish coexistence education have ignored the religious dimensions of this topic, which is increasingly absurd. I argue that it is impossible to understand Arabs in Israel without coming to grips with how much their religious identity is central to who they are.

In addition to two essays by two Jewish rabbi-educators who have specialized in Jewish-Muslim relations, you will find in this section essays by five leading Arab Israeli and Palestinian Muslims, who provide the reader with insights into the philosophy and behavior of religious and cultural Muslims in Israel and in Palestine. This is the first time that essays by most of these authors have appeared in print, and therefore this represents some very important new thinking in an essential emerging field of interreligious dialogue in Israel and the region. Learning to live with our Muslim neighbors is certainly one of the most important imperatives that we face.

Third, I have been engaged in trialogue among Jews, Muslims, and Christians in Israel for most of my career. I believe that this work is essential, since the three major monotheistic religions share so much in common, especially in terms of basic universal humanistic values. I share some of the lessons that I have learned in my essay in this section.

In addition, two leading scholars, one Christian and one Jewish, share some of their lessons learned from their many years of creating a new model of deliberation through their work as some of the leaders of the annual theology conference at the Shalom Hartman Institute in Jerusalem. My participation in these conferences for more than ten years has been one of the great intellectual and dialogical treats of my professional and personal life, which is why I am glad that this superb model can be explained to the world in this book.

I have added a fourth section to this book that I call "Educating for Peaceful Coexistence: Methodologies and Target Populations," which adds breadth and depth to this collection of essays. Some very creative work has been done with new methods, such as the Arab-Jewish circus of the Galilee and the use of film clips as texts to enrich our understanding of core issues in Israeli society. In addition, I have been witness to amazing educational experiments with religious Zionist educators, which have grown out of profound experiences with intensive dialogue among religious leaders, that are documented in one of the essays in this section.

Finally, in the concluding section, I chose to include two excellent essays by two long-time friends and colleagues that demonstrate how some rather remarkable Jewish educational and religious leaders have done pioneering work in reaching out to both the local and international communities. Not only have these two colleagues shown leadership in international interreligious forums, but they have also been among the consistent and committed leadership in interreligious dialogue and education in Israel.

This is the first such collection of essays since the book coedited by Yehezkel Landau and David Burrell, entitled *Voices from Jerusalem: Jews and Christians Reflect on the Holy Land* (1992), was published more than twenty years ago (also by Paulist Press). My hope is that you, the readers, will find this collection of essays meaningful and significant on a personal and professional basis. They are meant to inform the outside world of substantial programs and projects that have been going on for decades in Israel, usually under the radar, without much fanfare or publicity. In addition, I hope that you will be inspired by the idea that interreligious dialogue, education, and action can be a substantial force for reconciliation and peacebuilding in our troubled part of the world.

JEWISH-
CHRISTIAN
RELATIONS
IN ISRAEL

Jewish Points of View

JEWISH TOUR GUIDE, CHRISTIAN GROUP

Interreligious Encounter without Pretext

YISCA HARANI[1]

In recent years, the number of Christian tourists and pilgrims visiting the Holy Land has reached impressive numbers. Though these are not as high as those of the Christian visitors to Rome or Lourdes, the trend is clear: at times of stability and relative safety, more and more Christians wish to visit the holy places in the land of Jesus.

The increasing trend in Christian tourism is revealed by data collected by the Israeli Ministry of Tourism: in 2011, 2.8 million Christian tourists visited Israel (out of 3.45 million tourists and visitors), an increase of 26 percent compared to 2009. Thirty-one percent of the tourists that arrived in 2010 were pilgrims,[2] of which 30 percent were Catholics, 9 percent Protestants, 4 percent Evangelicals, and 23 percent other Christians (primarily Russian Orthodox) (see table in the appendix on page 15).

Following a policy change regarding visas, the number of visitors from Russia and the Ukraine has increased significantly. Tourism packages and discounted flights also affect the type of tourists arriving, and Christians from remote countries, such as Korea, Brazil, Nigeria, and Indonesia, who could not afford such a trip before, jump at the chance.

This chapter does not aim to analyze the question of believers' self-determination or the statistics regarding Christian tourists and pilgrims. Rather, it wishes to present the encounters between them and the Israeli Jewish tour guides as a *special and historic opportunity*. Since the Christian world comprises many different groups, these encounters change according to the nature of the faith and messages of the pilgrim's or tourist's church, and also according to factors such as land of origin, education, and level of familiarity with modern interreligious dialogue.

Certain groups, such as Evangelicals, ask in advance for Jewish tour guides and even expect them to be well versed in Judaism and observant Jews. Other groups approach tourist agencies that work mainly or primarily with Arab tour guides (both Christian and Muslim), and others request Christian or Messianic Jewish tour guides.

Most of the Christian tourists, however, do not ask in advance for a Jewish tour guide and their visits do not include preplanned interreligious interactions. For the most part, the tour guide is hired as a professional, and so the group finds itself faced with a Jew.[3] The encounter between them throughout the days of the trip spontaneously reveals the opinions and questions of Christians. The spontaneity of the encounter, in contrast with interreligious events and conferences that bring together people who seek this kind of interaction, is free of the conventions that characterize interreligious dialogue. These conventions that are applied to encounters between Christians and Jews in interreligious dialogue aim for sensitivity, care, and goals such as sharing and mutual respect. The primal nature of the guide-group encounter is an *encounter without pretext*. This is in contrast to the elite nature of the formal dialogue. The groups of Christians who travel to the Holy Land for a tour and find themselves guided by Jews (or Muslims or Druze, who are not addressed in this chapter) encounter the interreligious reality in passing and express in a rudimentary and sometimes crude way their attitudes and impressions, each group according to its character and the dynamics of the journey. The joint journey in the country becomes an anthropological lab and a unique opportunity to discover how Judaism and the Jews were and are perceived by different communities. Similarly, it is possible to explore the responses and attitudes of tourists toward Israelis, "Israelism," Israeli politics, and the Israeli state, but that would be a different study. Nevertheless, the distinction between the categories of "Jews" and "Israelis" is sometimes blurred, and therefore certain responses to Judaism are actually responses to Israel and Israeli identity, and vice versa.

While the attitudes of tour guides toward the Christian groups they work with have been studied recently, the attitudes of Christian groups

4

toward the tour guides were not. The responses, questions, and conversations described in this paper are based on my notes taken during
the past twenty years, in which I have worked as a trainer of and advisor to tour guides who have shared their experiences with me. (The
tour guide names appearing in the article are abbreviated to the first
letter, to preserve their anonymity.) My central claim is that the interreligious encounter between Christian tourists and Jewish tour guides,
which takes place statistically between hundreds of thousands of
people, for the duration of hours or up to two weeks, represents in a
wide and varied way the knowledge, relationship, and change that each
of the sides undergoes.[4]

THE UNIQUENESS OF THE
JEWISH TOUR GUIDE/CHRISTIAN TOURIST
ENCOUNTER IN THE HOLY LAND

Guiding Christians on Holy Land tours has traditionally been the
role of priests and monks (although in the twentieth and twenty-first
centuries, nuns have also been very active in guiding pilgrims), when
the possibility of Christians being guided by Jews was practically
unlikely and spiritually "inappropriate."[5] This situation changed with
the training of Jewish tour guides even during the times of the British
Mandate, and more so since the establishment of the State of Israel. The
number of tour guide licenses held by Jews gradually became larger
than those held by non-Jews, and the ability of monks and priests to
serve as tour guides without the state license has been limited. Some
groups receive guidance from clergy operating according to a special
license and agreement with the State of Israel. Entitled "spiritual ani-
mators," they are sanctioned to guide groups only at sites related to particular religions, but the number of these are limited and most tourists
are not guided by them.

Throughout history, the possibility that specifically Jews would
guide tours to the land of the Bible was a remote one. This was not just
for practical reasons, but also out of principle—it was difficult to expect
that the experts on the land of Jesus would be those mentioned in the
Christian texts as those who rejected the gospel and rejected Jesus. The
situation today is that the guides who are the interpreters and experts

of the routes of Jesus, Mary, and the early Christians are primarily Jews. This absurd situation, which for certain Christians used to be shocking, strange, and even perverse, has become the norm, and most Christian groups that have reached Israel in the past sixty years have encountered Jewish tour guides.

THE ADVANTAGES OF A JEWISH TOUR GUIDE FOR GUIDING CHRISTIAN GROUPS

For many Christians, the encounter with the Jewish tour guide might be the first prolonged encounter they have with a Jew, and a rare opportunity also to hear both explanations and personal stories. The tour guide becomes, willingly or unwillingly, an "ambassador" of the State of Israel, of the Jewish people, and the people's tradition. A tour guide can make an excellent impression on the people he or she guides, and thus create a positive impression and a continued interest in Jewish-Christian dialogue. Additional advantages of a Jewish tour guide are the deep familiarity of the Jewish and Israeli tour guide with the landscape of the country, especially if he or she grew up in Israel, was educated in Israeli schools, or served in the army (in addition to military training in the geography of the land, the army dedicates a full educational day a week to knowledge of the country); the familiarity of the Jewish-Israeli tour guide with the Bible in general and in the source language in particular is a main advantage (this also is the result of the educational system in Israel, which stresses biblical studies).

KNOWLEDGE ABOUT CHRISTIANITY AMONG JEWISH TOUR GUIDES

At school, the Jewish pupil hears very little about Christianity, if at all. For many of the tour guides, studying Christianity during the training course undertaken in order to receive a guide license is a first and rare opportunity to become acquainted with the world of Christianity. In the past few years, the time dedicated to this subject has been doubled from twenty academic hours to forty. In addition, as part of the training course for tour guides, intensive tours of Christian sites in Israel are undertaken, and sites that have a biblical context relevant to

Christians are discussed. The additional knowledge is acquired by the tour guide via in-service training seminars offered by the Ministry of Tourism—day-long seminars that deal with a variety of Christian topics—and the tour guide can also take part in a specialized course on Christianity that focuses on the study of Christian hermeneutics, taught by theologians and clergy. Experience from guiding is also translated into knowledge and enriches the tour guide with knowledge and text analysis learned from group leaders, preachers, pastors, and priests. When guiding Christians, the Jewish tour guide may serve as a source of knowledge and inspiration to Christians in general and to the clergy accompanying them. Many groups admire and are even amazed at the proficiency shown by the Jewish tour guides in their knowledge of Christianity (for example, a priest thanked M at the end of a tour for "teaching all of us not only about Judaism but also about our own faith").

DIFFICULTIES ENCOUNTERED BY CHRISTIAN GROUPS

The issue of guiding tours focusing on a religion that is not the religion of the tour guide is relevant to other places in the world (e.g., a Muslim tour guide explaining the importance of Christian sites in Turkey or a Christian guide offering tours to the Hindu temples in India). The case of guiding Christians in Israel, however, is different in several ways:

1. The Jews of our times are identified as part of the same ethnic-religious collective as the Jews of the Scriptures. Unlike the Italian tour guides and the people of modern Rome who are not identified with the Romans of the New Testament or the murderers of Christian martyrs in the city of Rome (and are, of course, not identified with the murderers of Julius Caesar), the Jew is perceived in history (whether erroneously or on purpose) as part of the same historical collective that rejects the Messiah Jesus and his gospel.

2. The journey of pilgrimage is meant to be a journey of awakening of personal faith and salvation. The Jewish tour guide who shows the Holy Sepulchre to a group but rejects,

by his or her own faith, the verity of the resurrection of Jesus, or guides tours of the Basilica of the Annunciation while in his or her mind is skeptical of the possibility of Mary's virgin birth, creates an implicit (or explicit) conflict. Therefore, it is reasonable to claim that such a person is unfitting to lead the believers as a tour guide as they follow in the footsteps of the one the tour guide rejects. A Muslim guiding Christians in the holy places might also cause a conflict within the Christian group, but the respect to Jesus and Mary that is part of the Qur'an and the New Testament serves as a common denominator and allows for alternative discourse.

3. Some Christians, mostly Evangelicals, claim that the State of Israel, from a theological perspective, means the fulfillment and realization of the prophets' visions, and that Jewish sovereignty stems from the Scriptures. For them, the guide exemplifies and represents the realization of the divine plan for Jews living in Israel. A Jewish guide who does not believe in the Scriptures literally or does not believe that Israel is the realization of a divine plan (or who does not believe in God) might disappoint these Christians, who expect him to represent the object of their faith.

4. For other Christians,[6] Jewish sovereignty over a country as a realization of the Scriptures is impossible, and they may feel conflicted when faced with a Jewish-Israeli tour guide as a representative of Jewish sovereignty in the country, especially if his or her explanations include statements in this spirit.

5. Jews are a minority in most parts of the world, and the Christian tourist typically does not experience life as a minority (as does the Arab Christian in the Middle East in general and Israel in particular). Upon arrival in Israel, Christian tourists find themselves deposited in the hands of a Jewish tourism professional, not always by choice. The reversal of sociological statuses in itself creates a cognitive dissonance. The intensive work of Christian and Muslim

tourism professionals and tour guides, the demand for which is dramatically increasing in recent years (especially by social justice tourism, liberal Protestant groups, and Catholic groups), should be noted. But they are still a minority in the field and cannot meet the demand for tour guides.

Between cognitive dissonance on the one hand, or ambivalence on the other, the encounter between the Jewish tour guide and the Christian tourist is unlike any other encounter. The difficulties presented above indicate that Christians touring Israel are challenged from the very first day. This encounter can be exploited and leveraged for interreligious dialogue.

PERCEPTIONS AND ATTITUDES REFLECTED IN TOURISTS' QUESTIONS

The tour guide accompanying a group during the days of its tour provides information voluntarily and regularly throughout the tour. He or she can form impressions of the tourists' knowledge and attitudes primarily based on their questions, terminology, and phrases. The questions concerning visible differences are obvious: many of the tourists are surprised to discover rectangular objects placed on the right side of the doorframe (*mezuzot*) or threads trailing out of men's clothes (*tzitziyot*), and wonder at the different menu served on the Sabbath in their hotel's dining room and the absence of milk in their coffee when they are offered meat meals. Most tourists are interested in finding out why Jews "shukkle" when they pray, which seems to them strange. Questions about matters of faith, culture, or metaphysics typically arise after a more prolonged acquaintance with the tour guide, or when prompted by the sites or explanations. A tour guide learns with experience which questions arise at which stage of the tour, but doesn't always reply the same way, especially when he or she finds it difficult to answer. Out of dozens of questions, I have selected five that prove particularly challenging to tour guides and are indicative of the tourist's perception of the "Jew."

1. Do You Believe that Jesus Is the Messiah?

Nine out of ten tour guides have been asked by tourists whether or not they are Christians and believers in Jesus Christ. The question does not arise without context—it follows the guidance and explanations provided by the tour guide at the Christian sites. The question, "Do you believe in Jesus Christ?" arises, among other reasons, due to the enthusiasm of the tour guide, who tends to praise and excite in order to please and delight his or her group, and possibly also because he or she finds the topic of great interest. After the sites are presented as the authentic places in which the miracles and events took place, and excerpts of the New Testament are read aloud, the listeners wonder whether they are faced with a Jew or a "believer."

Tour guides faced with this question for the first time may be amazed or embarrassed, and sometimes feel distress about letting down the asker by admitting that for themselves, Jesus is not their Messiah or savior. With experience, tour guides come up with different versions of replies: "I believe that he was a good Jew / that he was a moral man / that he was like a prophet / that he was a man of vision / that he was a regular Jew / that he was one of hundreds of Jewish tragedies." One tour guide (A) said that he was so afraid of losing his group's love (an Evangelical group) that he answered with the words, "Pray for me." A number of tour guides conducting tours in Russian have reported that they do not identify themselves as Jews at the beginning, and give the impression that they're not Jewish, in order to not embarrass the group or lose its sympathy (as reported by D concerning all of the Russian groups).

2. Why Do You Not Believe in the Messiah?

The question, "Do you believe in the Messiah?" does not necessarily lead to the answers yes or no. Often, after a Jewish tour guide is revealed as a "nonbeliever" in one form or another, the question of *why* is raised, or, in a more direct way, "How can you read the Scriptures and not accept the Messiah?" The tourist may accept the explanation and justification offered by the guide, but may also become frustrated or interpret the reply in the spirit of the stereotype of "recalcitrance." In some cases, tour guides said that the group gathered around them and started praying for them "to accept the gift of faith." One tour guide was standing with her group in the "dungeon" of the high priest's house on Mount Zion when the preacher asked her in front of the entire group, "Do you love Jesus?" (as reported by P, who was working with an Evangelical group).

Christians' confusion when faced with the Christianity-expert guide's lack of faith is demonstrated by the following: in the conversations of a priest with one of his groups, without the presence of the guide, he explained that "God is preventing the tour guide from accepting Christianity at this stage, so that he will continue his blessed work of bringing Christians' hearts closer to the people of Israel" (as reported by Y, working with German Pentecostals. The pilgrims' frustration and this analysis were shared by the priest with the tour guide after years of working together).

The frequency of such questions is correlated with the denomination of the group: Catholics ask it less, Orthodox and Evangelical Christians ask it more.

3. Why Did the Jews Kill Jesus?

A tour that follows the arrest, trial, beating, and death of Jesus is an extraordinary situation, if guided by a non-Christian. In addition to the experience of becoming reacquainted with the charged story of Jesus' suffering, another experience is created—that of believers in Jesus (the group) being led along the way by the "other" tour guide, the representative of the "Jews."

The tour guide describes well the loneliness of Jesus in the Garden of Gethsemane at nighttime, his loneliness in the dungeon of the house of the high priest, and the wickedness of those who shouted for him to be crucified, adding the historical and social context. The Jewish tour guide explains the situation thoroughly, but does analytical historical discussion satisfy the group? But for groups experiencing the Via Dolorosa, it may become apparent that the teacher is not really crying for the death of Jesus, and does not explicitly see the wrongdoing and catastrophe as taking place "for us and with us to blame" (neither collectively nor as an individual). The texts of the passion of the Christ are dramatized in some way or another in the Via Dolorosa processions or are read out loud. Those walking in the footpath of this sad story do not ignore the question arising from every story of injustice—why? And also—who's to blame? Jewish tour guides will attempt to emphasize the empathy of the Jews (primarily the women) who stood grief stricken at the side of the road and at the foot of the cross and dared to reach out a helping hand (M, when she guides French or American groups, takes care to stop at stops 5, 6, and 8 to stress the sympathizing bystanders).

Sometimes out of certainty and innocence, the question is posed in the second person plural pronoun: "So why did you kill Jesus?" (as reported by N when guiding a group from Nigeria). Sometimes the question is "said" more than "asked," and so the asker makes explicit the feeling of pain, frustration, and possibly anger: "So why did you kill Jesus?!" (as reported by K when guiding Brazilians). In groups from the center or west of Europe, the phrasing is typically more historical and general: "Why do you think the Jews wanted the death of Jesus?" (as reported by D when guiding a French group). The tour guide, who claims to be an authority on understanding the history of the area and the period, is asked to provide an explanation. But the rational historical explanation is often met by lack of trust: Is the tour guide being apologetic and avoiding a more accurate statement defining the role of the Jews?

4. Is the Holocaust Punishment for the Jews Killing Jesus?

The question of the existence of the Holocaust in a world where there is a good and kind Creator continues to challenge theologians and people of faith. Although they are not necessarily students of theology or philosophy, pilgrims sometimes raise the possibility that the Holocaust took place as a punishment for the refusal of the Jews to acknowledge Jesus (as reported by D when guiding Russians, and A when guiding Indonesians).

5. Why Do You Think Anti-Semitism Exists?

The question of the formation and existence of anti-Semitism in the world still fascinates researchers of different disciplines. Although this question is studied and discussed when visiting Yad Vashem, this kind of question does not necessarily imply an intellectual interest in the answer, and may reveal implicit anti-Jewish concepts and attitudes. When the question, "Why do you think there is anti-Semitism?" is asked with the question, "Why do you think they say that the Jews control the world?" the tour guide may get the feeling that the asker is not really asking a question but expressing an opinion (as reported by B when guiding South Americans).

FAITH AND POLITICAL REALITY: COMPARING THE SCRIPTURES WITH THE POLITICAL REALITY

One of the deepest desires of believers walking in the footsteps of Jesus and Mary in the Holy Land is to better understand the character of Jesus of Nazareth, and they would like to come closer to the man who has become a savior for them. The reality of the land in modern times might lead to disappointment: the modernization, the commercialization, the gap between expectation and realization, and so forth. The tour guide for the most part attempts to reach a compromise between previous expectations and reality—for example, by explaining that walking the Via Dolorosa during Passover in the time of Jesus resembled the crowded reality of a city of tourism or pilgrimage. In the face of the greed of the shopkeepers, the tour guide presents the reality of shopping, selling, and commerce during the temple period. The stories of Herod and the rulers that followed him are compared to politicians and people of power as examples of power and injustice who ill-treat the common people today.

The Jewish-Arab conflict also enters into contemporary reality, heaping facts and difficulties upon the baffled tourist: Who versus whom, who's right and who's to blame, and whom do we support? Some tourists make a distinction between the political conflict and the religious history of the area. Within the context of the comparative discourse ("Then is similar to now"), there are groups in which the comparison between the days of Rome and the high priesthood is drawn with the "Israeli Occupation" as a form of power and aggressiveness, an example of leadership sinning by stealing from the poor, oppressing people of morality and spirit, and using curses and lies to achieve their rule (as reported by G guiding British and Irish groups). The figures of Israeli soldiers stationed around the Old City, carrying clubs or guns, play into the hands of the comparison between that time

13

and the present: the war of the just is doomed to failure in the face of steel and hard souls. This narrative, which juxtaposes good versus evil, weakness versus strength, and decency versus wickedness, may be formulated and disseminated in the Palestinian public (translated into art in the posters of the crucified Palestinian, the slogan "Jesus at the checkpoint," etc.), but is also prevalent in the internal discourse of the visiting groups.

The Jewish tour guide, who frequently seeks to make comparisons between the past and the present, tries acrobatically to use the element of comparison, but without making clear parallels when it comes to the question of who is the victim and who is the victimizer in our times. Many groups tend to draw a parallel between the authoritative rule of Herod and the priests and the aggressiveness of the Israeli rule. It is too simplistic to see the suffering of Jesus persecuted by the Jews, flogged, and executed, in the suffering of the Palestinian people today. The question is to what extent the tourist making such comparisons expresses a preconceived grudge toward the Jews in general and the Israeli rule in particular. Making the connection between the early victimizers and those of our times implies systematization and thus strengthens those who blame the Jews as persecutors of Jesus.

SUMMARY

The most intensive interreligious encounter, at least quantitatively, apparently takes place in the arena of tour guiding in the Holy Land. The Jewish tour guide, whether good and well-learned or not, finds himself or herself facing a challenge, and so too for the Christians the encounter is a challenge, the difficulty of which is attested to by the comparisons and questions the tour guide is asked. Via this kind of encounter, it is possible to get to know directly and reliably what different Christian groups know and think about Judaism. It is also possible to map churches or countries that have a more vocal approach and stereotypical concepts to match (for example, D guides Russian groups and was asked "whether the Protocols of the Elders of Zion were written on Mt. Zion").

My claim is that the duration of the encounter and the amount of participants justify a large-scale study about the concept of the Jew in the Christian world. These golden opportunities become in the field,

APPENDIX: RELIGION BY DENOMINATION (TOURISTS, NOT INCLUDING ONE-DAY-ONLY VISITORS)—2010 STATISTICS.

Religion / denomination	Number of tourists 2010	Percentage out of all tourists	Percentage of pilgrims out of the total of tourists of this denomination	Number of pilgrims out of the total of tourists of this denomination	Percentage of pilgrims out of the total number of tourists	Percentage of pilgrims of this denomination out of the total number of pilgrims
Jewish	653,984	24%	8%	52,319	2%	6%
Protestant	235,109	9%	55%	129,310	5%	15%
Catholic	810,924	30%	52%	421,680	15%	49%
Evangelical	99,067	4%	68%	67,366	2%	8%
Other Christian—primarily Russian Orthodox	623,139	23%	24%	149,553	5%	18%
Muslim	28,233	1%	31%	8,752	0%	1%
Other	40,792	1%	33%	13,461	0%	2%
Unaffiliated	237,118	9%	4%	9,485	0%	1%
Total	2,728,366	100%		851,926	31%	100%

de facto, interreligious encounter and dialogue, which may lead to respectful public diplomacy and deeper, truer acquaintance. Just as it is essential to educate the tour guides about Christianity, it is necessary to educate the groups. Neither of them begins the journey with the intent of having a fruitful interreligious encounter, but in effect, this is what happens, and the sounds of the interreligious encounter will echo for a long time in the ears of both sides.

Notes

1. Translated from the Hebrew by Rakheli Hever. The writer is thankful also to Dr. Jackie Feldman and Dr. Amos Ron for reading the article and sharing their experience.

2. The use of the term *pilgrims* is more characteristic of Catholics. There are Evangelicals who consider "pilgrimage" anathema as a Catholic term, even though their behavior is almost identical.

3. Given the need for a licensed guide from the Ministry of Tourism, the demographics in Israeli society, as well as the language and orientation of the guide course.

4. The dynamics of change of perceptions on both sides deserves special attention outside the scope of this article.

5. A reversed reality took place in the early Byzantine period (fifth and sixth centuries), when Jews as natives and "guardians of Scripture" were the preferred verifiers of Christian truth.

6. Especially those who still accept replacement theology.

IN THE SHADOW OF HISTORY: ISRAEL-VATICAN RELATIONS 1948-1973

The Israeli Perspective[1]

AMNON RAMON

On January 14, 1952, the Prime Minister of Israel, David Ben-Gurion, found time to write a letter to the Research Department of the Ministry of Foreign Affairs, pointing out that "it is strange that you use the term 'Holy See' without quotation marks, as if the term were acceptable in Hebrew. Let us leave that usage to the Catholics. Is there no non-Catholic term for the Vatican?"[2]

Two weeks later, Ben-Gurion offered the following remarks in the Knesset (Israel's parliament): "There are greater forces in the world that are hostile to us, not necessarily our neighbors alone. There is a great religion in the world that has an historical account with us about what transpired in this eternal city [Jerusalem] 2000 years ago...and the delegates of that religion will not forget that we rejected their Messiah, and therefore were decreed to wander among the Gentiles forever. And they cannot come to terms with the fact that after centuries of wandering we have returned to our own land, renewed our independence and Jerusalem is once again the capital of Israel."[3]

These sentences reflect the complex attitude of the leaders of the young state, first and foremost Ben-Gurion, toward the Catholic Church and the Holy See. Until recently not a little research has dealt with the impact of historical relations between Christians and Jews on the attitude of the Vatican toward the State of Israel. In this paper I would like to focus on the other side, the Jewish-Israeli side, asking—following the study by Uri Bialer[4]—to what degree the religious-historical relations between Christians and Jews influenced the attitude of the leaders of the State toward the Catholic Church and the Vatican in the first twenty-five years of the existence of Israel.

The leaders of Israel, the land of the Jewish people, which for centuries was a minority dependent on the good graces of Christian and Muslim rulers, found themselves in 1948 in the role of the "Caesar," expected to deal with the affairs of local Christian communities, relations with international Christian bodies (mainly the Vatican), holy sites, and the vast church property that remained within the boundaries of the young state. Most of the leaders of the state were aware of the influence of religious-historical residue in the attitude of the Christian world toward Israel. However, they themselves were also not free from the influence of Jewish notions about Christianity and the Christian world. The fact that most of the Christians in the country were Arabs, regarding whose loyalty to the state the Israeli leadership had some doubts, increased the problematic nature of the relations between Israel and the local Christian communities. This problem was compounded after June 1967, when, after the Six-Day War, the Jewish state came to rule the most important holy sites to Christianity and the centers of the different churches in the Holy Land.

This study is based mainly on documents from the Israel State Archives in Jerusalem, supplemented with documents from the United States National Archives in College Park, Maryland, and the National British Archives in London (PRO), that I used for my PhD dissertation. I am curious, of course, to know how these matters appeared from the point of view of the Vatican, but for that we shall have to wait until the documents in the archive of the Holy See, here in Rome, are made public.

It is apparent from the documents that the leaders of the Zionist movement, from Herzl to Ben-Gurion, were, of course, aware of the theological opposition of the Catholic Church to the establishment of a Jewish state in the Holy Land. Already in 1899, after meeting with the Nuncio Taliani in Vienna and Oscar Straus, the American ambassador in Constantinople, Herzl, who had the greatest awareness among Zionist leaders of the influence of the Catholic Church and the Holy See on the European powers, wrote the following: "I considered only Rome to be a serious opponent....Only Roman Catholicism is as ecumenical as

Judaism. Rome is the rich brother who hates the poor brother; the other [Orthodox] churches are national, and can therefore dispense with Jerusalem as an Archimedean point of leverage."[5] And indeed the confrontation that Herzl anticipated between the Vatican and the young State of Israel did take place fifty years later.

From the Israeli point of view, the hostility of the Vatican toward the Zionist enterprise and its opposition to the establishment of the State of Israel was expressed in two actions taken by the Vatican toward the end of the 1948 war: the first was severe criticism of Israel for the violation of churches and Christian holy sites by soldiers of the Israel Defense Force in its earliest stage; the second, demanding that the international community force Israel and Jordan to carry out the internationalization of Jerusalem, in accordance with the November 1947 United Nations decision on the partition of Palestine. These demands by the Vatican reached a climax in the summer of 1948, on the basis of hard facts: in Jerusalem, and elsewhere, desecration and looting by Israeli soldiers did take place. Nevertheless—from the Israeli point of view—these events were exploited by Catholic propaganda in order to present the young state in the most negative way and to try to force it to agree to internationalization, of which the Vatican became a keen supporter from October 1948. The most important act of the Holy See was drafting its own diplomatic corps, as well as the entire Catholic world's approval of the resolution on internationalization of Jerusalem in the United Nations General Assembly on December 9, 1949. The Vatican saw internationalization as a way to save at least Jerusalem from the fate of partition of the Holy Land and to change the Holy City and its surroundings into a *Corpus Separatum* under UN auspices, supervised by the "enlightened" Christian world. The resolution on internationalization was approved, as is well known, by an exceptional coalition, including countries considered Catholic, the countries of the Communist bloc, led by the Soviet Union, and the Arab and Muslim states. In the eyes of the leaders of Israel it was the Vatican that was the central factor in creating this "unholy" alliance.[6] Looking back, it seems that the Vatican's success in December 1949 was exceptional and resulted from an unusual coincidence; subsequently the Holy See never achieved such an international diplomatic success.

At any rate, the decision by the General Assembly was regarded by the leaders of Israel as evidence of the power of the Vatican and the

Catholic Church. Prime Minister Ben-Gurion announced, as a countermeasure, that he was moving the government ministries and the Knesset to Jerusalem (in the course of December 1949); Foreign Minister Moshe Sharett joined the Prime Minister in declarations that made it clear that they understood the motives of the Vatican and the dangers they harbored. On December 13, 1949, Ben-Gurion claimed in a Knesset debate that "the power of world Catholicism, which for very many years had not displayed the power it revealed on this occasion, [drafted] about 30 nations throughout the world, and it is evident that this resulted only from its pressure since there are states that changed their mind in the course of the day."[7] He predicted that the decision to make Jerusalem the capital "will be used as a weapon by the Vatican" because "they have an old account with the Jews for two thousand years." He also expressed his suspicion that the Vatican would demand Nazareth as well, since "that same Jew of 2000 years ago is associated not only with Jerusalem."[8] In a government meeting later, Ben-Gurion claimed that "the Vatican does not want Israeli rule here [because] it has an 1800-year old dogma to which we gave a mortal blow by establishing the State of Israel."[9]

Moshe Sharett claimed that the resolution to internationalize Jerusalem "contained settling an account ever since the crucifixion of Jesus, an event that happened here in Jerusalem, if I am not mistaken 1916 years ago."[10] The Foreign Minister, who took part in the meeting of the General Assembly, testified regarding its discussions that "in the end it was an entirely subjective feeling, but I sensed blood in the hall. I felt as if it was said that these Jews need to know once and for all what they have done to us [the Christians] and now there is an opportunity to let them feel it and that is the whole matter."[11]

The words of Sharett and Ben-Gurion reflect the depth of historical residue felt by the Israeli leadership toward the Catholic Church and the Vatican. Many of the decision makers in Israel attributed nearly unlimited powers to the Vatican, and they seem to have brought this image from their Eastern European upbringing. In Israel the Vatican was considered a central force on the world scene, seeking—together with the United Nations, the Arab states, and the entire international community—to make Israel give up its control over Jerusalem and withdraw from much of the territory it captured in the 1948 war. This concept of aggrandizing the power of the Vatican greatly influenced, in my opinion, Israel's policy toward the Catholic Church in the subsequent years. With regard to everything related to the subject of Jerusalem, paradoxically, it was the external pressure from the Vatican and the United Nations that drove Ben-Gurion to determine, officially and definitively, that Jerusalem was the capital of the Jewish state. In the 1960s Abba Eban (the first Israeli ambassador to the UN and also the first ambassador in Washington) claimed that UN measures led to the declaration on Jerusalem "as an integral part of the state and its capital while many of Israel's leaders regarded Jerusalem as an educational and cultural center, but not necessarily, and perhaps not even ideally—the capital of the state."[12]

These events of late 1949 had, in my opinion, a crucial influence on the relations between Israel and the Vatican in the following years. The adherence of the Vatican to the internationalization plan (until 1967) and the Israeli refusal to discuss the matter led to the failure of any significant rapprochement between the two sides. At Israel's initiative, a number of attempts were made in the fifties to break the ice, but the response of the Vatican was a cold shoulder. Two examples elucidate this.

The first incident was the question of the performance of the Israel Philharmonic Orchestra before Pope Pius XII in May 1955. The Vatican agreed to the appearance of the orchestra "as a tribute to the Catholic Church for saving Jews during the Holocaust." Eliyahu Sasson, the Israeli representative in Rome, was even willing to allow the orchestra to perform before the pope on the Shavuot (Pentecost) holiday, claiming that the performance was without charge. Foreign Minister Sharet rejected the idea of performing on the holiday "even before the throne of honor."[13] Finally the orchestra performed Beethoven's Seventh Symphony before the pope on May 12, 1955. The performance raised hopes in Israel of improved relations with the Vatican, but these were dampened by the report in the Vatican newspaper, *L'Osservatore Romano*, on the next day, reporting that "his holiness met with Jewish musicians from 14 different nations," without any mention of the State of Israel.[14]

Another initiative was the decision to dispatch to the Vatican in early 1957 Maurice Fisher, one of the notable early diplomats in the Israeli foreign service, who was well versed in Christian affairs ever since his stint as an officer in the Free French army in Lebanon during World War II. On January 1957, Fisher departed, full of good will, for a six-week mission to Rome, in order to try to establish the first direct ties with the Vatican. Despite his many attempts and efforts, however, Fisher was unable even to arrange a meeting with a representative of the Secretariat of State.[15] Fisher's failure in Rome found expression in the harsh words against Israel of Domenico Tardini, the Pro-Secretary of State, made to the French delegate to the Vatican in November 1957. Tardini said that "there was no real need for this state, the creation of which was a grave mistake on the part of the Western powers and the fact of its existence is a perpetual cause for dangers of war in the Middle East. Since Israel is a fact, it cannot be destroyed, but every day we pay the price of this mistake."[16] One year later Tardini expressed his fear that Israel would overtake a disintegrating Jordan and rule over all the holy sites of Christianity.[17]

The first buds of change appeared only upon the death of Pius XII in October 1958. The election of the new pope, John XXIII, who was thought to be more favorably inclined toward the Jewish people and Israel, and who had close ties with Maurice Fisher from their days of service together in Paris, raised new hopes in Israel.[18] Fisher met with the pope in February 1959 and held a number of meetings in Rome until the middle of 1962. It quickly turned out, however, that despite the Israeli hopes, even the new pope could not improve relations, while the basic interests of the Vatican (primarily concern for the fate of Christian communities in the Middle East and Vatican ties with Arab countries and the Third World) did not allow this.[19] From here on the subject of relations with Israel became a low priority on the agenda of the Holy See. Pope John XXIII focused his efforts on preparations for the deliberations at the forthcoming Second Vatican Council (Vatican II).

The meeting of the Council in 1962–65, and mainly its promulgation of the *Nostra Aetate* declaration in October 1965 (in the formulation of which Jewish organizations and the Israeli embassy in Rome were involved), were the beginning of a long historical process that brought about a change in the attitude of the Catholic Church toward Judaism and the Jewish people.[20] However, the impact of the declaration on relations between the Vatican and Israel in the short term was slight. From the Israeli point of view, the Vatican negated entirely the political implications of the document, out of fear of harming its relations with Arab states and the Third World. The visit of Pope Paul VI to the Holy Land in January 1964, during a break in the deliberations of the Council, did not constitute a significant turning point in Israel-Vatican relations.[21]

A significant improvement in Israel-Vatican relations took place, in my opinion, only after the 1967 war. Israel's taking control of the West Bank and East Jerusalem, in which the important holy sites of Christianity and church centers are found, forced Israel and the Vatican to adjust themselves to an entirely new situation. Israel's leaders, who had endured the "trauma" of the Vatican campaign and the internationalization of Jerusalem plan from the early years of the state, suspected that the capture of East Jerusalem and its incorporation into Israel in June 1967 would lead to a revival of the internationalization plan and that it would receive enthusiastic support from the Christian world. However, the different international constellation in 1967—and mainly the international (and even Vatican) recognition that the plan was no longer feasible—actually led to a degree of rapprochement between Israel and the Vatican. Both local church leaders and the heads of the Vatican understood that Israel was the dominant force in Jerusalem and the West Bank, a fact that could no longer be ignored.[22]

The director general of the Prime Minister's Office, Yaakov Herzog, who had conducted the contacts with the Vatican after the 1948 war, said,

> And now when I came to them twenty years later [in 1967], the cardinals sat there and held a great debate on the future of Jerusalem. I saw that something had changed there. They tried to convince me that during the world war they had saved Jews...; they tried to present a moderate image. They looked for ways to touch our hearts. I sat and wondered at the miracles and marvels, that this enormous fortress in control of 600 million Catholics, whose orders traverse continents and peoples, and now Jerusalem is in our hands—and it does not rise up against us.[23]

On the other hand, the new status of Israel after the Six-Day War enabled the Israeli government to adopt a more tolerant policy toward local and international Christian elements (mainly the Vatican). Against the background of the opposition of the international community to the annexation of East Jerusalem, the Israeli authorities regarded Christian elements as a moderating force and even an ally, in opposition to the Palestinians and the Muslim world, which could provide Israel with a modicum of international legitimacy for its rule in East Jerusalem and the holy places. This tolerant policy found expression in a number of measures that Israel carried out: declarations by the heads of state and legislation of the Preservation of Holy Places Law in late June 1967, which promised strict preservation of holy places and nonintervention in their administration; the Israeli initiative to grant generous reparations to churches (including Catholic bodies operating in Jerusalem) for damage in the 1948 and 1967 wars; refraining from appropriation of church-owned land, return of the Notre Dame complex to the Holy See in 1971, and encouraging the opening of Christian institutions in Jerusalem such as the Tantur Ecumenical Institute and others. These steps reflect Israeli self-confidence after the 1967 war, and are a counterpoint to the "defensive" Israeli approach after the 1948 war. It seems that the influence of the religious-historical residue diminished in the years after the 1967 war, and considerations of Realpolitik became predominant.[24]

The change was apparent also in the position of the Holy See and the first measures it took after the war: Pope Paul VI met with the Israeli ambassador in Rome, Ehud Aviel; a special envoy of the Vatican Secretariat of State, Monsignor Angelo Felici, was sent for talks with Israeli leaders in Jerusalem; the Apostolic delegate in Jerusalem, Augustin Sepinski, who had refrained before the war from any contact with representatives of the Israeli government, met with the heads of the Ministry of Foreign Affairs, and when he concluded his term, even with the President of the State. His replacement, Monsignor Pio Laghi, who arrived in Israel in August 1969, developed close ties with ministers and high officials who dealt with Christian affairs on behalf of the Israeli government. These ties reflected the change in Vatican policy toward Israel after the war. In fact, from the point of view of the Israeli authorities it could be said there were de facto diplomatic relations between Israel and the Vatican during Laghi's tenure (1969–74).[25]

On the interstate level, the Holy See and Israel conducted a number of contacts—mainly between Yaakov Herzog and Ehud Aviel with Monsignor Augustino Casaroli, the Deputy Secretary of State. These contacts led to a certain softening in the Vatican position toward the State of Israel and its control of Jerusalem. The new position of the

Vatican, the influence of which is felt to this day, emphasized that the holy sites should benefit from a special statute with international guarantees, and the need to maintain the special historical and religious character of the city, in addition to the obligation to protect the civil and religious rights of the religious communities that live in the city.

In the wake of the new reality and the formulation of the Vatican's new position, negotiations started in February 1968 between Israel and the Holy See on a secret agreement regarding the holy sites. The understanding on the basis of which the negotiations were conducted was that a formal agreement between Israel and the Vatican was impossible as long as the major questions of the status of the territories, Jerusalem, and the Israeli-Arab conflict were unresolved. Both sides understood that Arab pressure and primarily concern for the fate of Christian communities in Arab states prevented any formal recognition of Israel by the Vatican and even more so recognition of Israeli control of East Jerusalem. This understanding led to the formulation of a more modest approach that sought to reach an agreement between the parties on the status of the Christian holy places in Jerusalem for an interim period until a permanent solution would be achieved. In accordance with this approach, the Israeli Foreign Ministry, starting in March 1968, prepared the first draft of a secret agreement, at the center of which was the Israeli willingness to grant the Christian holy places in Jerusalem diplomatic status (which was later changed to "special status"), including full autonomy to the Christian communities to administer them "according to the existing rights and customs." All of this was in addition to granting the status of heads of diplomatic legations to the heads of Christian communities in Jerusalem.[26]

The negotiations that began between Israel and the Holy See revealed that the gap between the two sides was too wide to be bridged even by a secret agreement. The representatives of the Vatican wanted to reinforce the status of the holy places by international guarantees and to extend the special status to include holy sites within the pre-1967 borders of the State of Israel. Likewise the Vatican objected strongly to Israeli actions to "change the character" of Jerusalem and restrict the freedom of action of Christian and Muslim communities in the city by Israeli rule. Since the gap between the two sides was so great, it is not surprising that the Vatican decided to freeze the negotiations with Israel in September 1968. However, the "understanding" between the sides that the Vatican would not raise the subject of Jerusalem in international forums and that Israel on its part would maintain its relatively tolerant policy toward the Christian communities and the holy places remained almost intact.[27]

Despite the freezing of the negotiations about the holy sites, however, some signs indicated modest improvement in Israel-Vatican relations without official declarations. Among these were the frequency of meetings between the Israeli ambassador in Rome and the deputy Secretary of State of the Vatican, exchanges of messages between the pope and the president of Israel, and improvement of relations between Israeli authorities and the apostolic delegate in Jerusalem. These signs were, first of all, the result of the strengthening of Israel's position in the international arena in the wake of the Six-Day War and the inability of the Vatican to ignore this development. At the same time the gradual theological change in the attitude of the Church toward the Jewish people after the promulgation of *Nostra Aetate* also had some impact. The visit of the Israeli Foreign Minister, Abba Eban, to the Vatican in October 1969 was a continuation of this process of semi-normalization between the states, without formal diplomatic relations. But simultaneously Vatican identification with the difficult plight of the Palestinian refugees was increasing, leading to closer ties with the Palestinians and the PLO.[28]

In early 1973 both sides initiated another step toward improved relations. On January 15 Prime Minister Golda Meir met with Pope Paul VI for the first time, in a meeting that went on for an hour and quarter. The audience included all of the important topics on the agenda between the two states—the Palestinian refugee problem, the Arab-Israeli conflict, aspirations for peace, the Jerusalem question, and the situation of Christian communities in Israel. This meeting reflected the major changes that had transpired in the relationship between the parties since 1967. On the subject of Jerusalem and the holy places, the Vatican took a more positive position toward Israel than in the past. However, the issue of Palestinian refugees brought to the fore historical residue: The pope claimed that "if a solution is not found for the Palestinian refugee problem, the tragedy will continue, not only for them but for others as well" and "the Jews have a special obligation because of history."[29] The response of Prime Minister Meir was sharp and in character: she recalled her earliest childhood memory—the pogrom in Kiev, asserting "when we were merciful and when we did not have a homeland and when we were weak—that is when they took us to the Nazi crematoria." She concluded, "We will not allow another Holocaust to take place," reminding the pope "that she herself asked the Arabs in November 1947 to agree to compromises just as we agreed to compromises …, but the following day they [the Arabs] killed Jews."[30]

Thus the visit demonstrated the great progress in the relationship between the two parties since 1967, but also the complexity of the relationship and the existence of historical residue. The predominant approach in the Israeli Foreign Ministry after the visit was to refrain from negotiations with the Vatican on "small subjects" (out of fear of losing bargaining chips in future negotiations) and to wait until the initiative to formalize relations comes from the Vatican and not from the Israeli side. At the end of September 1973, Michael Pragai, of the Ministry of Foreign Affairs in Jerusalem, wrote to the adviser on Vatican affairs in the Israeli embassy in Rome that "in our relations with the Vatican it seems the best way to deal with it, is not to sign any partial agreement, but to wait until conditions ripen for a comprehensive settlement."[31]

Twenty years passed, the conditions ripened, and in late December 1993 the fundamental agreement between the State of Israel and the Holy See was signed. Nevertheless, the complex nature of Israel-Vatican relations, the special bilateral ties, and the religious-historical issues—as they developed in the first twenty-five years of the state—remain with us to this day.

Notes

1. The article is based on a lecture given in a conference on the relationship between Israel and the Holy See held in Rome in June 2012. For a detailed presentation of the subject, see my PhD dissertation: Amnon Ramon, "'There Is a Major Religion in the World with Which We Have an Historical Reckoning…'—Israeli Policy toward the Christian Churches and the Question of Jerusalem 1948–1973," (University of Haifa, 2007 [Hebrew]), and my book: *Christians and Christianity in the Jewish State* (Jerusalem: Jerusalem Institute for Israel Studies, 2012 [Hebrew]).

2. The Ben-Gurion Archives (online): http://bengurionblog.blog spot.co.il/2009/05/blog-post_12.html.

3. Knesset Minutes ("Divrei HaKnesset"), 11:1186.

4. Uri Bialer, *Cross on the Star of David: The Christian World in Israel's Foreign Policy 1948-1967* (Bloomington: Indiana University Press, 2005).

5. Herzl's diary, quoted in, Sergio I. Minerbi, *The Vatican and Zionism* (New York: Oxford University Press, 1990), 97.

6. Ramon, *Christians and Christianity in the Jewish State*, 19-23.

7. The Minutes of the Knesset Foreign Affairs and Defense Committee, 13/12/1949, Israel State Archives, Jerusalem (ISA) 7561/12.

8. Ibid.

9. The Minutes of the Cabinet Meeting, 27/12/1949, ISA, 25-26.

10. Ibid., 3.

11. Ibid.

12. Michael Brecher, "The Political Struggle over Jerusalem," in *Jerusalem in the Modern Period*, ed. E. Shaltiel (Jerusalem: Yad Izhak Ben-Zvi and Ministry of Defence, 1981 [Hebrew]), 399.

13. Moshe Sharett, *Yoman Ishi* (personal diary), ed. Yaakov Sharett, vol. 4 (Tel-Aviv: Sifriyat Ma'ariv, 1978), 4:998.

14. Meir Mendes, *Le Vatican et Israel* (Paris: Cerf, 1990), 122.

15. Summary report on the mission of Fisher to the Vatican (15/1/1957-8/2/1957), ISA (Foreign Ministry Archive) 3102/19; PRO FO 371/142295 13/3/1959; Bialer, *Cross on the Star of David*, 56–59.

16. M. Fisher to L. Cohen, 15/11/1957, ISA (Ministry of Foreign Affairs [MFA] Archive) 273/15.

17. R, Kagan to M. Fisher, 9/12/1957, ISA (MFA Archive) 273/18.

18. Mendes, *Le Vatican et Israel*, 123-24.

19. E. Sasson to M. Fisher, 28/12/1959, ISA (MFA Archive) 3102/20.

20. Ramon, "There Is a Major Religion in the World," 104-19; Bialer, *Cross on the Star of David*, 72–90.

21. Ramon, "There Is a Major Religion in the World," 107-19.

22. Ramon, *Christians and Christianity in the Jewish State*, 92–94.

23. Yaakov Herzog, *Hen Am Levadad Yishkon* (a people that dwells alone), (Jerusalem, 1974 [Hebrew]), 15-17.

24. Ramon, *Christians and Christianity in the Jewish State*, 70–88.

25. Ibid., 94.
26. Ibid., 93–94.
27. Ibid., 94.
28. Ibid.
29. A. Najar to the Prime Minister, 16/1/1973; A. Najar to S. Dinitz, 20/1/1973, ISA (MFA Archive) 5342/19.
30. Ibid.
31. M. Pragai to Z. Ne'eman, 23/9/1973, ISA (MFA Archive) 5342/23.

JERUSALEM
A Journey into "the Between"[1]

DANIEL ROSSING

Using the ancient hermeneutic tradition of *gammatria*, in which each letter in the alphabet has a numerical equivalent, Jewish teachers and preachers throughout the ages derived insights—some playful, some profound—from the fact that different Hebrew words have the same numerical value. Thus, for example, *yain* (wine) and *sod* (secret) are equal, which suggests that if one imbibes too much wine, too many secrets might pour out.

On a somewhat more serious plane, we find that *yerushalaim* (Jerusalem) has the same numerical value as *perush*, "interpretation." Indeed, the Holy City is an icon that invites and inspires many different interpretations and understandings, not only among its residents, but no less in the hearts and minds of the endless stream of pilgrims and visitors who flock to Jerusalem, seeking inspiration and insight. Each distinctive community and tradition in the city is a living witness to the multicolored rainbow of God's covenant with universal humanity. The texts, or narratives, of the diverse groups are living "sites" on the worldwide web of faith; every site in the city, whether ancient or modern, is an open "text" waiting to be read and interpreted, to instruct and inspire.

My own particular perception of the Eternal City is inspired by thirty years of encounter with its myriad layers of history and tradition, and above all with its mosaic of diverse religious, cultural, ethnic, and national communities. It is informed also by the experience of having served as a frequent mediator between communities in moments of conflict or crisis. For me Jerusalem is the city of "the between"—between creation and redemption, between heaven and earth, between dream and reality, between past and future, between tradition and modernity, between the planted area and the desert, between settled and nomadic life, between West and East, between majority and minority.

To truly enter Jerusalem is to leave the alluring arena of *either-or* dichotomies and embrace the sometimes frustrating but always rewarding realm of *both-and* dilemmas. Zion, like Zionism, is the challenge of living in the creative tension of the between. The city invites all who set foot in her gates to celebrate creation and seek redemption, to grasp heaven and earth at once, to elevate reality with dreams and ground dreams in reality, to faithfully recall and respect the past and fervently reach out to the future, to join tradition and modernity in a fruitful marriage, to find security in one's particular theological or ideological home without being afraid to wander in the open spaces of our universal humanity, to infuse the fixed structures of the Occident with the flowing rhythms of the Orient, to be empowered and powerless in the same moment.

The very name of the city in Hebrew—*yerushalaim*—seems to point to *both-and* life in the between. It has a special plural ending (*aim*) that is used almost exclusively for things—especially parts of the body—that function most naturally and effectively in pairs: *oznaim* (ears), *ainaim* (eyes), *sfataim* (lips), *yadaim* (hands), *raglaim* (legs), and so on. Clearly one would never consider choosing one ear or the other, one eye or the other, one hand or the other, one leg or the other. We need both of them, for without one or the other our hearing or sight or speech or movements would be distorted and impaired.

In the case of the parts of our bodies, the Divine Creator has coordinated the pairs so that they complement one another and function in harmony. But with regard to the above-mentioned pairs—and many others—that feature so prominently in our lives, as they do in the life of Jerusalem, it is our God-given task as cocreators with the Master of the Universe to coordinate the elements and ensure that they function in harmony and effectively complement one another. Let us explore but two of the many facets of the between that one encounters in Jerusalem and from which we can gain vital insight for our personal lives and our faith communities.

The first facet concerns memory of the past and visions of the future. In many respects, that which makes each community in Jerusalem distinct and different is its unique memory of the past. Jerusalem holds within it nearly four thousand years of history. No one can recall each and every detail of his or her individual life history, let alone all the details of four millennia of history. Our memories are by nature and necessity always selective. What we choose to remember is what makes us distinct and different. And so it is also with the diverse groups in Jerusalem; each group remembers and observes different milestones along the long timeline of Jerusalem. As you move about the city from community to community, you quickly sense not only that Jerusalem is a world in a city, but also that you are traveling in an exhilarating time warp. In Jerusalem the centuries run concurrent rather than consecutive; the passion for past and future eras impregnates the present with meaning.

About six years ago Jews remembered and celebrated the three-thousandth anniversary of King David. Christians recently recalled and commemorated the two-thousandth anniversary of the birth of Jesus. Muslims look back to and faithfully observe other events and dates. Even within one faith community, different groups evoke and emphasize different eras. Among the Christians, the Greek Orthodox vividly recall the Byzantine Empire that ruled and left its imprint on the city during the fifth and sixth centuries. The "White" Russian Orthodox look back with pride and longing to the nineteenth century and the widespread activities of the Russian Church in the Holy Land in those days, the architectural evidence of which is markedly present in the city to this day. Armenian, Coptic, Syrian, and Ethiopian Orthodox Christians, like the diverse Catholic and Protestant communities, recall still other significant dates and events. All share the common memory of "this do in remembrance of me."

Furthermore, different members of one community may recall the same specific era or event in different ways. On the festival of Hanukah, some Jews stress the military victory of the Maccabees, while others emphasize the miracle of the one small jar of oil that sufficed for eight days. In our modern-day return to Zion, different groups of Jews recall different historical precedents and models for entering Zion. Some remember the entry into the land in Joshua's time by military conquest, consecrating and sanctifying the land by purging it of idolatrous desecrations. Others look back to the return from Babylon with Ezra and Nehemiah, not as a conquering army but with the sponsorship of the superpower (Cyrus) of that time. Both models are part of the tradition; both figure in my dialogue with my tradition.

Jerusalem is the capital of memory. No other city in history has been the subject—and object—of so much memory and longing. Its landscape is punctuated by mountains of memory: Mount Moriah—for Jews the Temple Mount and for Muslims the Al-Haram Al-Sharif; the Hill of Golgotha/Calvary—for Christians the traditional site of the crucifixion; Mount Herzl—*har hazikaron* ("the mountain of memory") of modern Israeli-Jewish identity, which includes the Yad Vashem Heroes and Martyrs Memorial to the Holocaust, the national cemetery, and the military cemetery of Jerusalem; and the Mount of Olives, which figures so prominently in the messianic visions of all three faiths in the city.

Parallel to and intimately wedded with the diverse memories of the past of the various communities are the different lofty visions of the future that the city has inspired over the ages. Our massive edifices of memory buttress the many different eschatological skyscrapers—visible only to the eye of the respective believer—that rise along Jerusalem's horizon. The city's stones vibrate with future shock.

Unless creatively and constructively coordinated through *both-and* dialogue, the different memories of the past and visions of the future can easily generate unhealthy competition and destructive conflict in which various groups hurl their particular milestones at one another, or try to crush one another under the weight of their respective eschatological structures. Memory quickly becomes a prisoner of *either-or* warfare, with each group locked in its solitary cell, unaware of the other languishing nearby. Each fettered memory cries out to God and to all who pass by to give ear to its historic case and look with favor upon its vision of the future.

But mother Jerusalem waits with divine patience, passionately pleading with all who love her to seek the peace of Jerusalem by pursuing the path of dialogue. In the between, interfaith and intercultural dialogue is in essence a peace process, a way of living creatively and constructively with the inherent tensions of the between. It is a process in which there are very few, if any, easy answers or magical solutions, but many profound questions and dilemmas shared by all.

Dialogue summons residents and visitors alike to seize the endless opportunities that Jerusalem offers to encounter the many "others" that populate the city. Only through the encounter with the "other" can we truly and fully fathom the infinite depths of our own unique otherness, our own particular memories and visions of the future. Mother Jerusalem waits patiently, constantly challenging us to recall the example of our common father Abraham, who, after concluding his own special covenant with God (Gen 17), did not withdraw from the broad open spaces of humanity into the seclusion, security, and solace of his tent, but rather sat in the door of his tent in the heat of the day, his mind and heart open to others, without regard for whether they share in his particular covenant. His reward was a son—a future.

A second facet of the between to which I would like briefly to draw attention emerges from my day-to-day encounters in Jerusalem with the many "others" outside my own tradition. It concerns the issue of minority and majority status and roles in Jerusalem. On the surface it would seem that the traditional roles have been reversed: in the local setting of Jerusalem, Jews have suddenly become the majority vis-à-vis Christian and Muslim minorities. But the reality is more complex because we live simultaneously in multiple contexts—local, regional, and international. In large measure due to the extraordinary international attention focused on Jerusalem, one cannot live in the city as if one were on an isolated island. The regional Middle East context and the international context are as ever present as the local context.

As a Jew, I am the majority in the local context, but at the same moment I am a tiny minority in the regional and international contexts, struggling for national liberation and seeking the recognition and acceptance that had been denied me for two thousand years, and which still is not given easily by either the Muslim majority in the Middle East or by some segments of the Christian majorities in the West. The Muslim in Jerusalem is highly conscious of being part and parcel of the dominant majority in the region, and this majority consciousness makes all the more difficult the Muslim's struggle with the sometimes harsh realities of being a minority in the local context of Jerusalem. The different Christian communities are tiny minorities in Jerusalem, collectively constituting less than 3 percent of the total population. But in varying degrees they are conscious of, and draw strength from, their links with large Christian majorities in the West.

Each group in Jerusalem is thus both a minority and a majority, both powerless and empowered, at one and the same moment. This facet of the between presents us with a unique situation and an urgent challenge. We need to be far more attentive to it, for if we are, rather than being a source of confusion and conflict, it will help to remove, on the one hand, the sting of arrogance and triumphalism, and on the other, the bitterness of absolute defeat and subjugation, which for centuries have severely poisoned our relationships and produced so much enmity and strife.

Jerusalem is "the between" par excellence. But the between is not unique to Jerusalem. The between is at the very core of our lives and our faith. It is the heart of our interpersonal and intercommunal relations, and above all of our relationship with God. Whether one affirms the "already" of a Christian's firm faith in the incarnation or the "not yet" of the Jewish people's steadfast faithfulness to God's enduring covenant, we all live between the not yet and the already, between creation and redemption, between past and future. We must never think that we are totally powerless nor imagine that we are all powerful. The words of the rabbinic sage Hillel address us from the midst of the between: "If I am not for myself, who will be for me? And if I am only for myself, who am I? And if not now, when?"

We are constantly challenged—now!—to make pilgrimage to Jerusalem, to respond to the command to "go up," not as a temporary escape from the demands of daily life, but as a timeless journey into the between, into the heart of life and faith. Jerusalem pulsates with the life blood of the between, and as such has the potential to infuse all who join together and come to her (Isa 60:4) with new life and new insights into the life of the between. To journey into the between is not simply a matter of transportation, but indeed an occasion and opportunity for transformation.

Notes

1. An earlier version of this article appeared in *Pilgrimage in a New Millennium: Spiritual Reflections from Christians and Jews in the Holy Land*, published by the Interreligious Coordinating Council in Israel, 1999.

JEWISH-CHRISTIAN RELATIONS IN ISRAEL
Too Many Walls, Not Enough Bridges

FAYDRA SHAPIRO

Not that long ago, I took a taxi from the college where I work to Nazareth for a meeting at the Catholic vicariate there. I explained to the driver clearly where I wished to go, but as we approached Nazareth he took a wrong turn and headed for the mostly Jewish neighborhoods of Upper Nazareth. When I stopped him and explained the mistake, he shook his head—he was not willing to take a religious Jewish woman to Nazareth itself. "What could a [Jewish] religious woman possibly want there?!" he asked.

It's the kind of question I often feel hovering over my passion for Jewish-Christian relations, particularly here in Israel. Encouraging and facilitating Jewish-Christian relations in Israel presents special challenges and opportunities, and that is all the more so to be involved as an Orthodox Jewish woman.

In many ways, I arrived at this moment by accident. As a university professor in Canada, my field was a social-scientific approach to contemporary Jews and Jewish life. Back in the early 2000s I found myself hearing more and more about something strange and exotic—Evangelical Christian supporters of Israel. Using the cover of the academy to satisfy my curiosity, I started fieldwork and soon enough I knew that Christian Zionism would be my next major research project. Over the years I wrote a number of academic articles and became very involved in the world of Jewish-Evangelical encounter. In order to do so, I began teaching and researching issues in contemporary Jewish-

Christian relations more broadly. Then—together with my family—we made Aliyah (came up to live in Israel) and chose to live in the Galilee. Yezreel Valley College is located in the fertile plain that lies just south of the lower Galilee, lying between the hills of Nazareth and the Gilboa mountain range in northern Israel. It is the land where the earliest Zionist pioneers drained swamps and built up agricultural settlements, the earliest being Merhavia, established in 1911. In the same way, and seized by that pioneering spirit, Yezreel Valley College has worked tirelessly since its founding in 1965 to build up the Galilee and the State of Israel by offering excellent public higher education to some five thousand Israeli students each year. Its location on the road between the modern Jewish city of Afula and the ancient Christian and Muslim city of Nazareth positions the college to stand as a cultural meeting point in the north. In 2011, in keeping with its pioneering roots and its commitment to intercultural encounter, Yezreel Valley College boldly decided to invest in a new project. I was delighted to be asked to head up the first program in an Israeli academic institution dedicated to studying and fostering Jewish-Christian relations.

Moving across the world to a new culture at midlife presented some serious challenges for any family. One of the challenges I found most enticing was in finding that my field of study was quite different in Israel from what it was in North America. In short, the major issues and contours of Jewish-Christian relations in Israel are quite different from the ones that characterize the North American scene.

North America has seen some fifty years of productive dialogue between Jews and Christians. Following World War II it came to be understood that the evil of the Shoah, with its annihilation of six million European Jews, required significant work to understand the role of Christianity in normalizing anti-Jewish ideas. That consciousness evolved into investigating how Christianity needed to take responsibility for anti-Judaism in the church and move in more productive directions in its relationships with Jews and Judaism.

Taking the lead in this difficult process of reevaluating historic relations with the Jews was the Roman Catholic Church. Among other sweeping developments that were adopted through the Second Vatican Council (1962–65), the document *Nostra Aetate* started official Jewish-Christian relations onto a new path. A scant seventeen sentences of this short Declaration of the relations of the church with non-Christian religions is devoted to the issue of the Jews. These sentences boldly assert the spiritual bond between Jews and Christians and the Jewish root of the church (making use of the root and branch imagery of Rom 11), assert that God still holds the Jews "most dear," insist that Jews cannot be held collectively responsible for the crucifixion, decry anti-Semitism, and urge efforts that would encourage "mutual understanding and respect." The document passed on October 28, 1965, by a vote of 2,221 bishops to 88. This early effort spawned an ongoing project that included the establishment of a Pontifical Commission for Religious Relations with the Jews (1974) that has published additional Guidelines (1974) and Notes (1985) that continue the work of *Nostra Aetate*.[1] The Holocaust was singled out for sustained condemnation in *We Remember: A Reflection on the Shoah* (1998), and centers for promoting Jewish-Christian relations sprang up and now flourish at numerous Catholic institutions of higher education. And while there have been criticisms from all sides about different aspects of this ongoing interfaith work between the Roman Catholic Church and the Jews, there is little doubt that the relationship underwent significant change in the second half of the twentieth century.

The unique dynamics that play out in Israel, however, create a significantly different environment for Jewish-Christian relations, with its own modes of encounter and areas of concern, with different possibilities for changes, different constraints, and different challenges from those experienced by its North American counterpart.

THE CHALLENGES OF JEWISH SOVEREIGNTY

The reentry of the Jews into history with the State of Israel is no doubt a spectacular achievement. Some two thousand years of forced diaspora life, characterized by relative powerlessness and often in Christian lands, ended with the birth of the modern Jewish State of Israel. Here, we Jews find ourselves not only comprising the majority of the population, but also in possession of sovereignty and the ability to legislate for our citizens and residents.

Unsurprisingly, nobody in Israel has ever gingerly approached me after a talk, eyes wide, to tell me with shy awe that they've "never met a Jew before." Jewish holidays are *the* public holidays. In Canada, where Jews are a small minority concentrated in a few large urban centers, it was not uncommon for people to have never had much interaction with Jews or Judaism before. In Israel, however, the inverse dynamic holds sway. At the Galilee Center for Studies in Jewish-Christian Relations, we regularly work with Jews who have never (knowingly) met a Christian in their lives. Jews in Israel tend to know very little about Christian life and traditions, except through the combination of American television and the public education system, which tends to result in thinking that the most important aspects of Christianity are Christmas and the Crusades. Jews in North America come across the New Testament in every hotel room. Jews in Israel might easily never come across a copy of the New Testament in their lives.

This new balance of power has the ability to help us rewrite some of our basic scripts in Jewish-Christian relations. First, it offers us the opportunity and challenge to reenvision the Jews as something other than perpetual victims. Jewish-Christian relations in the Christian West are built on the history of the Jew as the marginalized Other, and on recent efforts to rectify that history. In Israeli Jewish-Christian relations, anti-Semitism need not be the overwhelming issue. (The fact that it still remains a significant issue is testimony to the post-traumatic historical stress carried by Jews, existential threats to Israel, and our deep sense of ourselves as a minority.) Yet the promise of independence and the fact that there is no history of local Christian persecution of the Jews allows Jews the possibility of rethinking their relations with Christians from a different platform.

Equally important is that this new economy of power encourages us to reenvision Christians as something other than powerful persecutors. All of a sudden Christians in Israel share some significant dynamics with Jews in Europe or North America as a small minority wrestling with the challenges of maintaining a distinct culture and religion amidst the Jewish majority.

This relatively new and heady experience of sovereignty brings with it responsibility, and for the first time in recent history, Jews find themselves face to face with the question of how to protect minority rights in a state that strives to successfully balance its Jewish and democratic commitments. The challenge of Jewish power and its implications for Jewish-Christian relations is one of the unique and most challenging aspects of this kind of work in Israel.

RELIGION IS NEVER "JUST" RELIGION

Here in Israel, Jewish-Christian relations are at least as much about Jews and Christians as about Judaism and Christianity. Jews and Christians in Israel regularly attend different schools, read different newspapers, live in different neighbourhoods or villages, and speak different languages from one another. The distance between Jews and Christians here is only somewhat a function of religious difference. In Israel religion is never "just" religion; rather, religion is deeply intertwined with ethnicity and, as such, politics.

Around the world Jews are ethnically Jewish and (overwhelmingly) practice some variation of Judaism. Christians practice the religion of Christianity and are of many different ethnicities. But here in Israel the ethnicity of most Christians—about 80 percent—is Arab. Thus Arab Christians will often feel themselves to be caught in the uncomfortable situation of being read as "Other" from all sides: for Jews, they are Arabs and, for Muslims, they are Christians.

But it's not "just" ethnicity either. Jews in Israel are also Jewish Israelis and Zionists. In a conflict zone of competing claims and narratives, Jewish-Christian relations themselves easily become fraught with political interests concerning what kinds of Jews and Christians, allied in what kinds of ways, and for what kinds of causes.

For good or for ill, in Israel everything is political, everything either is, or is read as, a "statement." How you dress, where you live, what youth group your children attend, what music you listen to, they all say something—real or imagined—about you and your priorities, ideology, and self-definition. This means, for example, that the old adage "Don't judge a book by its cover" really doesn't play out here in Israel, where people make judgments about each other very quickly based on certain cues. Those quick judgments, often about things that really matter, can end up hindering our best efforts to build relationships. But when approached with care and conscious questioning, those assumptions can also encourage a deeper dialogue.

Based on my dress and choice of headwear, I am often expected to hold certain religious, political, and social attitudes. I've had many Christians surprised to find that I'm neither ignorant about nor threatened by Christianity as an "Orthodox" Jew. I read the New Testament. I'm happy to discuss Jesus. And I even engage with Jesus-believing Jews (with whom I totally disagree). Doing Jewish-Christian relations while looking as "traditional" as I do serves to unsettle stereotypes and allow a little light to creep into the social categories we take for granted.

This prevalence of politics in Israel also means that things we might think of being "just religious" are inherently "political" here. For example, how we read the Bible matters here a great deal. Questions that are most often consigned to theological seminaries in North America concerning the nature of chosenness, God's promises of restoration, and the relationship of the New Testament to the Old Testament take on a real urgency here in modern Israel. Here, where the Israel-Palestine "conflict" suffuses so much of what we do, reading the Bible plays a different role in Jewish-Christian relations because of its political implications from its role in North America.

DO JEWISH-CHRISTIAN RELATIONS REALLY MATTER?

In some ways the third challenge is the most fundamental. In Israel, the importance of building better Jewish-Christian relations is in no way self-evident. I've been challenged about this very issue by all kinds of Israelis. Most often this involves Jews insisting that Jewish-Christian relations do not need any attention and that in Israel we need to work (only) on Jewish-Arab (so often read as just Muslim) relations. For many here, it is Jewish-Arab issues that demand investment because those are ostensibly the *real* issues we face. For many in Israel, Christians and Jewish-Christian relations are not a significant enough issue or a large enough demographic in contemporary Israel to warrant our attention and our energy.

I imagine that the Christian clergy members being spat on, the faithful whose holy sites are vandalized, and the believers who watched their Scriptures ripped up by a member of parliament, who then posed for pictures, might think differently.

I always find this argument, particularly when it comes from academics, to be especially bizarre. I can handle Jewish ambivalence about Christians and Christianity. I get that. But to suggest that Jewish relations with Christians and Christianity are somehow irrelevant to us in Israel because there are so few of them here evokes a certain Soviet-style understanding where value is measured by usefulness to the state. It's a little like saying we needn't study history because it's about dead people, or the moon because it's so very far away. Funnily enough, this version of "why do Jewish-Christian relations" is just a variation on the conservative (religious) argument sometimes heard here, which wonders why Jews ought to know anything about Christianity at all.

Many religious Jews are suspicious and concerned about the assumptions and implications of interfaith work generally. It should come as no surprise that their specific discomfort with Christianity is even stronger. We're a majority in Israel, the argument goes, and finally our children can be raised *really* Jewish, untainted by these foreign influences. So why on earth would we want them to know anything about the New Testament? We've related enough to Christianity; now let's just do Jewish-Jewish relations.

Yet Jewish-Christian relations are unique, and uniquely important, both in humanity and also in service to the State of Israel.

First, there are no two religions that share as broad a textual foundation as do Judaism and Christianity. While both religions have their own interpretations and texts, the fact that both religions engage and interpret the Hebrew Bible, however differently, makes their relationship uniquely close.

Second, because it grew out of a Jewish context, Christianity is deeply and passionately interested in Jews and Judaism. The problem of dealing with its Jewish roots has plagued and inspired Christianity for its entire existence in an effort to assert, at the same time, continuity with and difference from Judaism. Similarly, Christianity is theologically preoccupied with the matter of the Jewish people and what their chosenness implies for the status of Christianity.

Of course the Christian "problem" with Judaism is different from the Jewish "problem" with Christianity. The former is mostly theological and tends to worry about ideas. The latter is overwhelmingly historical and worries mostly about security of persons and communities. In different ways, Christianity and Judaism are deeply and necessarily entangled with each other, in history and today.

Through the issue of the Shoah, Jewish-Christian relations serve also as an important case for opening up some of the most crucial conversations in our world today, about difference and genocide, and about —as Rosemary Radford Ruether titled her book—faith and fratricide.[2]

Let us not forget that it was also the Jewish-Christian crucible that formed the basis for Western civilization. A thorough understanding of how Judaism and Christianity develop and relate to each other helps us to ask legitimately all kinds of good questions about the contours of this process and the product that emerged.

Finally, it requires little imagination to see that Jewish-Christian relations really are of serious importance for all of us here in Israel. It is in the Christian world that Israel finds some of its staunchest critics and some of its most powerful allies. The bitter debates within mainline denominations over boycotts and divestment and the platform given in the Christian world to groups whose Palestinian liberation theology too often conceals insidious anti-Israelism and latent anti-Semitism are ultimately about Jewish-Christian relations. And yes, they have everything to do with Israel.

Jews and Christians have their own problems, issues, texts, theologies, and traumas to work through. They share much, and of course they differ greatly. Thinking carefully together about Jewish-Christian relations and striving to build better relationships between Jews and Christians is not to suggest that Islam is unimportant or Muslims not critical conversation partners for Jews (and Christians). But twentieth-century developments in Jewish-Christian relations are less than fifty years old. They are still young and fragile, requiring careful care and a protected space in which they can grow.

We hold in our hands the priceless privilege and responsibility to nurture those developments and tailor them for work with Jews and Christians here in Israel. At the Galilee Center for Studies in Jewish-Christian Relations, we recognize that Jewish-Christian relations are about far more than just theological differences. Issues like politics, ethnicity, history, and culture are all significant issues that require us to draw on many fields of study and approaches to investigate and address.

Due in part to the growth of boycott and divestment movements on North American campuses and scholarly associations, we increasingly hear calls for maintaining a clear separation between the academy and politics: the idea that institutions of higher education should be about teaching academics and not teaching political activism.

Those of us who were trained in the academic study of religion know the argument—and the temptation—extremely well. We've spent years learning how to separate our academic interests and our private commitments, looking down our noses at institutions like seminaries who (we were taught) sought to muddy the academic waters with things like beliefs and commitments. We were taught to be critical thinkers whose analyses necessarily stood apart from political, moral, or religious causes. This was "academic," requiring us to leave our personal religious beliefs at the door. Religious practice and activism was just more data for us to study, and certainly not to be taken seriously as part of the academic project.

However, a vision of studying Jewish-Christian relations that is not at the same time deeply committed to building better relationships between Christians and Jews is both intellectually dishonest and morally adrift. Studying people without actually striving to make a difference in their lives seems, particularly in conflict zones like the one I live in, to be an irresponsible use of privilege. Equally, activism without continuing education and information will fail to develop and reach its full potential. Accordingly, my work with The Galilee Center for Studies in Jewish-Christian Relations at the Yezreel Valley College is at the same time academic in orientation and also committed to building better relationships between communities on the ground. We embrace a vision in which academia and community efforts can be used to richly inform and inspire each other.

My work at this new center has at its core a vision of bringing disparate worlds together, of being cognizant of the walls that exist and recognizing their value for definition and boundaries, while at the same time working to build bridges among religions, cultures, and people. While that is most obviously addressed to Jews and Christians, it is actually a more robust encounter that includes the interaction of students and clergy, Israelis and foreigners, academics and laypeople. At least as important are our efforts that bring together different kinds of Jews and different kinds of Christians, and seeking in Jewish-Christian relations an opportunity for healing and reconciliation within religious communities.

At the Galilee Center for Studies in Jewish-Christian Relations, we bring scholars, academic tools, students, and the campus environment to help us actualize that very vision of an Israel and a world with more bridges. So in answer to the taxi driver's unexpected question—what could a religious woman possibly want there—the answer is clear and unambiguous: she seeks to build the kind of world that God himself envisioned, one of diversity and respect, difference and engagement between his beloved peoples.

Notes

1. "Guidelines and Suggestions for Implementing the Conciliar Declaration *Nostra Aetate* No. 4" (1974), "Notes on the Correct Way to Present Jews and Judaism in Preaching and Teaching in the Roman Catholic Church" (1985).

2. Rosemary Radford Ruether, *Faith and Fratricide: The Theological Roots of Anti-Semitism* (New York: Seabury Press, 1996).

JEWISH-CHRISTIAN RELATIONS IN ISRAEL

Christian Points of View

FROM A CULTURE
OF FEAR TO A
CULTURE OF TRUST
Facing Extremism in the 21st Century

MUNIB A. YOUNAN

On August 7, 2012, Wade Michael Page walked into a Sikh Temple in Oak Creek, Wisconsin, killing six persons with an automatic rifle. On the very next day, 540 miles away in Joplin, Missouri, a mosque was burned to the ground. Why would someone attack a religious building or people at prayer?

Many see such religion-related violence as correlated to the terrible events of September 11, 2001. Yet similar acts were perpetrated earlier, such as the Babri Mosque attack by Hindus in Ayodhya, India, in December 1992, or the massacre of Bosnian Muslims by Christians in Srebrenica in July 1995. It is, sadly, a worldwide phenomenon. On July 22, 2011, Anders Breivik set off a bomb in Oslo and went on a shooting rampage at a political camp for youth, killing seventy-seven because of his hatred of Muslims and multiculturalism. On Easter Sunday 2012, thirty-nine people were killed in a car bomb near a church in Kaduna, Nigeria. The horrendous nature of this deed is only multiplied by the fact that the bomber was targeting Christians at worship on the most sacred day of the year. With increased mobility and immigration, people are living in fear of the other—the other who is often unknown.

Here in the Middle East, the potential for catastrophe is like a cloud that hovers over us every day that we strive to live in peace and understanding. When the Arab Spring dawned, many were filled with hope because of the focus on human rights and democratic ideals such as freedom of speech, expression, religion, and the equality of women. Many were encouraged because the methods and means were nonviolent. Now the voice of the people is silenced, and we are all watching carefully how events will unfold in the region and beyond.

In Israel and Palestine we could cite plenty of examples for all sides over the course of the past century. Although it is relatively "quiet," the occupation remains. Although the majority of Israelis and Palestinians *say* they want peace, we still remain in a state of conflict where extremists continue to push the possibility of peace further out of reach. School children in southern Israel continue to be forced into underground shelters by rockets launched from Gaza. In the West Bank, rightful owners of the land are terrorized by settlers who claim all the land as a "divine gift." Today, the most serious challenge to peace has become those settlers who are using the slogan "price tag" as a threat to anyone who challenges them. Over the last year, a wave of mosques and private property have been vandalized and set on fire, all with "price tag" graffiti and slanderous and threatening words toward Arabs, and even against Jews who question such extremism. Some say there is no other altercation in which religion is abused more than the Palestinian-Israeli conflict. It is self-evident that the Holy Scriptures are unfortunately misused for these purposes of escalating conflict instead of building unity and trust.

As the world grows smaller through international travel, technological advances, and instantaneous communication, it seems that we are fomenting a culture of fear in which the other is perceived as a threat. What is the role of religion in all this? Throughout history, religion has helped people to deal with their fears. "Do not be afraid!" is a declaration that occurs frequently in the Bible. Even the term *religion* has the root meaning of binding people together, not tearing them apart.

Can religion help us to get beyond this culture of fear that pervades the twenty-first century? Or is religion the problem? Some suggest that one religion is to blame for the strife we experience. Yet from the examples above, it seems like all people of all religions need to look inward, to see where each of us has contributed to the problem, to ask for forgiveness from God and one another, and to seek reconciliation, so that we all can live together in peace. We need to be honest with one another. We need to discuss how religion has so often caused problems for us and divided us. When this is done properly, perhaps we will learn how religion can help us to live together. Religion can help us to move from a culture of fear to a culture of trust. We should also understand that no single religion has a monopoly on extremism—all religions have adherents who use their doctrinal beliefs as a rationale for inhumane behavior.

A CULTURE OF FEAR

Following the Oslo attack by Anders Breivik, the Islamic Council of Norway and the Church of Norway Council on Ecumenical and International Relations issued a "Joint Statement Opposing Religious Extremism" in which they noted characteristics of religious extremism, namely, that extremists see themselves as the sole interpreters of their own religion and that the concepts of human dignity and human rights apply only to them. They see no reason for dialogue. Extremists are convinced that there are groups of people with whom it is impossible to coexist and that they must therefore oppose or remove, either from society as a whole or from their particular locale. As a result they turn to terror or other forms of compulsion in order to enforce the implications of their religious views on others.[1]

These findings are similar to those of others who have studied religious extremism. Throughout the last two decades of the twentieth century, the esteemed Lutheran historian Martin Marty of the University of Chicago undertook the five-volume *Fundamentalism Project*,[2] in which he found, common among all religions of the world, a movement that presents a militant opposition to modernity. Dr. Marty also found that this phenomenon is characterized by a strong rejection of religious and cultural pluralism, a belief that one's own way is the only way, the adherence to a rigid set of rules and laws, and a following of strong individual leaders or a group of insiders who interpret these rules for all. Perhaps the most important points are that a culture of fear is present among people regardless of their religious affiliation and that there are individuals among all religions who fear the other, who promote an attitude of mistrust and separation, and who turn to hatred and violence against innocent victims—all in the name of religion. The problem, as the Norwegians have declared in the wake of their own tragic encounter with terror, is not religion, but religious extremism.

This tendency of adherents of various religions to turn to hatred and violence was addressed shortly after 9/11 by Dr. Charles Kimball, who served as Director of the Middle East Office of the National Council of Churches in the United States and later as a university professor. Shortly after September 11, Dr. Kimball traveled across America, trying to help people understand that it was not the average Muslim neighbors who were to blame for these attacks, but individuals who were on the fringes of Islam, namely, Muslim extremists. In his book *When Religion Becomes Evil: Five Warning Signs*,[3] Kimball argued that the problem is not Islam, or Judaism, or Christianity. The problem is when certain individuals, claiming to be speaking for God or defending God-espoused doctrine, act counter to the core teaching that love for God shows itself in respect for the other. He writes,

> Whatever religious people may say about their love of God or the mandates of their religion, when their behavior toward others is violent and destructive, when it causes suffering among their neighbors, you can be sure the religion has been corrupted and reform is desperately needed.

Clearly Kimball sees individuals as the culprits who misrepresent religious teachings, or who take them to the extreme. Yet he does not let others off lightly when it comes to responsibility. He continues, "Conversely, when religion remains true to its authentic sources, it is actively dismantling these corruptions."[4]

The moderates within Christianity, Judaism, and Islam also bear a responsibility—namely, to ensure that they remain "true to its authentic sources" and "to dismantle these corruptions." When mainline Christians, Muslims, and Jews—especially their leaders—remain silent and timid about these core values, they allow themselves to be held hostage by the extremists, and they contribute to the problem.

This is the reason that I call on religious leaders to be prophetic. Religious leaders from every faith and ethnicity must have the courage to stand up and say to their own extremists that any violence done in the name of God or religion is blasphemy. We as religious leaders need to become more engaged and to speak out more forcefully to "dismantle the corruptions" and give a vision of life together in all its diversity in the whole globalized world. Instead of dividing the world on the basis of religion, we must rightly practice religion so that it might be a uniting force against the evils of the world. We must lead by example so that the adherents of the Abrahamic faiths can see our good works and give thanks for the gift of peace that passes mere human understanding and creates harmony in diverse communities.

A CULTURE OF TRUST

Within the world of Islam, King Abdullah II of Jordan took the lead in calling for tolerance and unity. This began with a Ramadan sermon in November 2004 by Chief Justice Sheikh Iz-al-Din al-Tamimi that became known as "The Amman Message." Later in July 2005, two hundred Muslim scholars from over fifty countries came together in Amman to endorse it.[5]

Unfortunately, following the events of September 11, 2001, mainline Christian leaders were perhaps a bit too timid—there is no question that their views were spoken, yet they were drowned out by others. For example, Rev. Franklin Graham, the son of the respected American evangelist Billy Graham, publicly declared that Islam was an "evil and wicked religion."[6] This careless act of dangerous rhetoric threatened to create a rift even among moderates at a time when unity of purpose and compassion was crucial.

Such religious views played into the political views articulated by Bernard Lewis and also Samuel P. Huntington in *A Clash of Civilizations*,[7] which were influential in the Bush White House. The Christian piety of this American president gave way to the voice of his vice-president, who declared that the United States had to "work the dark side," using "any means at our disposal" and "without any discussion." The world was soon divided between the bifurcation of the so-called axis of good and the axis of evil.

I am convinced that as religious leaders we must continually, and unequivocally, speak with one voice for an ethic of nonviolence and together combat extremism. To take up the cross of Jesus and to follow takes seriously his command to love our enemies and to turn the other cheek. Mahatma Gandhi said, "I object to violence because when it appears to do good, the good is only temporary; the evil it does is permanent."[8] The way of nonviolence means holding steadfastly a candle of light even in the darkest part of the night.

During the midst of the Civil Rights movement nearly four decades earlier, Rev. Dr. Martin Luther King Jr. wrote,

Returning hate for hate multiplies hate, adding deeper darkness to a night already devoid of stars. Darkness cannot drive out darkness; only light can do that. Hate cannot drive out hate; only love can do that. Hate multiplies hate, violence multiplies violence, and toughness multiplies toughness in a descending spiral of destruction.[9]

It is no accident that King titled his book *The Strength to Love.* "Working the dark side" is a sign of weakness. Hating the other only shows our own inadequacies. The only answer is love.

What is the essence of religion? When a young man approached Jesus asking what are the greatest of commandments, Jesus responded very simply: love of God and love of neighbor as self (Matt 22:37–40). This came from the Jewish Torah and was quoted by Jesus' contemporary Rabbi Hillel. Islam teaches the same principle. Building on this ethic of love, John teaches, "Those who say, 'I love God,' and hate their brothers or sisters, are liars; for those who do not love a brother or sister whom they have seen, cannot love God whom they have not seen" (1 John 4:20).

In reaction to the negative responses following September 11—including the "war on terror," the profiling of Arabs and Muslims, the wars in Iraq and Afghanistan, and the continuing growth of hatred and suspicion—138 Muslim scholars from all Islamic countries and regions in the world met in September 2007 to produce *A Common Word between Us and You,* expressing what they saw as fundamental Muslim teaching and also the main common ground between Christianity and Islam. According to their statement, the most fundamental common values between Islam and Christianity, and the basis with the highest potential for future dialogue and understanding, are the shared emphases on love of God and love of neighbor. *A Common Word* documents these shared emphases by referencing significant passages in the Qur'an and the Bible. Rather than engage in polemics, the signatories have adopted what they see as the traditional and mainstream Islamic position of respecting the Christian Scripture and calling Christians to be more, not less, faithful to it.

Another important initiative is the *World Interfaith Harmony Week*, proposed by King Abdullah II of Jordan and adopted by the United Nations General Assembly in October 2010 to be recognized each year in the first week in February. When His Highness Prince Ghazi of Jordan, Special Adviser on Religious Affairs to King Abdullah II, presented the initiative before the UN General Assembly, he stated, "The misuse or abuse of religions can...be a cause of world strife, whereas religions should be a great foundation for facilitating world peace. The remedy for this problem can only come from the world's religions themselves."

This is the reason that we must seek the common values of love, coexistence, accepting the other, peace, forgiveness, justice, and reconciliation that can change the culture of fear into a culture of trust. Only a culture of trust can make our world into a safe haven for all. In this way we may together combat all kinds of anti-Semitism, Islamophobia, Christianophobia, and xenophobia, in order that religion will be the true source of understanding, forgiveness, and reconciliation in every civilization and culture.

Following the July 2011 massacre in Oslo, at a memorial service for the victims, Prime Minister Jens Stoltenberg said, "My greatest thanks goes to the Norwegian people, who appeared responsible when needed, who kept their dignity, who chose democracy." He reaffirmed the need for "dialogue and tolerance" in the land, and he expressed the hope that when political work resumed, leaders would "behave with the same wisdom and respect as the Norwegian people." The chief of police also added, "We do not want barbed wire, roadblocks and weapons as part of everyday life in Norway."

This reflects the words of Rev. Dr. Martin Luther King Jr., also echoed by those of Desmond Tutu in the midst of apartheid in South Africa:

Goodness is stronger than evil;
Love is stronger than hate;
Light is stronger than darkness;
Life is stronger than death;
Victory is ours, Victory is ours;
Through God who loves us.[10]

Let us commit ourselves to continue to work for a transformation from a culture of fear to a culture of trust.

THE ROLE OF EDUCATION: BOUND TO LIVE TOGETHER

In a 2006 Gallup poll, American respondents were asked, "What could western societies do in order to improve relations with the Muslim or Islamic world?"[11] The top three answers were:

Better Understanding of Each Other's Beliefs (18 percent)
Improve Education (14 percent)
Work Together (9 percent)

In a sense these three answers speak to the importance of education in improving relations. The answer "Control or stop extremists and terrorists" finished a distant fourth with only 6 percent agreeing. At the same time, 56 percent admitted that they knew "not much" or "nothing at all" about the opinions and beliefs of people who live in Muslim countries. A survey from the same time by the Council of American-Islamic Relations found that only one in five Americans could give the name of one Muslim whom they knew fairly well. Those who had Muslim friends had a much higher opinion of Muslims than those without.

Education is the primary transformative power that can build truth among peoples. This is what we are noticing in the Arab Awakening, that the power of education can transform the whole Middle East into a modern civil society that respects human rights, women's rights, freedom of religion, freedom of expression, and other democratic principles.

What do we find among Palestinians and Israelis today? If we took surveys, how well would Palestinians say they knew Israelis when the bulk of their contact is with soldiers? How well would Israelis say they knew Palestinians when they are divided by the wall and when Israelis are forbidden by their own government from entering the Palestinian cities? As for relations between Christians and Muslims, we are in a better position because we have lived side by side in the Holy Land for centuries. Our relations are not always free from difficulties, but from youth we have learned to respect each other and to work out our problems in a civil way.

I still remember the day in 1967 when I had my first encounter with a Jewish person; I was born in the Old City, separated from West Jerusalem by barbed wire and the "no man's land." My feelings were filled with fear and apprehension, compounded because these first Jews entering the Old City carried weapons. Through Jewish-Christian dialogue, especially in the Jonah group, Rabbis Ron Kronish, Naama Kelman, Levi Weiman-Kelman, David Rosen, and others have become not only trusted dialogue partners, but my dear friends. Yet, the truth is that we are only a small minority who have had the opportunity for such edifying encounters.

This is the reason that our educational systems must provide curricula that portray the other accurately and foster respect and understanding. In my own church, the Evangelical Lutheran Church in Jordan and the Holy Land (ELCJHL), education is considered our direct mission and our strength. Among our stated goals are:

1. To develop wholesome, creative, and innovative students through a holistic approach to education that addresses their needs and develops their talents, competencies, inclinations, and ability to cope in an ever-changing world.
2. To integrate peace education and culture, reinforce democracy, and encourage tolerance, coexistence, love, and respect toward others.

Only when students from different religions study together, play together, and participate in extramural activities together during their education years will they have the skills to work together and contribute together to society as good citizens when they are adults.

This was the view of Gandhi: "If we are to teach real peace in this world, and if we are to carry on a real war against war, we shall have to begin with the children."[12] In the same way, Nelson Mandela said, "Education is the most powerful weapon you can use to change the world."[13]

The same ideas must follow also across lines for Palestinians and Israelis. This is the goal of the Council of Religious Institutions of the Holy Land (CRIHL),[14] a council that is made up of leaders of all three major religions in the Holy Land: the Chief Rabbinate of Israel (including both Ashkenazi and Sephardic Chief Rabbis), the Heads of the Local

Churches of the Holy Land, the Ministry of the Islamic *Waqf* at the Palestinian Authority, and the Islamic Shariah Courts of the Palestinian Authority. By our own participation in this council, we have gained appreciation for each other and work to remove stereotypes, and to stand together to oppose statements and speeches that support extremist ideas.

Over the past several years, the council has worked together to support the production of an analysis of how Palestinian and Israeli school textbooks depict the other so both Israeli and Palestinian education ministries can work toward a curriculum based on mutual respect. The publication of "Victims of Our Own Narratives: Portrayal of the Other in Israeli and Palestinian School Books" is a watershed moment in the parallel narratives of the Holy Land. Using the latest empirical methods, we discerned the manner in which the books we are handing to our children are shaping their attitudes and comprehension of those around them. The results of the study indicate that there are two conflicting narratives between Palestinians and Israelis, and the values of coexistence are lacking. For example, the study revealed a serious lack of information in all the textbooks about the religions of other peoples. The textbooks did not promote or recognize the diversity within the walls of the Old City, nor did the textbooks advocate for unfettered access to the holy sites of the various faiths. How can we hope for our children to live in peace if we do not plant seeds of hope in them when they are young? Now that we have this analysis in hand, we can begin to address the issues therein and work toward giving our children—both Palestinian and Israeli—a more accurate and hope-filled picture of a future with peaceful coexistence. Our aim is to make the textbooks more inclusive, so that children will grow up with a knowledge and respect of their neighbor's faith and practice. In this way we as religious leaders have taken a stand that we believe can affect our society at its core, bring about better understanding among peoples and religions, resulting in justice, reconciliation, and peace among neighbors.

This fulfils the council's mission statement based on the core values of love of God and love of neighbor:

> As religious leaders of different faiths, who share the conviction in the one Creator, Lord of the Universe; we believe that the essence of religion is to worship G-d and respect the life and dignity of all human beings, regardless of religion, nation-

ality and gender....We accordingly commit ourselves to use our positions and good offices, to advance these sacred values, to prevent religion from being used as a source of conflict, and to promote mutual respect, a just and comprehensive peace and reconciliation between people of all faiths in the Holy Land and worldwide.[15]

When I am asked what will change the culture from one of fear to one of trust, I always say "Education, education, education!"

MAINTAINING HOPE IN THE MIDST OF THE ONGOING ISRAELI-PALESTINIAN CONFLICT

A resolution to the Israeli-Palestinian conflict will not result from merely good feelings and a positive attitude. We have to expect tough discussions and difficult decisions to be made by those in the political arena. My views on this have been consistent in support of the "two-state solution." This is the same basic framework that was set forth in the Oslo Accords signed in 1993 and strengthened in the "roadmap" proposed by the Quartet (the United States, Russia, European Union, the United Nations). This is the framework that has been at the heart of all negotiations between Israel and the Palestinians.

For me, this means consistent support for the following six points:

1. A two-state solution based on 1967 borders
2. A shared Jerusalem for Jews, Muslims, and Christians; for Palestinians and Israelis, as the Heads of Churches declared in 2006
3. An end to Israeli settlements in the occupied territories
4. A political solution for the Palestinian refugees
5. An equitable sharing of natural resources, especially water
6. Regional cooperation

The security of Israel is dependent on freedom and justice for Palestine. And freedom and justice for Palestine is dependent on the security of Israel. This is a symbiotic relationship, and a key formula for justice in the Middle East.

Currently the Israeli-Palestinian peace process seems to have been put on hold for various reasons. Some are saying that we must wait until the Arab Awakening resolves itself, and then the world will turn again to the Israeli-Palestinian question. I would suggest that there can be a two-track approach and that the world must continue to focus on Israel-Palestine while the developments of the Arab Awakening continue to unfold.

Most of all, *we must continue to offer a message of hope in the midst of difficult times.* This is what it means that our church in Jerusalem is located just a short distance away from the Church of the Holy Sepulchre. Living in the shadow of Golgotha and the empty tomb, we proclaim a message of hope because of our faith in a God who has defeated the powers of death and evil. We call upon our members to remain steadfast in the land, called to a vibrant witness and a creative ministry of service. These days, neither those in the political realm nor those in the media appear optimistic about a resolution in the near future. As for myself, I am neither optimistic nor pessimistic. Yet as a Christian I live in hope and continue to work for peace based on justice.

As a Palestinian, I want my children and grandchildren to live in peace with hopes and dreams, no different from Israelis who want their children and grandchildren to live in peace with their own hopes and dreams. As a Palestinian, I must grow in seeing the image of God in Israelis, just as Israelis grow in seeing the image of God in Palestinians. As a Palestinian, I must seek a just peace that respects the concerns of Israelis, just as Israelis must respect the concerns of Palestinians in achieving a peace based on justice and reconciliation based on forgiveness. Only then will the Holy Land be a promised land of milk and honey for both Palestinians and Israelis.

Notes

1. "Joint Muslim/Christian Statement Opposing Religious Extremism," Church of Norway, November 22, 2011. http://kirken.no /english/news.cfm?artid=363357.

2. Martin E. Marty and R. Scott Appleby, *The Fundamentalism Project,* 5 vols. (Chicago: University of Chicago Press, 1991–95).

3. Charles Kimball, *When Religion Becomes Evil: Five Warning Signs* (San Francisco: HarperOne, 2002).

4. Ibid.

5. "The Amman Message," http://www.ammanmessage.com /index.php?lang=en.

6. Mark Tessler, "Arab and Muslim Political Attitudes: Stereotypes and Evidence from Survey Research," *International Studies Perspectives* 4 (2003), 175.

7. Bernard Lewis, "The Roots of Muslim Rage," *The Atlantic Monthly* (September 1990); Samuel P. Huntington, "The Clash of Civilizations," *Foreign Affairs* (1993) and *The Clash of Civilizations and the Remaking of the World Order* (New York: Simon and Schuster: 1996).

8. Mahatma Gandhi, *The Essential Gandhi*, ed. Louis Fischer (New York: Knopf, 2002).

9. Martin Luther King Jr., *The Strength to Love* (New York: Harper & Row: 1963), 37.

10. Desmond Tutu, *An African Prayer Book* (New York: Doubleday, 1995).

11. Gallup, "Complex but Hopeful Pattern of American Attitudes Toward Muslims," March 23, 2006, http://www.gallup.com/poll /22021 /complex-hopeful-pattern-american-attitudes-toward-muslims.aspx.

12. *The Essential Gandhi.*

13. Nelson Mandela, as quoted in Reginald McKnight's *Wisdom of the African World* (Novato, CA: New World Library, 1996).

14. Council of Religious Institutions of the Holy Land, http://www.crihl.org.

15. See http://www.crihl.org.

AN ECCLESIAL COPERNICAN REVOLUTION AND THE BAT KOL INSTITUTE IN JERUSALEM

MAUREENA FRITZ

When Nicolaus Copernicus formulated a heliocentric cosmology that displaced the earth from the center of the universe, it caused a paradigm shift in humanity's conception of itself. With the publication and promulgation of paragraph 4 of *Nostra Aetate* on the relationship of the church with the Jewish people, a new major paradigm shift was set in motion, comparable in effect to the Copernican Revolution.

Pope John XXIII, who summoned the Second Vatican Council, set this shift in motion. *Nostra Aetate*, officially promulgated by Pope Paul VI on October 28, 1965, dealt with relations between the church and non-Christian religions. Paragraph 4 focused on the bond that ties Christians to the Jewish people. This new perception comprises the paradigm shift. It evoked a new interest on the part of the church for Jewish exegesis of the biblical texts and scholarly dialogue with Jews. The Bat Kol Institute in Jerusalem is an offshoot of *Nostra Aetate*. It is a place where Christians come to study the Word of God within its Jewish milieu. Face-to-face encounter between Christians and Jews raises questions that open unto new horizons.

"You will know them by their fruits. Are grapes gathered from thorns, or figs from thistles?" (Matt 7:16). These words of Jesus come to mind when we reflect on the history of anti-Semitism in the church and the church's vilification of Jews throughout the ages.[1] But an about-turn, likened to the Copernican Revolution, happened at the Second

Vatican Council with the publication and promulgation of paragraph 4 of *Nostra Aetate*[2] on the relationship of the church with the Jewish people. John T. Pawlikowski wrote:

> *Nostra Aetate*...represents one of the most decided shifts in Catholic thinking emerging from the Council....In making their argument for a total reversal in Catholic thinking on Jews and Judaism, the bishops of the Council bypassed almost all the teachings about Jews and Judaism in Christian thought prior to Vatican II and returned to chapters 9—11 of Paul's Letter to the Romans where the Apostle reaffirms the continued inclusion of the Jews in the covenant after the coming of Christ even though this remains for him a "mystery" that defies complete theological explanation. In one sense, the bishops in *Nostra Aetate* were picking up where St. Paul left off in the first century.[3]

An Ecclesial Copernican Revolution. Four major themes are emphasized in *Nostra Aetate*, paragraph 4 (1965), and the three major documents—*Guidelines* (1975), *Notes* (1985), and *The Jewish People and Their Scriptures* (2002)[4]—that interpret it. These themes are:

1. "The covenant with the Jewish people has never been revoked" (*Notes* '85, I.3). This quote is based on Romans 11:29 ("For the gifts and the calling of God are irrevocable"). *Nostra Aetate* is the first official Catholic document to make this statement. It signals a "hermeneutic of rupture"[5] in a long line of teaching, particularly evident when compared with such facts as the following:

    In the cathedral in Strasbourg (built between 1176 and 1439), two statues greet the visitor, one symbolizing the church; the other, the synagogue. The triumphant church is portrayed as a beautiful woman wearing a royal robe with a crown on her head. In her right hand is a staff; and in her left, a chalice. The synagogue is portrayed as a defeated woman, her head is bowed, her staff broken, her eyes blindfolded, and the Torah is slipping from her hands.

    In the wood carving on the benches of Erfurt Cathedral in Thuringia, Germany (most of which dates from the fourteenth and fifteenth centuries), Ecclesia, the church, is riding on a horse and is attacking the synagogue with a lance. Her shield carries the Christian symbol of a fish. The synagogue is riding a pig and she is blindfolded.

In the church window of St. John's Church in Werben/Elbe River, Germany (around 1414–67), the left section of the window depicts the church riding a tetramorph (a creature with the heads of eagle, human, lion, and bull, symbolizing the four Gospels). She holds the staff of the cross and the chalice in her hands. The divine hand from heaven places a crown on her head. The right section depicts the synagogue as riding a donkey about to collapse. In her right hand she holds the head of a he-goat. Her crown is falling. She is blindfolded. The staff of her flag is broken. The hand of God holding a sword pierces her head in divine judgment.

2. Because of the unique relations that exist between Christianity and Judaism, "linked together at the very level of their identity...the Jews and Judaism should not occupy an occasional and marginal place in catechesis: their presence there is essential and should be organically integrated" (*Notes* '85, I.2).

Compared with past statements that expressed separation from Judaism, the links with Judaism are now stressed. One of many examples of the move toward separation of Christianity from Judaism was the fixing of the date of Easter. The date of the separation of Easter from the Jewish Passover took place during the First Ecumenical Council of Nicaea (325). An account of this event is given in the *Life of Constantine* by Bishop Eusebius of Caesarea (AD 263–339):

> It was...declared improper to follow the custom of the Jews in the celebration of this holy festival, because, their hands having been stained with crime, the minds of these wretched men are necessarily blinded....Let us, then, have nothing in common with the Jews, who are our adversaries...avoiding all contact with that evil way...who, after having compassed the death of the

> Lord, being out of their minds, are guided not by sound reason, but by an unrestrained passion, wherever their innate madness carries them...a people so utterly depraved.... Therefore, this irregularity must be corrected, in order that we may no more have any thing in common with those parricides and the murderers of our Lord...no single point in common with the perjury of the Jews.[6]

3. "Jesus was and always remained a Jew; his ministry was deliberately limited 'to the lost sheep of the house of Israel'" (*Notes* '85, III.20). The Jewishness of Jesus is emphasized. Today, if Jesus were alive and living outside Israel and applied for *aliya* (immigration), he would qualify not only because of his teachings as portrayed in the Synoptic Gospels but also because he was born of a Jewish mother. The new teaching elaborates on his Jewishness:

> [Jesus] was circumcised and presented in the Temple like any Jew of his time (Lk 2.21, 22–24), he was trained in the Law's observance. He extolled respect for it (Mt. 5.17–20) and invited obedience to it (Mt. 8.4). The rhythm of his life was marked by observance of pilgrimages on great feasts, even from infancy (Lk 2.41–50; Jn. 2.13—7.10, etc.). The importance of the cycle of the Jewish feasts has been frequently underlined in the gospel of John (2.13; 5.1; 7.2, 10, 37; 10.22; 12.1; 13.1; 18.28; 19.42; etc.)[7]

4. Recognition of the connection of the Jewish people with the Land. The Vatican *Notes* '85, VI.33 affirmed "the existence of the State of Israel" on the basis of "the common principles of international law." On December 30, 1993, the Vatican recognized the State of Israel, thus reversing its former position as expressed by Pope Pius X, who on January 25, 1904, told Theodore Herzl, who sought the Vatican's support for the State of Israel, "The Jews have not recognized our Lord, therefore we cannot recognize the Jewish people."[8]

Despite the scornful judgment of Pius X, Theodore Herzl did not give up. In late January 1904, after the sixth

Zionist Congress (August 1903) and six months before his death on July 3, he traveled to Rome and crossed the Tiber to the Vatican. Herzl first met the Secretary of State, Cardinal Merry del Val on January 22. According to Herzl's diary, the Cardinal said that "the history of Israel is our own history, it is our foundation. But in order that we should come out for the Jewish people in the way that you desire, they should first have to accept conversion." Three days later, Herzl met Pope Pius X (on January 25—a public holiday in Rome celebrating the Conversion of St. Paul!). Again from Herzl's diary: the Pope replied to Herzl's outline of the Jewish Return: "We are unable to favor this movement. We cannot prevent the Jews going to Jerusalem, but we could never sanction it....The Jews have not recognized our Lord, therefore we cannot recognize the Jewish people."[9]

The words of Pius X are relevant:

> No homeland for the Jewish people: Shortly after the 1897 Basle Conference, the semi-official Vatican periodical (edited by the Jesuits) *Civiltà Cattolica* gave its *biblical-theological* judgement on political Zionism: "1827 years have passed since the prediction of Jesus of Nazareth was fulfilled...that [after the destruction of Jerusalem] the Jews would be led away to be slaves among all the nations and that they would remain in the dispersion [diaspora, *galut*] until the end of the world." The Jews should not be permitted to return to Palestine with sovereignty: "According to the Sacred Scriptures, the Jewish people must always live dispersed and *vagabondo* [vagrant, wandering] among the other nations, so that they may render witness to Christ not only by the Scriptures...but *by their very existence.*"[10]

A Paradigm Shift. Nostra Aetate created a major paradigm shift that affects all of church teaching. *Nostra Aetate* is not in continuity with church teaching, as some insist on saying, but rather it is a radical break with its teaching on Jews and Judaism.[11]

What do we mean by paradigm and paradigm shift? A paradigm is simply the predominant worldview in the realm of human thought. A paradigm shift occurs when a current worldview, a thought system, is transformed into another. A major paradigm shift occurred when Copernicus (ca. 1600) discovered that astral bodies did not revolve around the earth, but the earth revolved around the sun. With that discovery, the earth and all those who dwelt upon it were shifted from center stage in the universe to the periphery, something that created a major crisis in human identity. Who was man? Who was woman? These questions struck terror in the hearts of many, who dealt with their fear by either denying the truth of the discovery or ignoring it.

Before the promulgation of *Nostra Aetate*, Christianity was presented as the new or the true Israel (*verus Israel*) that had superseded carnal Israel, the old Israel (*vetus Israel*).[12] As a result, *verus Israel* was inherently also *versus Israel*, i.e., anti-Jewish.[13] Now suppose that *Nostra Aetate* reverses this. Israel is back in the center and the church is on the periphery. Could St. Paul have envisaged such a system when he cautioned the church to recall that its members were wild olive branches grafted unto the olive tree of Judaism and to "remember that it is not you who supports the root, but the root supports you" (Rom 11:18)? Is this what the church is saying when it writes, "The Jews and Judaism should not occupy an occasional and marginal place in catechesis" but are central to its teaching (*Notes* '85, I.2)? Should the church not consider that if Jews and Judaism take on an importance for the church, then Jesus, too, "who was and always remained a Jew" (*Notes* '85, III.20) is there with them, not diminished but enhanced?

The Return of the Prodigal Son. Angelo Roncalli was elected Pope John XXIII on October 20, 1958. On March 21, 1959, only two months after announcing that a great council would be held, he ordered the removal of the word *perfidus* from the Good Friday prayer for the Jews. The next year, he greeted a delegation of American Jews with the biblical words, "I am Joseph your brother." He felt at home with his Jewish brothers and sisters. His comfort level with the Jews was an invitation to the whole church to follow suit.

Homecoming can be demanding. The homecoming of the church can be particularly demanding. Years of teaching rooted in a deficient and negative assessment of Judaism is not easily overturned. It could take years to reinterpret sacred texts and rethink Christian identity in order to rid the church of its bias against Jews and Judaism. The path home requires a commitment to Jewish studies and scholarly dialogue with Jews. Catholic documents, beginning with *Nostra Aetate*, lay particular stress upon study: "The Church, therefore, cannot forget that she received the revelation of the Old Testament through the people with whom God in His inexpressible mercy concluded the ancient Covenant. Nor can she forget that she draws sustenance from the root of that well-cultivated olive tree unto which have been grafted the wild shoots, the Gentiles" (*Nostra Aetate*).

Ten years after *Nostra Aetate*, *Guidelines '75* was published, emphasizing that "christians must therefore strive to acquire a better knowledge of the basic components of the religious tradition of Judaism; they must strive to learn by what essential traits Jews define themselves in the light of their own religious experience."

In another ten years, *Notes '85* was published, which stated, "Because of the unique relations that exist between Christianity and Judaism—linked together at the very level of their identity...—the Jews and Judaism should not occupy an occasional and marginal place in catechesis: their presence there is essential and should be organically integrated...with due awareness of the faith and religious life of the Jewish people *as they are professed and practiced still today*" (*Notes '85*, I.2, 3).

The Bat Kol Institute. The Bat Kol Institute is a daughter of *Nostra Aetate*. Founded on April 8, 1983, with headquarters in Jerusalem, it defines itself as "Christians studying the Word of God within its Jewish milieu, using Jewish sources." While the majority of its professors are Jewish with expertise in rabbinic, midrashic, and modern interpretations of Tanach, Christian professors of theology and Jewish studies are essential members of the staff.

What happens during the Bat Kol sessions is not just the development of a new positive understanding of the relationship between the church and the Jewish people, but a real homecoming experience in which participants encounter anew the God of Israel whose identity is not frozen in the pages of the Tanach (the Old Testament). The Tanach is a first record of Israel's encounter with God. Through continued interpretation of past and present encounters with God, understanding of God deepens and further encounter with God is facilitated.

Encounters with God are followed by interpretation. The Jewish dialectical method of interpretation broadens horizons for "seeing." It is a method, evident in the Talmud, by which opposing views are accepted and examined for aspects of truth in both. Examples of this are the discussions over the years between the Schools of Rabbi Ishmael and Rabbi Akiva on whether or not direct encounter with God is possible. According to the School of Rabbi Ishmael, direct encounter with God is *not* possible:

> To cleave to God! How is it possible "to cleave to God"? How is it possible to rise heavenward and to cleave to fire? Does not Scripture say, "the Lord your God is a consuming fire" (Deut. 4:24)? and "His throne was fiery flames"? (Daniel 7:9). It can only mean that we are commanded to cleave to the sages and their disciples. We are commanded to walk in God's ways: "After the Lord your God you shall walk" (Deut. 13:5). "The Holy and Blessed One said, 'If you fulfill my commandments you will become like Me.'"

The School of Rabbi Akiva, on the other hand, holds that direct encounter with God *is* a reality. It is possible

> to personally cleave to God with one's whole heart and soul, as do two lovers. The cleavage may be compared to two dates that are attached one to the other. "Blessed is the one who trusts in God and whose trust God is" (Jer 17:7). "My soul thirsts for God" (Ps. 42:3).[14]

The goal of interpretation and reinterpretation is revelation:

> Where necessary, we must clarify or correct our speech with other persons, reinterpret our sacred texts and traditional formulations, and adjust ourselves to what is being said to us in the present or formulated by writings of the past. We do all this for God's sake, for our words provide living habitations for Divinity in the world.[15]

The Jewish dialectical method of interpretation encourages participants to look anew at their own religious beliefs. Conscious that traditions may mask our thoughts and that glib pieties provide hiding places for courageous searching for truth, some dare to reexamine their own

New Testament texts: for example, Jesus as the only way to the Father (John 14:6 and 1 Tim 2:5–6), the parables attributed to Jesus with an anti-Jewish bias, such as the vineyard leased to tenants (Matt 21:33–43), and the anti-Jewish bias in the Passion narratives.

Besides reinterpreting texts, those engaged in dialogue with Jewish tradition and religious scholars find themselves in a rich garden of delights. Millennia of encounter with God and continued interpretations of these encounters open new vistas within the Godhead. A major insight into the God of Israel began with Moses's encounter with God at the burning bush and became a basis for understanding God. But Israel's encounter with God did not stop there. Continued encounters with God until today have led modern Jewish scholars to express the way of encounter with new words and new expressions. For example, Fishbane observes, "At certain unexpected moments we see what we have never seen before; we understand in a new way; we catch a glimpse that the 'merely other' of everydayness is grounded in an Other of more exceeding depths and heights."[16]

Applicants to Bat Kol come to Jerusalem to study books of the Bible: for example, the Five Books of Moses with Talmudic, Midrashic, Hassidic, feminist interpretations; the beauty and complexity of the psalms for today's audiences; the meaning of *teshuvah* (repentance), a concept that has been a central aspect of Jewish theology for two millennia. Scholarly and religiously inclined students appreciate the challenge of having their minds stretched. One participant wrote, "I learned to appreciate Torah from Jewish instructors, using Jewish methods of interpretation, within a Jewish cultural context. Although I had been an academic biblical scholar specializing in Christian Origins for many years and thought I knew quite a lot about the bible, I realized that I had missed a huge dimension of biblical understanding—the "fifth gospel" of the land of Israel, and the rich heritage of Jewish scripture study. The knowledge, methods, and perspectives I've learned at Bat Kol have affected every biblical studies course I have taught in the past several years. I've also used Bat Kol methods and materials in church-based Bible studies, both formal and informal, to the great appreciation of the participants—some of whom have gone out and bought their own Jewish study Bibles" (*Bat Kol Newsletter*, October 2012).[17]

Along with specific times of intense study of the Jewish sources, students continue the study of their own tradition. The Church, with new insights, encourages them to look anew at the Christian Scriptures:

> The Gospels are the outcome of long and complicated editorial work....The sacred authors wrote the four Gospels, selecting some things from the many which had been handed on by word of mouth or in writing, reducing some of them to a synthesis, explicating some things in view of the situation of their Churches....Hence, it cannot be ruled out that some references hostile or less than favorable to the Jews have their historical context in conflicts between the nascent Church and the Jewish community. Certain controversies reflect Christian-Jewish relations after the time of Jesus. (*Notes* '85, 29a)

One of the most challenging statements to come out of the church's teaching is its insistence on the Jewishness of Jesus: "Jesus was and always remained a Jew; his ministry was deliberately limited 'to the lost sheep of the house of Israel'" (*Notes* '85, III.20). Such a statement raises questions, not least of which is the question of the "newness" of Jesus.

Some question whether students should be exposed to dialogue with Judaism. The answer of most is a resounding "Yes." They admit that the new questions have shaken them up but lifted them out of their lethargy and their fixed ways of thinking and, thus, put new life into old wineskins.

Notes

1. Jeremy Cohn, *Christ Killers: The Jews and the Passion from the Bible to the Big Screen* (Oxford: Oxford University Press, 2007).

2. Vatican II documents are often referred to by the first words in the official Latin text. *Nostra Aetate* translates "in our time." The sixteen documents of the Second Vatican Council can be found at http://www.ewtn.com/library/councils/v2all.htm.

3. John T. Pawlikowski, "The Search for a New Paradigm for the Christian-Jewish Relationship: A Response to Michael Signer," in *Reinterpreting Revelation and Tradition: Jews and Christians in Conversation*, ed. John T. Pawlikowski and Hayim Goren Perelmuter (Franklin, WI: Sheed & Ward, 2000), 25–48, at 25.

4. The full titles of these documents are the following: "Guidelines and Suggestions for Implementing the Conciliar Declaration *Nostra Aetate*, No. 4 (1975)"; "Notes on the Correct Way to Present the Jews and Judaism in Preaching and Catechesis of the Roman Catholic Church (1985)"; and "The Jewish People and their Sacred Scriptures in the Christian Bible (2002)." They can be found by typing their titles into Google.

5. Others prefer to use the word *reform* rather than *rupture*. But is not a total reversal in Catholic thinking on Jews and Judaism more in line with rupture than with reform?

6. Eusebius, *Life of Constantine*, vol. 3, chap. 18.

7. *Notes* '85, III.20.

8. http://www.christusrex.org/www1/ofm/mag/MAen9901.html.

9. http://www.christusrex.org/www1/ofm/mag/MAen9901.html.

10. Quoted in David Creamer, SJ, "*Nostra Aetate*: Building Bridges of Friendship and Cooperation over Forty Years," *Perspective: A Semiannual Journal of Ignatian Thought* 8, no. 1 (2005).

11. "Map for the Journey of Faith," in *The Tablet: International Catholic Weekly*, 6 October 2012, 2.

12. *Nostra Aetate* states that the church is the new people of God (*Ecclesia...novus populus Dei*), but not that it is the new Israel.

13. On the history of Christian anti-Judaism, see, for example, Edward H. Flannery, *The Anguish of the Jews: Twenty-Three Centuries of Antisemitism. Revised and Updated* (New York/Mahwah: Stimulus, 1995); James Carroll, *Constantine's Sword: The Church and the Jews. A History* (Boston/New York: Houghton Mifflin, 2001); Robert Michael, *A History of Catholic Antisemitism: The Dark Side of the Church* (Palgrave Macmillan, 2008); and also chapter 2 in Paul O'Shea, *A Cross Too Heavy: Pope Pius XII and the Jews of Europe* (New York: Palgrave Macmillan, 2011), 27–51.

14. Abraham Heschel, *Heavenly Torah: As Refracted through the Generations* (London: Bloomsbury Academic, 2010), 193–95.

15. Michael Fishbane, *Sacred Attunement: A Jewish Theology* (The University of Chicago Press, 2008), 42–43.

16. Ibid., 35.

17. http://www.batkol.info/?page_id=474.

JEWISH-CHRISTIAN DIALOGUE IN ISRAEL TODAY
When Jews Are the Majority

DAVID M. NEUHAUS, SJ

Much of the work on Jewish-Christian dialogue has been based upon the experience of a Jewish minority living in the midst of a Christian majority, the predominant reality in Europe and North America, where Jewish-Christian dialogue is most developed. This fundamental encounter has given birth to a particular discourse that is dominant in the praxis and analysis of Jewish-Christian dialogue since the middle of the twentieth century. But what happens in Israel today when Christians are a small minority and are invited to dialogue with Jews who constitute the dominant majority in society? What might need to change in perspective, in focus, and in formulation within the context of the Jewish-Christian dialogue in Israel?

INTRODUCTION

One of the most impressive revolutions of the twentieth century was the one that changed the face of Jewish-Christian relations in Europe and North America. Long centuries of shared history were often marked by traumatic interactions: small Jewish minorities living in predominantly Christian countries were often marginalized, discriminated against, and even actively persecuted. The twentieth century saw anti-Jewish sentiment reach a pinnacle in the Nazi attempt to carry out the programmatic extermination of all Jews in Europe. Not only did the Nazis fail to carry out their plan, but instead the Shoah, as the genocidal program of the Nazis became known, provoked a wakeup call as the Christian churches conducted a profound examination of conscience and called on Christians to purify themselves of all anti-Jewish sentiment, to become aware of the Jewish roots of Christianity, and to work with Jews in building a better world.

Over the past sixty years, Jewish-Christian dialogue in Europe and North America has brought Jews and Christians ever closer together, as Jews and Christians recognize each other more and more as close allies in an increasingly secular world, defending together values rooted in their common heritage and working for a society founded on a shared ethical system. In addition, both Jews and Christians today recognize the essential contributions made by Christianity and by Judaism to the civilization that has come to be identified as Judeo-Christian, a society rooted in the shared Scriptures of Israel and Christianity. Today, a diversity of Jews encounter a diversity of Christians in order to discuss beliefs and theology, study their shared history together, and work alongside one another in order to build a better world. Not all misunderstanding has disappeared, but there is a palpable positive change in the way Jews and Christians relate to one another.[1]

The Shoah is not the only foundational element of Jewish-Christian dialogue in the modern age. Many Jews identify today with a national state—the State of Israel. The establishment of the State of Israel in 1948 led to a further shift in relations as many Jews immigrated to Israel, making the Jewish population of Israel one of the largest in the world. For the first time in the history of Christianity, Jews constitute a majority in one country in the world—a country that is intimately linked with both Jewish and Christian origins. Israel has become a central element in the dialogue between Jews and Christians on a number of different levels: theological, political, and historical.

This chapter will focus on relations between Jews and Christians in Israel rather than on Europe and North America, which have been at the center of the revolution in relations.

JEWS IN ISRAEL

The Jews, their faith and civilization, originated in the Middle East.[2] In this area, many centuries later, a Jew named Jesus called his fellow Jews to believe in him as Messiah and Savior, and his disciples formed a new community made up of both Jews and believers from the nations. Judaism and Christianity are thus Middle Eastern religions in their origins, although over the centuries these two faith communities became more and more situated in Europe. In the seventh century this area was conquered by Muslim armies, and soon after, Jews and Christians in the region became minorities living within an Arabic-speaking, Muslim majority, and were ruled for most of the period until 1948 by Muslim governors.[3] Two interludes in Muslim rule were the period of the Crusades (1096–1299) and the period of the British Mandate (1918–48), when Christian-dominated governments ruled the area.

Jews have always been an integral part of the Middle Eastern world. Like their Christian compatriots, many Jews in this Muslim world, while remaining faithful to the religion of their ancestors, adopted Arabic as their language and culture and contributed to the development of Arab civilization. There were vibrant Jewish-Arab communities in many Arab countries until 1948, including Iraq, Syria, Lebanon, Palestine, Egypt, Libya, Tunisia, Algeria, Morocco, and Yemen. There were also vibrant Jewish communities in the non-Arab Muslim world, most importantly in Turkey and in Iran. The year 1948, which saw the establishment of the State of Israel and the beginning of a series of wars between the new state and the surrounding Arab countries, also saw the rapid decline of the Jewish communities in the other countries of the Muslim world, where today sizeable Jewish communities exist only in Turkey, Iran, Morocco, and Tunisia.[4]

Today, one of the largest concentrations of Jews in the world is to be found in Israel.[5] After the establishment of the State of Israel in 1948, millions of Jews immigrated to Israel from the West and from the East. Jews in Israel are very heterogeneous. There are believing, practicing Jews and nonbelieving, nonpracticing Jews and many varieties in between. Well known is the division among ultra-Orthodox, modern Orthodox, traditional, Conservative, Reform, and Reconstructionist Jews. As important for understanding Jewish life in Israel are the diverse cultural backgrounds of the Jewish communities in Israel that originate in Western and Eastern Europe, West Asia and North Africa, North America, Latin America, and so on. A helpful distinction with regard to our subject is the distinction between Jews that come from the countries historically dominated by Christendom and those that come from the Muslim world. However, each community has its own history that shapes attitudes toward Christians and Christianity. The enormous diversity of the Jewish population in Israel is still apparent in a society in which more than half the Jews were born in other lands and migrated to Israel. Israel has been dominated politically, socially, culturally, and politically by elites whose roots are in Europe, particularly in Eastern Europe.

Jewish Israeli society is young and still in formation, and this does not always facilitate relations with those defined as outsiders. Close to 20 percent of the population of the State of Israel is made up of Muslims, Christians, and Druze, the majority of whom are Palestinian Arabs. It is also important to be aware at the outset that the historical context of European anti-Semitism and its culmination in the Shoah is formative for and remains at the forefront of the attitudes of many Jewish Israelis toward Christians.[6]

This chapter will thus focus almost exclusively on the relationship between Jews and Christians from the perspective of the reality in Israel, the dominant reality in the area of West Asia.

RELATIONS BETWEEN JEWS AND CHRISTIANS IN ISRAEL[7]

A large proportion of the world's Jewish population today resides in the State of Israel. Christians in Israel are a tiny statistical minority, officially less than 2 percent of the general population. They are also far from homogeneous; they include Orthodox (Greek, Russian, Romanian, and so forth), Catholic (Eastern and Latin Catholics), Eastern non-Chalcedonians (Syrian and Coptic Orthodox), and Protestants (Anglican, Lutheran, Evangelicals, and so on). This confessional complexity comprises only one level of diversity. Another level is the different origins of the Christians in Israel: indigenous, generally Arabic-speaking Christians (80 percent of Israeli Christians are Palestinian Arabs), Christians, generally foreign born, who are integrated within Jewish Hebrew-speaking society, and newer populations of migrants (foreign workers and asylum seekers). What are the relations between Jews and Christians in this area? In much of what follows, we will focus on the established churches composed of Arab

Christians, as they are the most vocal and visible of the Christian populations in the area.

Perspectives on indigenous Christian-Jewish relations in Israel must
be clearly distinguished from perspectives that are current in Europe
(and North America). From the European perspective, Jews and
Christians have been in a fruitful and passionate dialogue for the past six
decades. Documents like the Catholic Church's *Nostra Aetate* (1965) and
others issued by Anglican and Protestant communities have sown a new
consciousness among Western Christians about the Jewish roots of
Christianity and the fraternal relations that Christians seek with the
Jewish people. This dialogue has been powered by two strong motors.
One is the awakened sense of contrition among Christians with regard to
the tragic fate of the Jews in Europe during periods when anti-Judaism
and anti-Semitism dominated, culminating in the catastrophe of the
Shoah. The other is the embrace of the biblical and, by extension, the
Jewish heritage of the Church, and the fact that Jesus, his disciples, and
the early Church are part of a Jewish world that has bequeathed to the
Church a rich shared heritage, most importantly the Old Testament.

The context, and thus the perspectives, in Israel are quite different
for historical, cultural, social, and political reasons. A degree of animosity toward Jews is common among Arab Christians in Israel, where
Christians are a minority and most of them are part of a society that is
overwhelmingly Muslim. Jews are not generally perceived as the victims of centuries of marginalization and even persecution but rather as
the face of a problematic political reality, the State of Israel, with the
added complexity of the continuing occupation of Palestinian lands.
Furthermore, the Old Testament, rather than being held up as "a shared
heritage," provokes concern, particularly with regard to texts about
election, promise, and land. Many Christians in Israel fear a fundamentalist exploitation of these texts in the conflict between Arabs and
Jews over Israel/Palestine.

One can enumerate five characteristics of the particular context for
indigenous Christian-Jewish relations in Israel in contrast to the
European context:

1. Non-European, non-Christian context
    Contemporary dialogue between Jews and Christians
    has focused almost exclusively on historical relations

between Jews and Christians in the lands where Christians defined the culture, society, and power relations. In relation to these lands, Christians have realized that certain modalities of thought, action, and political practice marginalized and even excluded Jews (and other non-Christians), often accusing them of being outsiders because they did not share the Christian faith of their compatriots and adhered to religious practices foreign to Christianity. However, Israeli society and politics are predominantly formed by Jewish history, culture, and tradition. This means that indigenous Christians do not perceive many of the themes and emphases of the predominantly European and North American Jewish-Christian dialogue as directly relevant in the Israeli context.

2. The presence of Islam

Islam is the dominant religion in Arab society, and Muslims are the majority among the Arabs in Israel. Thus, for Christians, dialogue with Muslims is a priority in a way that is not self-evident in interreligious dialogue in Europe and North America. When dialogue with Jews exists at all, it almost always becomes a trialogue within the Israeli context because Muslims cannot be ignored. Within this context, it is important to note that in Israel/Palestine, Christian and Muslim Arabs, whatever their religious differences might be, live in a common society, speak one language, share one culture, and experience one sociopolitical reality. Whereas before 1948 Jewish Arabs were part of this milieu, most Jews in Israel are not fluent in the Arabic language and do not integrate into Arab society, culture, and tradition.[8]

Before 1948 there were important Jewish communities in the Arab world that lived profoundly embedded in the Muslim, Arabic-speaking world of West Asia (such as in Iraq, Lebanon, and Syria). Especially in modern times, Jews and Christians in these countries interacted in a variety of different domains, sometimes collaborating in political, social, and cultural spheres as members of non-Muslim minorities. Contemporary interreligious dialogue in Israel might hopefully reawaken an awareness of the Jewish presence in the area before the Israel-Palestine conflict, a time before the abyss between Jew and Arab, when some Jews were Arabs. The 2000 Synod of the Catholic Church in the Holy Land concluded that "in our countries, Muslims, Christians and Jews have lived together in fruitful social and cultural interaction, this being evident in the clear traces we find of this interaction in Arab civilization."[9] These traces include the contributions of prominent Jewish figures within Arab culture, whether in the medieval period (among the developers of Arabic language, thought, and science were Jews who worked alongside Muslims and Christians) or in modern times (there were also Jews among the writers, poets, musicians, journalists, film makers, political and trade union activists).[10]

Today, however, whereas relations with Muslims are fundamental to the Christians in Israel, actual, lived relations with Jews are often limited to the workplace, the market, law enforcement, and bureaucracy. This strongly affects the vision of relations with Jews and Judaism. What is still in its infancy is an overall understanding of how these two essential relationships—with Jews and with Muslims—can be coherently presented so that local Christians can be both faithful to the Jewish roots of the Church and participate in the rich dialogue with the Jewish people as well as engage in an absolutely essential dialogue with Muslims, with whom Arab Christians share a world.

3. The reversal of power relations

Many contemporary European and North American Christians, profoundly cognizant of their context, are sensitive to the marginalized and vulnerable status of the Jews in the history of the West. However, the Christians in Israel reflect on Christian-Jewish relations from the experience of the sovereignty of a powerful Jewish polity. Never before in history have Christians experienced Jewish sovereignty (this having been established for the first time in the

Christian era in 1948 with the creation of the State of Israel). For many indigenous Christians, the Jew is often first and foremost a soldier, a policeman, or a settler. Whereas European Christians, strongly influenced by the history of anti-Judaism and anti-Semitism, engage with Jews as a minority, marginalized and often traumatized, Christians in Israel are in a situation in which power relations are reversed. They do not feel responsible for the fate of Jews in Europe; on the contrary, they sense that they themselves are the victims of this history.[11]

4. The Israel-Palestine conflict as definitive

Whereas from the Western perspective, the watershed in Christian-Jewish relations was the Shoah, which provoked an awakening to a certain teaching of contempt for Jews in Christian circles, from the perspective of Christians in Israel, the question of Palestine is at the center of relations with Jews. Whereas dialogue from the European perspective often includes a focus on the struggle against anti-Judaism and anti-Semitism, within the Middle East context the focus on justice and peace is an essential element of any prospective dialogue between Catholics and Jews.

Furthermore, certain Christian-leading spokespeople have expressed explicit concerns that a predominantly spiritual-theological discourse on Jews and Judaism ignores the burning issue of justice and peace and the conflict between Jews and Arabs, Israelis and Palestinians.[12] The established Christian churches continually affirm their commitment to justice and peace, a commitment that provokes tension with Jews, insistent on recognition and even support for Israel as a Jewish state. Deep fissures mark many church communions as various, often opposing, tendencies emerge with regard to dialogue with Jews and questions of justice and peace in Israel/Palestine.

5. The place of the Bible

The shared biblical heritage is a fundamental principle in the Catholic-Jewish dialogue that has flourished since Vatican II. Within the context of the State of Israel, however, the experience of this shared heritage is not without its ambiguities.[13] The Bible has been used as a foundational text when it comes to establishing a contemporary Jewish claim to the land that Palestinians see as theirs. Zionism, the ideology of Jewish nationalism, often interprets the Bible as a legal, historical, or even divinely revealed title deed to the land. Texts in the Old Testament have too often been mobilized by political forces in order to legitimate control of territories and establish political rights. Furthermore, linking the modern State of Israel with the biblical Israel (as some Jews and Western Christian groups insist on doing) makes it even more difficult for the Christians in the Holy Land to read the Old Testament and appreciate the "shared heritage" of Christians and Jews because it would seem to promote a denial of the rights of Palestinians. For many, the use of the Bible to dispossess Palestinians and legitimate injustice is a major problem.

The Roman Catholic Holy See's Commission for Religious Relations with the Jews forcefully stated in 1985, "The existence of the State of Israel and its political options should be envisaged not in a perspective which is itself religious but in their reference to the common principles of international law."[14] An important, ongoing theological project is the rereading of the Bible, and in particular the Old Testament, within the context of contemporary Israel/Palestine with particular attention to the election of a people by God and the giving of the land to them. What does this mean for the Church today within the real context of the Israel/Palestine conflict?

Whereas Christians and Jews meet often in Europe and North America, the present political situation in Israel-Palestine does not facilitate dialogue between Jews (who are dominant in Israel) and Christians (the majority of whom are Palestinian Arab but who are minorities in both Israel and in Palestine).

PROSPECTS FOR DIALOGUE BETWEEN CHRISTIANS AND JEWS IN ISRAEL

In conclusion, little dialogue exists between indigenous Jews and Christians in Israel. Where dialogue does exist, it focuses less on theological, spiritual, and religious issues than it does on the conflict between Jews and Palestinians and the attempt to find solutions that might guarantee justice and peace as well as democracy and human rights. Jews and Christians do collaborate on these issues when their political positions coincide. The rich dialogue between Jews and Christians that has developed in the West has hardly any echo in Israel. Justice and peace, when they come, will perhaps reestablish a dialogue between Jews and Christians that will broaden perspectives beyond the European and North American arena. This dialogue will need to be open particularly to Muslims and the long centuries of shared history in the Arab world.

It would be wrong to conclude this chapter without mentioning the development of a new Christian, non-Arab population in Israel today.[15] Alongside the rooted Arabic-speaking Christians of the land, many of whom have emigrated from the Holy Land because of the difficult circumstances in the region, there is a steady immigration of non-Arab Christians into Israel. Many of these Christians are connected by family ties to Jews and have become Israeli citizens (mostly from the countries of the ex-Soviet Union), others migrate to Israel seeking work (large populations of East Asians, predominantly Filipinos, Thais, Chinese, and Indians) or political asylum (predominantly Africans). They constitute a new face of the Church in Israel. Their lives, integrated as they are in the Jewish population, open up new perspectives for a dialogue between a Christian minority living at the heart of Jewish society, adapted to this society's culture and language. These new Christians are yet to be fully integrated into the existing churches and develop their own perspectives on the dialogue with Jews, but it will undoubtedly be a fascinating and new outlook on Jewish-Christian dialogue.

Notes

1. For an analysis of contemporary Western dialogue with particular reference to the Catholic Church, see David Neuhaus, "Achievements and Challenges in Jewish-Christian Dialogue: Forty Years after *Nostra Aetate*," *The Downside Review* 439 (April 2007): 111–29; Neuhaus, "Engaging the Jewish People—Forty Years since *Nostra Aetate*," in *Catholic Engagement with World Religions: A Comprehensive Study*, ed. Karl Becker and Ilaria Morali (Maryknoll, NY: Orbis Books, 2010), 395–413.

2. In the biblical narrative, the sphere of Israel's origins is between Mesopotamia and Egypt. Abraham, father of Israel, left his home in Ur of the Chaldeans and centuries later Moses led the nascent people out of Egypt. Guided by God, both Abraham and Moses made their way to the land that is known today as Israel or Palestine.

3. Islam is part of the Jewish-Christian world in discourse, practice, and imagination. The Qur'an, foundational text of the Muslim community, takes for granted the Old Testament and the New.

4. A rapidly shrinking Jewish community of a few hundred still clings to its ancient home in Yemen, but the Jewish communities of Iraq, Egypt, Libya, Algeria, Syria, and Lebanon have all but disappeared.

5. There is a current debate among demographers and statisticians about where the largest Jewish population resides, in Israel or in the United States. At the core of the debate is the complex question, who is a Jew?

6. See David Neuhaus, "Jewish Israeli Attitudes towards Christianity and Christians in Contemporary Israel," in *World Christianity: Politics, Theology, Dialogues*, ed. A. Mahoney and M. Kirwan (London: Melisende, 2004), 347–69.

7. See, for particular focus on Jewish-Christian dialogue, Jamal Khader and David Neuhaus, "A Holy Land Context for *Nostra Aetate*," *Studies in Jewish Christian Relations* 1 (2005–6), 67–88; David Neuhaus, "Catholic-Jewish Relations in the State of Israel: Theological Perspectives," in *The Catholic Church in the Contemporary Middle East*, ed. Anthony Mahoney and John Flannery (London: Melisende, 2010), 237–51.

8. The rich Judeo-Arabic culture, which was very much at home in the Muslim-Arab world, has all but disappeared even among those Jewish migrants to Israel. Israel consciously identifies itself with the European-North American cultural orbit rather than with the world of her immediate neighbors.

9. Assembly of the Catholic Ordinaries in the Holy Land, *The General Pastoral Plan* (Jerusalem, 2001), 157.

10. A remarkable study of the Jewish Arab civilization before 1948 is Ammiel Alcalay, *After Jews and Arabs: Remaking Levantine Culture* (Minneapolis: University of Minnesota Press, 1993). The Arab world of Muslims, Christians, and Jews also resonates in much of the literary works of the great Franco-Lebanese writer Amin Maalouf.

11. Among Christian theologians, church leaders, and writers it is not uncommon to find reflections on the price Palestinians have had to pay for the sins of European Christians committed against the Jews. See, for example, Elias Chacour, *Blood Brothers* (Lincoln: Chosen Books, 1984), 120–24; Naim Ateek, *Justice and Only Justice: A Palestinian Theology of Liberation* (Maryknoll, NY: Orbis Books, 1989), 18–32; Michel Sabbah, *Pastoral Letter: Pray for the Peace of Jerusalem* (Jerusalem, 1990), 17.

12. This has been clearly enunciated in the Kairos document, which can be read on the website of its sponsors: http://www. kairospalestine.ps/. This document, composed by Eastern Orthodox, Catholic, Anglican, and Protestant church leaders and laypeople, has provoked much debate in the circles involved in Jewish-Christian dialogue. Some reactions can also be found on the Kairos site.

13. Latin Catholic Patriarch of Jerusalem Michel Sabbah composed an important pastoral letter on this theme: *Reading the Bible Today in the Land of the Bible* (Jerusalem, 1991). Other Palestinian theologians, such as Naim Ateek, Rafiq Khoury, Geries Khoury, Mitri Raheb, Viola Raheb, and Jean Zaru, have written extensively on the challenges in developing a Palestinian hermeneutic for reading the Bible. See also Alain Marchadour and David Neuhaus, *The Land, the Bible and History* (New York: Fordham University Press, 2007).

14. Commission for Religious Relations with the Jews, "Notes on the Correct Way to Present the Jews and Judaism in Preaching and Catechesis in the Roman Catholic Church" (Rome, 1985), no. VI.

15. Analysis of these little known populations in Israel can be found in David Neuhaus, "Qui est qui? Russes et juifs en Israël aujourd'hui," *Proche orient chrétien* 1–2, no. 58 (2008): 21–58; David Neuhaus; "La foi chrétienne et l'hébreu en commun," *La Terre sainte* 609 (September–October 2010), 80–281. More information can also be found on the website of the Saint James Vicariate for Hebrew Speaking Catholics in Israel: www.catholic.co.il.

CHRISTIAN-JEWISH DIALOGUE IN PALESTINE/ISRAEL

A Different Dialogue

JAMAL KHADER

PRELIMINARY NOTES

Christian-Jewish dialogue witnessed a new beginning after the end of World War II and the creation of the State of Israel. Jews had always lived in Palestine, together with Christians and Muslims. The dramatic events that took place in the Holy Land in the twentieth century shaped a different type of relations between Christian Palestinians and the Jews. With the loss of the war in 1948 by the Palestinians, and with it 78 percent of historic Palestine and the foundation of the State of Israel, the new relationship is based on conflict and bloodshed. Eighty-five percent of Christian Palestinians were forced to leave Palestine with the catastrophe of 1948. In 1967, Israel occupied the West Bank and Gaza Strip, so all the Palestinians live now under occupation or in the Diaspora (except for Palestinians who live as citizens in the State of Israel).

For the Palestinians, Jews are now the Zionists of the State of Israel who occupied our land and control our lives with a military occupation. Christian Palestinians joined the national struggle for the liberation of Palestine, with the PLO or within the civil society and especially within education. Christian reflection and theology were heavily influenced by their context, a context of oppression and occupation. Modern theological concepts, such as "the Jewish roots of our faith," "the Jewishness of

Jesus," and "the faithfulness of God to his people" seem a luxury for the Christian Palestinians' theology. In our context, we can hardly speak of a Christian-Jewish "dialogue"; we can only talk about Christian-Jewish relations within the context of the Palestinian-Israeli conflict.

Our side of the story is different from the regular discourse of the Western Christian-Jewish dialogue. Can both dialogues be complimentary and mutually enriching? Our side of the story is based on our experience; our Christian faith inspires us and guides us in our search for a better future in our country, Palestine.

Dialogue, Life Experience

When my bishop asked me in 2004 to join the Diocesan Committee of Dialogue with Jews, I accepted without hesitation. It was a learning process for me. We met every month, and the meetings were divided into two parts: a meeting with a Jew, and subsequent discussion. The Jew might have been an Orthodox, Reform, or Conservative Jew, chosen to enrich our understanding of Judaism. After a presentation from the guest (or the host), followed by a Q&A session, the committee continued the meeting to evaluate and discuss the topics presented by the guest. There I learned about the rich diversity among Jews, who have different views about religion and its relationship with politics and coexistence. Since I lacked direct contact with Jews, those meetings taught me that dialogue is not about discussing some abstract theological issues but about the relationship among religion, the vision of the world around us, and political realities.

Those meetings showed the human face of my "enemies" and their deep commitment to their faith. But it also demonstrated the ideological use of religion to justify political options. In one of the meetings, a Haredi guest explained that "human life is not my first priority, but my Jewish identity: land, people and Bible. For my Jewish identity, I have no conscience problem in killing." That was a shock for me.

Another experience led me to the Rainbow group, a group composed of Christian and Jewish intellectuals that began to meet monthly beginning in the early 1970s. The evening began with a lecture by a Christian or a Jew, followed by discussion. I was the only Palestinian in that group, as all the Christians were Western Christians, with their Western history and Western way of thinking. That sometimes made me the center of attention when there were issues related to the Palestinian situation. When the question of what Christian Palestinians think of Jesus as a Jew was raised, I was the only candidate to answer that question. This has been another enriching experience for me.

As chairperson of the Department of Religious Studies, the dialogue with Jews is an important topic in the curriculum. We have a few courses on the Bible, including two on the Old Testament, and a course on Judaism. No Jewish teacher would be able to teach that course, as Bethlehem University is in the Palestinian Territories, and by military law no Jew is allowed to enter Palestinian Territories. We are fortunate to have Fr. David Neuhaus to teach that course. Fr. David organizes a "Jewish weekend" for the students to visit a synagogue and the Holocaust Museum and to meet with Jews. Although the process of obtaining permits from the Israeli military authorities is long, painful, and uncertain, we were lucky a few times to allow our students to experience Judaism as a living reality. The Catholic Seminary in Bethlehem has a similar course, and they take part in similar activities.

One special moment for me was the visit to Auschwitz in July 2011. We spent the whole day in that horrible place, and I learned a lot about human suffering and how humans may be inhuman with a specific race or ethnicity. The lesson was, "This should never happen again, not to Jews or to anyone!"

This Side of the Story

The Christian-Jewish dialogue has represented a very positive development in the lives of the churches for the last sixty years. Unfortunately, this dialogue was motivated by the reaction that followed the Holocaust. In the West, this dialogue takes place between a Christian majority and a Jewish minority, where the minority suffered at the hands of the majority. In our context, the dialogue is conducted between a Jewish majority and a Christian minority, where this minority suffered and still suffers because of the majority. Let us remember that Israel is still occupying Palestinian Territories, preventing the independence of Palestine. As horrible as the Holocaust was, it is not part of our history as Palestinians; we suffered indirectly from the consequences, as victims of the victims of the Holocaust.

In the West, there are certain theologians who reviewed the relationship with the Jews and the way they read the Old Testament in order to avoid supersessionism. In dealing with the promises, the chosenness, and the land, they affirm that the Jewish people are still the people of God, and that the land is the promised one for the Jewish people. In pushing those arguments, they "try to attach a biblical and theological legitimacy to the infringement of our rights."[1] Those post-Holocaust theologies were not developed against the Palestinians, but mainly by ignoring them. The voice of Palestinian theologians, and especially the recent Kairos Palestine document, have been a challenge for them. Some received that document as a theological challenge; others attacked it or just ignored it. This "other side of the story" poses serious questions to those theologies.

The Christian fundamentalists, mainly in the United States and known as the "Christian Zionists," have an eschatological theology in which Israel plays a central role. In preparing for the second coming of Christ, they support the State of Israel financially, morally, and politically as God's instrument to defeat the "anti-Christ." That theology is a dangerous one for Israel, the Palestinians, and the future of peace in the Middle East. Another danger comes from the spreading of those ideas in other parts of the world such as Africa and Europe. For that theology, the Palestinian Christians do not exist or at best face the same choice as the Muslims: to convert to their version of Christianity or face the final judgment in the final battle of Armageddon.

Those Western theologies put the Christian Palestinians in an uneasy situation in which they needed to defend themselves and develop their own theology, and they took it seriously. Many international conferences were organized by local Christian organizations to face those challenges,[2] and the theological dialogue with Western churches helped a mutual enrichment.

What remains more important is the direct dialogue with Jews. The launching of the Kairos Palestine document in December 2009 led to an occasion for dialogue with Israeli Jews. The Kairos group met with Jewish rabbis and scholars in Jerusalem at the initiative of the ICCI (Interreligious Coordinating Council in Israel) and within the International Council of Christians and Jews (ICCJ).[3] Those meetings were very useful and traced a new way to continue: a common message of local Christians and Jews to promote shared values. This message requires more work to formulate.

Reading the Old Testament

Palestinian Christians always read the Old Testament (OT); the Bible tells our story with God, or the story of God with us and his salvation. We were in Egypt, we came to the promised land, and we were unfaithful to the law of God.[4] Then the All-Merciful God sent his Word, Jesus Christ, to fulfill the promises of the prophets. In that spiritual reading, we are the people of God; Abraham, Isaac, and Jacob are our forefathers, and the blessings of God continue in Jesus Christ.

With the foundation of the State of Israel in 1948, and especially with the occupation of Palestinian Territories in 1967, we were exposed to another reading of the OT: this is the "promised land" that "God gave to us, Jews." The reality on the ground changed; the new state is called by the biblical name *Israel*, the settlements on Palestinian lands are called by biblical names as well (Shilu, Beit El, Alon Moreh, etc.), and Jerusalem is called *Yerushalaim*, city of David. Some fundamentalist groups even used passages of the Bible in which God orders the killings of the peoples in the land to justify the use of violence against the Palestinians.[5] With the religious arguments used to occupy and colonize our land, we began to ask if the Word of God legitimizes our oppression and occupation. Is it true that God gave my land to another people? Is he the same God of Jesus Christ that we experience in our faith?

In several sessions of theological dialogue, I began to realize that the way Christians read the OT is different from the Jewish way, although Jews have several readings themselves. But what complicates things is to hear Western Christians adopting the Jewish literal reading of the OT. "God gave that land to the Jewish people": that is what a Dutch Christian told me in Utrecht in 2009. "That land" means here my land. How can I accept such a reading of the Bible? The Bible is and should remain good news, a liberating word, not an oppressive one. Msgr. Michel Sabbah, Patriarch of Jerusalem for the Roman Catholic Church, summarized the questions asked by Christian Palestinians in his pastoral letter *Reading the Bible Today in the Land of the Bible*:

What is the relationship between ancient Biblical history and our contemporary history? Is Biblical Israel the same as the contemporary State of Israel? What is the meaning of the promises, the election, the Covenant and in particular the *"promise and the* gift *of the land"* to Abraham and his descendants? Does the Bible justify the present political claims? Could we be victims of our own salvation history, which seems to favor the Jewish people and condemn us? Is that truly the Will of God to which we must inexorably bow down, demanding that we deprive ourselves in favor of another people, with no possibility of appeal or discussion? (No. 7)

Some Christian Palestinians wanted to avoid reading the OT and limit the Bible to the New Testament. Msgr. Sabbah answered this clearly in *Reading the Bible:*

For the Christian, the two Testaments form a single book, containing the whole of Revelation given by God for the salvation of humankind. No part of the Old or New Testament can be separated from it for any reason, whether political or otherwise. All of Sacred Scripture is the Word of God. (No. 9)

Several theologians made significant contribution to interpret the OT in ways that take into consideration the Palestinian situation.[6] A few theologians tried to read the Bible through the Canaanites' eyes; others interpreted it in an allegoric way; others appropriated the text as the history of salvation in its link with the New Testament.

In the Pastoral Plan of the Catholic Church[7] we read,

The Sacred Scripture includes the Old Testament, which constitutes a common ground for Christians and Jews,[8] despite the essential difference in its interpretation. Christians read the Old Testament in the light of the history of salvation which finds its fulfilment in Jesus Christ, who does not abolish the Law but rather fulfils it (Mt 5:17).

The Bible is always read and interpreted in a context; our context is one of occupation and oppression. How can our reading of the Bible be a liberating one, a "Good News"? The Kairos Palestine document offers a christological reading of the OT. It states that

Our Lord Jesus Christ…came with *"a new teaching"* (Mk 1:27), casting a new light on the Old Testament, on the themes that relate to our Christian faith and our daily lives, themes such as the promises, the election, the people of God and the land.[9]

The vision of the land in the Kairos is the universal mission of this land. This universality is not the opposite of "particularity" of the land. This land is particular to us: "Our presence in this land, as Christian and Muslim Palestinians, is not accidental but rather deeply rooted in the history and geography of this land, resonant with the connectedness of any other people to the land it lives in."[10] Without making this connectedness an exclusive claim, it affirms that "our connectedness to this land is a natural right. It is not an ideological or a theological question only."[11]

On the other hand, it is the land that God chose to sanctify with his presence:

[Our land] is holy inasmuch as God is present in it, for God alone is holy and sanctifier. It is the duty of those of us who live here, to respect the will of God for this land. It is our duty to liberate it from the evil of injustice and war. It is God's land and therefore it must be a land of reconciliation, peace and love. This is indeed possible. God has put us here as two peoples, and God gives us the capacity, if we have the will, to live together and establish in it justice and peace, making it in reality God's land: *"The earth is the Lord's and all that is in it, the world, and those who live in it"* (Ps. 24:1).[12]

Quest for Justice and Peace

After a session of dialogue between Christian students of the Department of Religious Studies at Bethlehem University and Jewish students of the Department of Religions at the Hebrew University, held at the Tantur Ecumenical Institute (between Jerusalem and Bethlehem), a Jewish student said, "That was my first time that I met Palestinians who are Christians; I thought they were all Muslims."[13] A Christian Palestinian student said that it was "her first time that she meets Jews who are not soldiers neither [sic] settlers"! As sad as it sounds, that is the reality of the relations between Palestinian Christians and Jews in the Holy Land.

The local church does not reflect on this dialogue from the same starting point as its European counterparts, strongly influenced as they are by the history of anti-Judaism and anti-Semitism. Christians in the Holy Land see themselves as free of the taints of anti-Semitic practice and policy and the responsibility for the fate of European Jewry. Not only are Christians few in number in the Holy Land, but Christians live as a minority face to face with a Jewish majority (those in Israel), under Israeli military occupation (those in the occupied territories). This is an absolutely unique historical situation. Nowhere else in the world do Christians experience directly the sovereignty and power of a Jewish polity and never in history have Christians experienced Jewish sovereignty and power, these only having been reestablished in 1948 with the creation of the State of Israel.

This unique situation must inform dialogue that takes place in this land between local Christians and Jews, especially in Israel. For many of the Holy Land faithful, unfortunately, the Jew is often first and foremost a policeman, a soldier, or a settler.[14]

The Christian-Jewish dialogue in the Holy Land has a different agenda from that in Europe or the West. We cannot discuss theology as an academic exercise with no regard for the political and human situation. Therefore, the two important and interrelated topics of justice and peace are a priority in the dialogue.

Common reading of the Bible helps both sides to listen to each other and can offer mutual enrichment. Any reading has its own implications. Fundamentalists have their own reading of the Bible: a literal reading without taking the context into consideration, with a selected choice of texts. Such readings ignore sociopolitical realities and result in an injustice for the Palestinians. Their theology of the land is focused on the biblical texts of the OT and interprets the creation of the modern State of Israel as the fulfillment of the prophecies of the Bible. Applying those readings to the present situation, the Israelites of the OT become the Israelis and the Philistines, the Palestinians. Such biblical theology denies the Palestinians, including the Palestinian Christians, their national rights and causes them a big injustice in the name of the Word of God.

The reality of the ongoing struggle has a negative influence on mutual relations. Christians in this region are united in fate with their Muslim brothers and sisters, carrying on their bodies the scars of exile and forced dispersion, confiscation of land and civil discrimination, and violation of legitimate human rights.

The mutual regard between Christians and Jews in our country is defined by different historical memories. Christians in our countries look on Jews through their painful experience in the modern period (the catastrophe of 1948, occupation, and so forth). Jews, on the other hand, look on local Christians through the perspective of their traumatic experiences in the countries from which they came (such as anti-Semitism and massacres of the Jews during the Nazi period), even though the people of our countries were not party to this, or through the perspective of their attitudes toward the ongoing struggle and tensions (violence). In both cases, we are confronted with wounded memories because of injustice, oppression, violence, and wars.[15] The political struggle and the concomitant continuous tensions make sincere action for truth, justice, and peace an essential element of any true relationship.

Kairos Palestine: A New Approach to Dialogue?

When Kairos Palestine was launched in December 2009, there were many reactions, including reactions from Jewish organizations. The document was written by Christian Palestinians and its first target audience was Christian Palestinians themselves. Nevertheless, the magnitude of responses was an occasion for a new kind of dialogue.

The Kairos document initiated a dialogue between Christian Palestinians and Jews; the first was between Palestinian Christians and Israeli Jews. Knowing the situation of the Palestinians, and worrying about the future of the country, a number of Israeli Jews wanted to understand better the message of the Kairos and, after expressing their concerns about a few things in the document, they are looking at ways to overcome their initial negative reactions to see the message of the document. Those were mainly religious Jews, including rabbis, especially working in the field of Christian-Jewish dialogue. That dialogue was welcomed by the Kairos group, and there are attempts to proceed with this dialogue. The official media, needless to say, was hostile to the document; and most Israelis just ignored it.

The second dialogue initiated by the Kairos document was with Western churches in the context of the Western Christian-Jewish dialogue. Up until that point, the dialogue had been carried on in the absence of the Palestinian Christians. Feeling the need to respond to the Kairos, the Western churches initiated a dialogue with the Kairos group, in Europe, in Palestine, or in the context of Christian-Jewish dialogue. The International Council for Christians and Jews (ICCJ) played an important role in this dialogue. Including the Christian Palestinians in that dialogue will not be an addition, but will play a role in changing the paradigm of this dialogue. Making amends for what Jews had endured in the countries of Europe cannot be made on our account and in our land; correcting an injustice cannot result in a new injustice.[16] The agenda of the Christian-Jewish dialogue in our context is different.

Unfortunately, Christian Zionists and many American Jews attacked the document as an anti-Semitic one that renewed the so-called replacement or supersessionist theology. Those attacks saw in the document a danger for Christian-Jewish dialogue, and any endorsement of the document by Christian churches was seen as a return to anti-Semitism. To link the Kairos to anti-Semitism or to supersessionist theology is clearly a misreading of the document; the same can be applied to the call to BDS (Boycott, Divestment, and Sanctions). It is not about delegitimizing Israel, because we want to live side by side with Israel in peace and security, but it is about delegitimizing the military occupation. We call upon Jews and Israelis to work together to end occupation and to establish justice in this land.[17]

Christian Palestinians are not "the small minority who struggles for its survival, caught in between two big majorities, Muslims and Jews." They are a living community that shares the sufferings and the hopes of the people and that carries out a mission to establish a new reality based on equality, justice, peace, and reconciliation.

JERUSALEM

In 1995 the Catholic Patriarchs of the Middle East declared,

God has set aside the region of the Middle East by making it the arena for His dialogue with all of humanity. In this blessed land the three monotheistic religions developed: Judaism, Christianity and Islam. Ancient and contemporary circumstances often placed members of these three religions in a situation of struggle and strife. All must work to overcome these difficulties, creating the necessary conditions for sincere encounter and working for the benefit of the human person in our area and throughout the world.[18]

In 2001 the Assembly of Catholic Ordinaries in the Holy Land wrote,

Jerusalem is the place *par excellence* where this historic reconciliation should be accomplished on the basis of truth, justice, and peace. Thus, Jerusalem will be transformed from a place of conflict and tension into a place of dialogue and reconciliation, far removed from all monopolization, exclusivity, and obstinacy, in a spirit of frankness, understanding, and openness. In the midst of all this, our churches are called to define a form of coexistence, witnessing, before God and humanity, to a new form of relationship among human religious groups for the glory of God and the service of humanity.[19]

In 2009 Kairos Palestine stated,

Jerusalem is the foundation of our vision and our entire life. She is the city to which God gave a particular importance in the history of humanity. She is the city toward which all people are in movement—and where they will meet in friendship and love in the presence of the One Unique God....Today, the city is inhabited by two peoples of three religions; and it is on this prophetic vision [of Isaiah 2:2–5 ("They shall beat their swords into ploughshares, and their spears into pruning hooks.")] and on the international resolutions concerning the totality of Jerusalem that any political solution must be based. This is the first issue that should be negotiated because the recognition of Jerusalem's sanctity and its message will be a source of inspiration towards finding a solution to the entire problem, which is largely a problem of mutual trust and ability to set in place a new land in this land of God.[20]

In the midst of suffering and a politically desperate situation, we dare to keep our hope alive; we dare to believe in a better future, for us and for our opponents. Dialogue in our situation is not an academic exercise; dialogue is a vital activity of the church as part of its mission in building the kingdom of God.

CONCLUSION

Everyone agrees on the importance of dialogue; in our diverse world, we need to talk to each other, to resolve our problems and prevent any conflict. However, dialogue is not always easy.

At the same time, dialogue should reflect a specific context and influence that context. There is no abstract interreligious dialogue. Christian-Jewish dialogue in the Holy Land is necessarily influenced by the Palestinian/Israeli conflict and the religious dimension of this conflict. The task of dialogue is to examine the nature of the conflict and mainly the religious implications, and then try to find a common ground to work for justice, peace, and reconciliation (in that order). Dialogue for the sake of dialogue is not worth all the time and energy it requires. On one hand, this dialogue cannot be a political dialogue, even if the conflict is; and on the other hand, it cannot be an abstract theological dialogue as if the conflict does not exist. A fruitful Christian-Jewish dialogue needs to find its way by focusing on religious texts and values with the suffering human beings in mind. Moreover, justice and peace are more than biblical notions to be discussed; rather, they are values that need to inspire people of faith and beyond.

As people of faith, we believe that a better future is possible; we believe in a just and loving God, Creator and Father of all human beings created in his image and likeness, regardless of their race, color, sex, or religion. Dialogue reminds us of the plan of God to all his children to live together in peace and harmony. May dialogue help us in fulfilling the plan of God of us in this region.

Suggested Readings

Assembly of Catholic Ordinaries in the Holy Land. "Relations with Believers of Other Religions." Chap. 13 in *The General Pastoral Plan*. Jerusalem, 2001.

Kairos Palestine. "A Moment of Truth: A Word of Faith, Hope, and Love from the Heart of Palestinian Suffering." Jerusalem, December 15, 2009. http://www.kairospalestine.ps.

Khader, Jamal, and David Neuhaus, SJ. "A Holy Land Context for *Nostra Aetate*." *Studies in Christian-Jewish Relations* (E-journal of the Council of Centers in Jewish-Christian Relations) 1 (2005–6): 67–88, http://ejournals.bc.edu/ojs/index.php/scjr/article/view/ 1360.

Sabbah, Patriarch Michel. "Pray for Peace in Jerusalem." Pastoral letter, 1990.

————. "Reading the Bible Today in the Land of the Bible." Pastoral letter, 1993.

————. "Seek Peace and Pursue It: Questions and Answers on Justice and Peace in the Holy Land." Pastoral letter, 1998.

Notes

1. Kairos Palestine, "A Moment of Truth: A Word of Faith, Hope, and Love from the Heart of Palestinian Suffering," (Jerusalem, December 15, 2009), 2.3.3. The document can be found at www.kairo spalestine.ps.

2. For example, Sabeel Center, Dar Annadwa, Bethlehem Bible College, the Kairos group and Al-Liqa' Center organized several conferences on those topics.

3. In July 2010 in Istanbul (Turkey) and July 2011 in Cracow (Poland). See http://www.iccj.org/Rev-Dr-Jamal-Khader-Promised-Land-Land-of-Israel-Land-of-Palestine-Holy-Land.3341.0.html.

4. See Deut 6:21–25.

5. See for example: Exod 23:23–33; Josh 6:17–21; 8:20–29; 11:21–25.

6. For example: Naim Ateek, *Justice and Only Justice. A Palestinian Theology of Liberation* (Maryknoll, NY: Orbis Books, 1989); Mitri Raheb, *I Am a Palestinian Christian* (Minneapolis: Fortress Press, 1995); Salim Munayer, "Reading the Old Testament in Palestine" and "Palestinian Church Reads the Old Testament: The Triangle of Ethnicity, Faith, Land—and Biblical Interpretation," *Communio Viatorum* 46, no. 1 (2004): 34–62.

7. "Relations with Believers of Other Religions," chapter 13 of *The General Pastoral Plan*, Assembly of Catholic Ordinaries in the Holy Land (Jerusalem 2001).

8. Patriarch Michel Sabbah has said, "The whole of the Bible, the New Testament and the Old (also known as the Torah), is the Word of God, revealed for the salvation of humankind. The two Testaments are intimately connected with one another and they cannot be separated under any pretext" (*Reading the Bible Today in the Land of the Bible*, §35).

9. Kairos Palestine, "A Moment of Truth," 2.2.2. (Emphasis in original.)

10. Ibid., 2.3.2.

11. Ibid., 2.3.4.

12. Ibid., 2.3.1. (Emphasis in original.)

13. That same student admitted that he had just finished his military service in the Palestinians Territories a few weeks earlier.

14. Jamal Khader and David Neuhaus, SJ, "A Holy Land Context for *Nostra Aetate*," *Studies in Christian-Jewish Relations*, E-journal of the Council of Centers in Jewish-Christian Relations 1 (2005–6): 67–88. http://ejournals.bc.edu/ojs/index.php/scjr/article/view/1360.

15. "Relations with Believers of Other Religions."

16. Cf. Kairos Palestine, "A Moment of Truth," 2.3.2.

17. Cf. Ibid., 5.4.2.

18. Catholic Patriarchs of the Middle East, "Together in Front of God. Christian Muslim Coexistence in the Arab World," Pastoral Letter, 1994, n. 42.

19. "Relations with Believers of Other Religions."

20. Kairos Palestine, "A Moment of Truth," 9.5.

JEWISH-MUSLIM RELATIONS IN ISRAEL

Jewish Points of View

RELIGIOUS AND CULTURAL DIVERSITY AMONG MUSLIMS IN ISRAEL

Implications for Jewish-Muslim Dialogue

RONALD KRONISH

INTRODUCTION

Often there seems to be great curiosity and even greater ignorance in the Western world concerning the religion and culture of Islam, particularly as practiced among Arab peoples. The myth produced and perpetuated in the Western media—and in Israel—suggests that all Arab Muslims are three things: fanatics, terrorists, and religious fundamentalists.

This media tendency is particularly troubling in light of the fact that the overwhelming majority of the Palestinian Arab citizens of Israel[1] are Muslim.[2] My aim in this chapter is to explore beyond this unidimensional media stereotype and to understand Muslim Israelis from a broader, multidimensional perspective.

Information was gathered for this chapter by interviewing and working with Muslim Israeli professionals from a broad spectrum of religious beliefs, each by methods appropriate to our individual backgrounds. I brought the insights gleaned from more than three decades of experience living and working in Israel in the field of interreligious and intercultural education, and the curiosity of a Jewish Israeli wishing to learn more about his Muslim neighbors and fellow citizens. Researcher Joanna Arch, who was trained in qualitative research methods at Wellesley College, conducted ten in-depth interviews with Muslim Arab Israeli citizens from diverse religious and cultural practices. Since then, I have conducted additional interviews and had many conversations with Muslims in Israel about their identity, and have traveled several times with Israeli Muslims on speaking tours, where I have heard them explain their identity to foreign audiences.

Interviewees included Muslim Arab community leaders, educators, religious leaders, scholars, businesswomen, and legal professionals. All were professionals with university degrees from secular or religious universities and all but one were citizens of Israel. We did not aim to represent a typical cross section of Muslims in Israel in our limited number of interviews; this was impossible with our finite resources and knowledge of what a "typical" cross section might contain. Our goal was simply to interview a religiously diverse cross section of Muslim men and women. Thus, this article offers an impressionistic reflection rather than a definitive statement, and should be read as a work in progress rather than as the final word.

METHODOLOGY

The primary question of the interview—"Among Muslims in Israel, what do you see as the differences and similarities in religion and culture?"—sparked a range of responses. A few interviewees did not see any religious or cultural diversity within their communities at all. The majority did, but they did not always define disparate observance levels using the same labels or parameters. For example, one claimed that 70 percent of Muslims in Israel were secular in practice, another said 20 percent, and three others claimed that Muslims who defined themselves as secular could not be Muslims at all.

When probed more deeply, however, the collective responses of our Muslim colleagues revealed an increasingly lucid (and complex) picture of diversity in everyday religious and cultural practices among Muslims in Israel, which we attempted to organize in the categories outlined below. Given the lack of consensus on the number (and existence) of distinctive types of Muslim identity, these categories strive to convey a diversity of responses. They are strictly de facto in nature and do not stem from legitimization within Islam of religious and cultural diversity. In addition, approximate percentages of the numbers of Israeli Muslims who "fit" into a particular descriptive category were offered by some interviewees. These percentages serve as "guesstimates" rather than as empirical data, as we begin to paint a picture of the diversity of the Muslim Israeli community from within.

RELIGIOUSLY "EXTREMIST" MUSLIMS OF ISRAEL

Israeli Muslims who are "fanatically religious," in the words of Dr. Mohammed Hourani, a veteran Israeli Muslim educator and interreligious activist,[3] are those "who perform prayer five times a day, who visit Mecca more than once in a lifetime, who keep Islamic life in the most traditional way. The women cover their faces and wear long clothes and keep a distance between themselves and others."

The core division between what the late Dr. Mithkal Natour, a professor of Islamic law and an experienced Israeli Arab educator,[4] called "the two parties [of Israeli Muslims]—the extremists and the common people," is based on strictness of religious observance and attitudes toward the Western world. Religiously extreme Muslim Arab Israelis are more pious, more strict in religious observance, more traditional (and non-Western) in dress, and more immersed in Islam, than less observant Muslim Israelis. Although there are differences in level of observance, those with whom we spoke did not talk about theological differences.

Most of those who were interviewed emphasized that the number of Muslims in Israel who are extremely religious is relatively small. "There are very few among the Palestinian Muslims of Israel who are extreme...no more than five to seven percent maximum," said Dr. Aziz Haidar, a research fellow in sociology at Hebrew University's Truman S. Institute for the Advancement of Peace.[5] It seems that highly religious Muslims are concentrated in the central "triangle" area northeast of Tel Aviv and Jaffa.

Moreover, many argued that there is a distinction between degree of religiosity and involvement in politics among Israeli Muslims.

Mufada Rahman, a businesswoman with close friends from a wide range of religious observance levels,[6] pointed out, "There are many pious Muslims not involved in politics, who are very religious out of love [for God]. If a Muslim is involved in politics, it's because he likes it, not because he is a Muslim. There is a difference between a Muslim and a politician." In other words, some very pious Muslim Israelis are involved in politics, and some are not. Those who are drawn to politics are often involved in the Islamic Movement.

THE ISLAMIC MOVEMENT

Although Islam is a religion and not a political movement, the Islamic Movement in Israel, which first emerged in 1971, combines the two. The movement incorporates adherence to strict Muslim observance and opposition to Western culture into what noted educator Dr. Marwan Darweish[7] called "a political movement, a new analysis of the situation." Their slogan, according to Darweish, is that "Islam is the solution for everything."

Unlike the Palestinian terrorist organization Hamas, which operates in the West Bank and Gaza and whose members are mainly refugees in the territories (now partially under Israeli rule and partially under Palestinian rule), the Islamic Movement is nonviolent in its orientation and is led and supported by Israeli citizens. Its leaders often publicly denounce acts of violence by Hamas and other terrorist groups and participate in the Israeli democratic process at local and state levels.

Some of the interviewees drew a parallel between the leadership of the Islamic Movement and the Jewish religious political party Shaas. Darweish observed, "The leader of Shaas said he has more in common with the leaders of the Islamic Movement—[both are] very much into tradition and family."

Although most of the Islamic Movement's following is drawn from the more religiously observant sectors of Israeli Muslim society, there appears to be a notable difference between the politics and religious practices of the voters. According to Darweish, "My guess is that there are more [Muslims in Israel] who are secularist-traditionalists than there are people in the Islamic Movement. They may vote mostly for the Islamic Movement, but that's politics....There is no way they're all practicing Islam in an extreme way." Other interviewees made similar statements. In sum, just as pious Muslims are not necessarily politically involved, it seems that voters for the Islamic Movement are not necessarily religiously committed.

TRADITIONAL MUSLIMS OF ISRAEL

A number of the interviewees distinguished between moderately religious Israeli Muslims and a less consistently religious group, which they labeled "traditionalist" Muslims. Sociologist Dr. Haidar, who wrote a book (in Arabic) about the identity of Palestinian Arabs in Israel, states that among the Muslims of Israel,

> There are forty to fifty percent who live according to…Muslim [standards] in some ways and Western standards in others. They give more freedom to women, to their children, they go to movies, to the beach, and to the university. They live according to Israeli Western standards. At the same time, some pray at the mosque on Fridays. Most fast on Ramadan. They celebrate Islamic feasts by eating and drinking alcohol. It's a very interesting phenomenon.[8]

In terms of self-identity, Dr. Haidar emphasized that this traditional group of Israeli Muslims is "mostly nationalist—they define themselves more as Palestinian or Arab than as Muslim….At the same time, [they] observe some Islamic tradition." Perhaps the best parallel to this middle-of-the-road Muslim group are traditional (*masorti*) Jews in Israeli society, who often identify more as Israeli than as Jewish and who do not strictly observe Shabbat and Jewish holidays, but maintain some degree of Jewish tradition in their homes.

A few Muslim Israelis self-identified as secular Muslims even though within our categorical scheme they exemplified the "traditional" category. For example, Howla Sadi, who served as the Director of the Curriculum Department for Israeli Arab Schools in the Israeli Ministry of Education,[9] defined herself as "secular" because

> I try to give some Muslim things new meanings for this life. I do the things I believe in. I do some of these things to be part of the community. When I was a student in the university, I

didn't have time [to observe], so I stopped. Then, when I had children...I [again] began to pray and fast. And I never tell my children to do that, it's their choice.

When asked about the modern significance that she attaches to Muslim traditions, she responded, "Let us take fasting. For me the social [meaning] is to feel like the poor people everywhere...it makes you more aware to help these people. You bring the family together...and feel a part of the Islamic community everywhere." Thus even though Sadi considered herself to be "secular," she performed selected traditional Muslim rituals. However, she did so for the sake of cultivating social consciousness, family togetherness, and links to Muslims worldwide, rather than out of a sense of religious obligation.

"SECULAR" MUSLIMS OF ISRAEL

In the interviews, the question of "Secular Muslims—do they exist?" arose many times. "What do we mean by secular?" was asked. A few had never before heard of the term *secular*, but all had something to say about secularism once we defined it as "nonbelieving." One of the leading Muslims in Israel with whom we spoke (and who preferred to remain anonymous), stated,

> If you say you are secular, you can still be Jewish....If I take this model and try to put it in Muslim ideology, it does not work because if you are secular, you do not belong. From the religious point of view, you cannot be a Muslim [if you are secular]....If [a Muslim] says that he is secular, he does not understand Islam....He is thinking in the language of Judaism or Christianity.

Mohammed Hourani also stated that "we do not have the concept of *secularism* in Islam." Similarly, there seems to be no notion of ethnic Muslim identity among the Arab Muslims of Israel. Thus, on a theoretical level, there appears to be a mutually exclusive, either/or relationship between secularism (defined as "nonbelieving") and Islam as religion. Issa Jaber, now the head of the Local Council of the Israeli Arab town of Abu Ghosh, just west of Jerusalem, who is an active educator for Arab-Jewish Coexistence in Israel,[10] stated, "We have no religious or secular people, only very good Muslims or less good Muslims."

However, from a more pragmatic, de facto perspective it seems that some Israelis both behave as secular people and self-identify as Muslims. Dr. Haidar discussed Israeli Muslims who are secular in their style of life and in their behavior: "They have many jokes about the religion and the sheiks and are not at all religiously observant." Mohammed Hourani explained the complexity of this position: "Because of political and social circumstances, I can in a practical way behave as a secular [person], but I cannot declare myself as one because secular in Islam means that you are...not just out of Islam, it's also understood as being a path that is anti-Muslim." Thus "secular" Muslims generally are a silent minority. They are nonexistent in "Muslim consciousness, in the political awareness," said Dr. Marwan Darweish. But though they do not participate in community religious events, secular Muslims "participate in the social sense" within Muslim communities in Israel, says Dr. Haidar.

Dr. Haidar explained that "if you ask these people what they are, they say 'human being' or some start with 'Arab' and identify with fellow Arabs on grounds of pan-Arab nationalism or Palestinian peoplehood."

However, as another interviewee who wished to remain anonymous explained, Muslim-born Israelis who are neither religious nor traditional "still call themselves Muslim...because it distinguishes [them] from Jews and Christians. On their Israeli identity card it says *Arab*, which means that Jewish Israelis assume that they are Muslim."

We encountered an exception to this in Muslim-born, secularly educated Dr. Haidar, who did not identify himself as Muslim at all. He stated, however, that his complete lack of attachment to Islam is unusual for Palestinian Arabs in Israel because some remaining belief in Islam as a religion usually remains. For example, secular-identified Muslims may turn to Islamic concepts when struggling to explain metaphysical questions of life and death, and they often resort to traditional Muslim practices when there is a death in the family. Thus, the intersections of Muslim, Palestinian Arab, and Israeli identities are particularly complex for secular-identified Muslims.[11] Living as an Arab Muslim citizen within a Western nation that defines itself as "The Jewish Nation" sometimes seems, ironically, to facilitate both the adoption of a secular lifestyle and the inclusion of "Muslim" in one's self-definition.

Estimated percentages of Muslims in Israel who lead secular, nonobservant or anti-observant lifestyles ranged from 10 to 20 percent. According to Dr. Haidar, many of them are university educated. Geographically, secular lifestyles tend to be more pervasive among Muslims in the Galilee than in the "triangle" area of Central Israel.

Haneen Majadleh,[12] who gave a lecture to the Interreligious Coordinating Council in Israel (ICCI) in the fall of 2013, defined herself as a secular Muslim. She does not practice the rituals of the religion, nor is she a believer. Rather, she is a complete secularist in her outlook as well as a feminist, and she thinks that more and more young Muslim women who are educated in Israeli universities are leaving the old religious fold in order to be more modern, advance their careers, and be active in social and educational issues in Israeli society and in Palestinian communities within Israel. She admitted, however, that she is still the exception rather than the rule, and that many of the young people with whom she grew up in the Israeli Arab village of Baka-al Gharbiya remain traditional and stay in the village. She, on the other hand, has lived in Jerusalem ever since she began her studies in the field of social work at the Hebrew University, where she is currently completing her doctorate.

MUSLIMS OF ISRAEL IN THE CONTEXT OF THE LARGER MUSLIM ARAB WORLD

Because I work primarily with Muslim Arabs in Israel, I cannot know the extent to which the outline of religious and cultural diversity presented here is unique to them. In the interviews, the question of the uniqueness of Muslims in Israel often provoked complex, ambivalent responses. A few began with statements such as, "I don't know why you're asking about Muslims in Israel because there is no difference between Muslims in Israel and Muslims in the rest of the Muslim world. We are all one people, one nation. We cannot be spoken of in isolation."

At some point, however, nearly everyone stated ways in which the Muslim Arabs of Israel are different from other Muslim Arabs or other Muslim non-Arabs. One of our interviewees, for example, pointed out the uniqueness of being a minority in a non-Muslim and a non-Arab state. Indeed, Kadi Iyad Zahalka has stressed many times in his lectures and writings and conversations with me that there is something very special about being a Muslim in a non-Muslim state. In fact, he argues that in some ways, Israeli Muslims have more freedom of religious expression than Muslims in England or the United States, and the fact that the State of Israel provides religious sharia courts for Israeli Muslims is totally unique in the world.[13]

In making a similar point, Mohammed Hourani described the historical and political context of Muslim Israelis:

Because of the political and social circumstances, some Muslims are secular. For years they lived in isolation from Muslims all over the world. Until 1977, when Saudi Arabia and Jordan accepted Muslims to revisit Mecca and Medina, it was impossible for Muslims in Israel to visit any other Muslim country. Muslims in Israel from 1948–1977 tried to be part of the social life, problems, prosperity, economic, and social life of Israel. Because of this situation, this kind of pluralism was created, which is part of the general way [in Israel].

Issa Jaber said that in Abu Ghosh, his village west of Jerusalem, "We have been isolated for so long. We mostly keep in touch with Arabs within the Green Line, and that is mostly commercial [rather than] social contact. But other Arabs connect in daily life together." Geographic isolation and life in a Western democratic state has cultural consequences. In the words of one of our interviewees, "When my five-year-old son watches TV, he sees Israeli kids and American programs. He has no proximity to his own culture."

Many argued that the Western, secular, democratic influence within Israeli society facilitated the development of the "secular Muslim" identity discussed above. Muhammed Hourani stated,

The circumstances around us are very important for people in this land because I can't speak of myself as a Muslim as if I was in Saudi Arabia, Iraq, Jordan, or Egypt. Here we are talking about a democratic state....In religious society, you are under the pressures of the consensus around you [to be outwardly religious]. In secular [Israeli] society, you can behave as an individual, you can express yourself as an individual. This is the difference. If I was in Jordan or Saudi Arabia, I should accept the religious concepts and behave according to the expectations of the people around me. I would not be allowed to have these kinds of digressions.

Some of the more religious interviewees described the lack of Muslim religious unity in a different way: "[Muslims all] are supposed to be the same way," lamented Dr. Mithkal Natour, "but we are living in the West, not the East."

In addition to external pulls toward religious pluralism, Muslims of Israel may also be influenced by diversity from within the Israeli Arab minority, which includes a heterogeneous mix of Christians, Muslims, Druze, and Circasians. Marwan Darweish, among others, argued that this internal religious diversity "makes for more of a tendency toward secularism" because unlike Arabs in Muslim states, Arabs in Israel do not always connect on the basis of shared religion but rather on shared ethnicity or nationalism.

SUMMARY AND CONCLUSION

In this chapter I have attempted to convey the religious and cultural diversity among Muslim Arabs of Israel by describing four different orientations toward religious observance and identity within their community. These categories emerged from interviewing and from working over many years with Muslim Israelis from a diverse range of religious practices. Moving from most to least religiously involved, we began with "extreme" Muslims, whom we characterized as religiously observant in the strictest sense. Our interviewees emphasize that this group is not necessarily involved in politics; most of the highly devout Muslims in Israel observe "out of love," according to businesswoman Mufada Rahnian.

"Moderate" Muslims maintain high levels of regular religious observance, but are not as strict or conservative in their practice of Islam and are more open to Western culture. Many of the men wear Western clothes and attend secular universities in Israel and abroad.

Several interviewees estimated that approximately 30 percent of

Muslims in Israel are extremely or moderately religious, with moderates outnumbering extreme Muslims. "Traditional" Muslims in Israel maintain practices and attachments to Islam that are often completely transformed by modernity and are motivated by a desire to foster family and community ties more than by religious belief. "Traditional" Muslims such as Howla Sadi follow Muslim rituals as they see fit, and affix personally meaningful modern interpretations to them. In other words, they are selective about what they like from the traditions of Islam, and they ignore or reject those customs that no longer make much sense to their modern sensibilities. Estimated numbers of traditionalists among Muslims of Israel range from 40 to 50 percent.

The diversity of opinions regarding the notion of "secular" Muslims of Israel indicates the breadth of the perspectives on Islam within the Israeli Muslim community. Within Islam's religious and cultural consciousness, the notion of "secular" Muslims is in theory nonexistent; if you declare you are a nonbeliever, you cannot be a Muslim.[14] It is a fact, however, that some Muslim-born Israelis lead highly secular lifestyles, do not observe any Islamic obligations, and still identify as "Muslim."

Dr. Haidar estimated that 10 to 20 percent of Israel's Muslims fit this description. The degree to which these secular tendencies among Muslims are relatively unique to Muslims in Israel (among Muslims in the Middle East) was also a point of heated discussion. Many blamed or credited the largely Western, democratic, secular-influenced society in Israel and the relative isolation of Israel's Muslim Arabs from other Muslim Arab societies for the secular lifestyles of some Israeli Muslims. Some also pointed to the internal religious diversity of the Arab minority in Israel, which includes Muslims, Christians, Druze, and others.

Exploring religious and cultural diversity among Muslim Arabs of Israel holds implications for interreligious and intercultural dialogue and education in Israel and abroad. The multiple, complex dimensions of Muslim practices in Israel presented here provide evidence to counter the distorted Western media presentation of Arab Muslims as fanatic terrorists, and helps to erase the well-documented tendency in social psychology to view "out groups" in a homogenous manner.

Within Israel, such findings challenge Jews to orient ourselves toward a multifaceted mindset when entering into serious dialogue (and simply living) with our Muslim Arab neighbors. Now that we are conscious of the fact that any single Muslim Israeli is but one in a diverse group of individuals who often speak with different voices about their common religion and culture, we will be able to enter into dialogue with our fellow Muslim citizens without preconceived notions or outdated stereotypes.

Jews who engage Muslims in serious, systematic, and sensitive dialogue, as I have been doing for more than twenty years, will now be able to do so with a greater awareness of diversity within Islam in Israel than was heretofore the case. Moreover, they will find many parallels to Jewish diversity. Indeed, we discovered through this research that just as we have Haredi, modern orthodox, traditional, and secular Jews in Israel, virtually the same breakdown exists de facto in Israel's Arab Muslim society.

Moreover, it is important to state that Jewish-Muslim dialogue should be one of the major imperatives on our interreligious agenda now and in the years ahead. It is impossible for us to understand fully our Muslim (or Christian or Druze) Palestinian Arab neighbors if we only view them in ethnic or nationalistic or cultural terms. The religion of Islam, in its diversity, plays a central role in their lives. Accordingly, it is incumbent upon Jews in Israel, and abroad, to understand much more about how Islam is actually understood and practiced in this country and region in order to be able to live in peaceful coexistence, now and in the future.

Notes

1. There is little consensus on the question of identity among the Palestinian Arab Israelis with whom we work. In attempting to capture the diversity of self-definitions we encountered, we use identifier phrases such as *Muslim Israeli*, *Muslim Arabs of Israel*, *Muslim Arab Israelis*, and so forth, interchangeably in this paper.

2. According to Israel's Central Bureau of Statistics, the Arab population in 2013 was estimated at 1,658,000, representing 20.7 percent of the country's population, and the Muslim community represents about 70 percent of that number.

3. Mohammed Hourani, former head coordinator of the Arab Language and Literature program at David Yellin College in Jerusalem, completed a doctorate in education at Sussex University, United

Kingdom. He was born in the village of Dir-el-Assad in the Galilee and now lives with his family in East Jerusalem.

4. Mithkal Natour, PhD, served as the former Director of Arab Education for the Municipality of Jerusalem and as a lecturer in Islamic Law at the Islamic College of Baqa-Al-Gharbiah. He lived in Jerusalem where he practiced Islamic Family Law.

5. Aziz Haidar, PhD, a Research Fellow at the Harry S. Truman Institute for the Advancement of Peace, Hebrew University, completed a book on Palestinian identity in Israel (in Arabic).

6. Mufada Rahman, BA, Hebrew University, works as a business-woman in an Israeli insurance company. She was born in Abu-Ghosh, where she still resides.

7. Marwan Darweish, PhD, was born in the village of Um-al-Fahm in central Israel and served as an educator in Israel before moving to England.

8. Consuming alcohol is forbidden within Islam.

9. Howla Sadi, the Director of the Curriculum Department for Israeli-Arab Schools in the Israeli Ministry of Education, holds an MA in education from Hebrew University. She was born in northern Israel in the village of Ibilin and now lives in Jerusalem.

10. Issa Jaber, who lives in Abu Ghosh, was the Director of the Department of Education Abu Ghosh Local Council. He is now the mayor of the town, is active in the Association of Jewish-Arab Coexistence in the Judean Hills, and also serves as cochairperson of ICCI. He was educated at universities in Israel and Turkey.

11. For an in-depth discussion of the complexities of Palestinian Arab Israeli identity in general, see David Grossman's *Sleeping on a Wire: Conversations with Palestinians in Israel*, trans. Hain Watzman (New York: Farrar, Strauss, and Giroux, 1993).

12. Haneen Majadleh is a social worker living in Jerusalem, working on a doctorate at Hebrew University. In addition to her practical work as a social worker, she teaches sociology and research methods at Al-Qassemi College of Education in Baka-Al-Gharbiya and is a frequent lecturer on women's issues in Islam in Israel.

13. Kadi Iyad Zahalka is the kadi of the sharia court in Jerusalem. Prior to this he served as the director of the Shari'a Court System in Israel. He has an LLB from Tel Aviv University and his PhD is from Hebrew University in Jerusalem on "The Doctrine of Fiqh al-Aqalliyāt

(Muslim minority jurisprudence) And Its Implications for the Muslims in Israel." He has written two books on sharia law and the courts system and he serves as the chairman of the Shari'a Court Committee of the Israel Bar Association.

14. Under some extreme interpretations of Islamic law, those who declare they are nonbelievers must be stoned to death. However, this is not practiced in Israel.

ESTABLISHING A RELIGIOUS PEACE

MICHAEL MELCHIOR

BACKGROUND—THE NEED FOR RELIGIOUS PEACE

Religious identity and tradition have long been considered the main obstacles to peace between Israel and the Palestinians, and a main factor in many of the conflicts throughout the Middle East. It is perhaps understandable that until now, attempts to solve the Israeli Palestinian conflict have avoided these core issues. Politicians and policymakers alike have consistently viewed them as so complicated or emotionally loaded that addressing them would only hinder the political process, if not cause it to (often quite literally) blow up.

Yet I have always believed that ignoring the religious existential components of the conflict and the core identities and narratives of the peoples involved will not make them disappear, but rather will maintain the accepted "norm" that religion is the problem rather than the solution. More important still is that the opposite of what politicians and policymakers have believed is actually true. That is, any political process disconnected from these narratives will have a very limited chance at success.

Through my years living in Israel and working in government, I have learned that the general approach to the peace process as a secular process, as a very Western way of looking at peace, is the wrong approach. This is something that I have argued about with my secular friends on both the Israeli and Palestinian left as well as those in Europe and America.

I was a supporter of the political peace process from the beginning of the Oslo meetings in 1993, when, as the Chief Rabbi of Norway, I was involved with and very close to Norwegian policymakers. I was supportive, but skeptical throughout, and shared that view with many others. I was afraid then—and I remain so now—that it would not succeed if we don't change the narrative of the peace by including the right people, groups, and ideas in the process. Without religious authorities involved talking openly about their respective narratives and why religious teachings themselves compel us to make compromise for the sake of peace, there will be no way that society as a whole, on either side of the conflict, will see the peace process as credible or acceptable.

One often hears the simplistic claim that these groups or narratives are irrelevant. The dichotomous thinking of the Western world is that religion is something that belongs to the private sphere—to the home, the synagogue, the church, and the mosque—and has nothing to do with the public sphere. That is how Western policymakers look at the world, and therefore the religious narrative has no place in political peacemaking or in the world of conflict resolution.

For many years it has been a commonly held belief that religion often played a role in instigating and perpetuating conflict but could have no role in bringing about peace. Therefore, if we could ignore the identity, the ethnicity, the culture of the peoples in the region, then these issues would simply become nonfactors and disappear. I believe that this kind of peace becomes a "peace of interests" and not a "peace of values." There is a significant difference in the substance of these two types of peace. Interests are temporary and can, and often do, change, whereas values tend to have permanence. Look, for example, at the peace made between Egypt and Israel. This is a peace that was signed into being by two leaders, but the peace has certainly not trickled down to the people. I only hope and pray that our countries' interests do in fact remain aligned.

The view of analysts or policymakers who are more in tune with the reality of the situation is different from the view of those who see religious groups and narratives as irrelevant. They will admit that there may be a need to address the existential issues, but they argue that the best solution is for the politicians to conclude a "quick-fix" peace deal and only afterward will it be necessary or appropriate to deal with the existential issues. "You are right," they will tell me, "you can't just make the issues go away, but we will deal with them in a later phase." Yossi Beilin, for example, argued that "we will do it like in South Africa. We will solve the problem, then we will create a Truth Commission and deal with the substantial issues there."

My claim is that those who make this argument have not learned the lessons of history well. In South Africa there was a lengthy and important process dealing with the identities of the two parties, not the least of which was their collective religious identities. This process, through which issues of legitimacy and identity were addressed in order to create a political process, was led by impressive religious leaders such as Bishop Desmond Tutu.[1] It wasn't that de Klerk and Mandela woke up one day and simply decided to sign an agreement that would change reality. There was a process that dealt with the religious and cultural identities of the populations in a peaceful and dignified way and that dealt with the narratives of the people. The Truth Commission would not have been possible if it had been disconnected from the issues that legitimatized it and created justice for both populations. This is not what has happened here in our conflict in the past, nor is it happening now.

If Prime Minister Netanyahu and President Abu Mazen were suddenly to announce today that we have crossed the Rubicon and cut a deal, it would be so totally disconnected from any narrative that exists that it would likely be impossible to implement. No one would have enough faith in the other side to trust that they are truly ending the conflict and will truly make the concessions necessary. The Oslo peace process had great support throughout the world and in the region. It had great energy and much financial support. Why did it fail? And why have all the other processes since then also failed, despite all the effort and resources invested in them? Is it because peace is the wrong goal? My claim is that it is because certain components necessary to secure the very foundation of the political process have been missing from the start. In many cases, leaders have not only ignored the foundational components of religion and tradition, they have actively worked to remove them from the process.

There are many battles being fought in our area. This is true not only for Israel and Palestine; it is true for the whole region. One battle is for the character of our societies: What kind of society do we want to have? There are those who want religion to have a greater role and those who want society to be totally secular. Fighting for one or the other is a completely legitimate battle, and there are many different opinions and arguments to be made for each side.

The problem is that political leaders have often tried to combine one battle with another—namely, secularization versus traditionalism on the one hand and peace on the other. If the peace process is defined as a "secular" process, it will inevitably alienate the key constituencies in this conflict. Major parties and group identities will coalesce around their positions and see others, within their own societies as much as from without, as the enemy and will work to sabotage whatever possible solution is reached.

Fighting both these battles at the same time can only lead to everyone losing. One cannot fight the battle for secularization of society while doing so under the guise of seeking peace with one's external enemies. This is what happened here in the 1990s on both the Jewish and the Palestinian sides.

During the tragic election campaign between Netanyahu and Peres in 1996, Yossi Sarid,[2] one of Israel's most brilliant politicians, said on national television, "Just as we led Rabin to a platform of peace, we will run Peres on a platform of secularization." That sentence alone may have lost Peres that election, which he otherwise should have won. It forced many middle-of-the-road religious voters to say we cannot vote for Peres. "If we cannot have a traditional society, if we have to have a secular society like Yossi Sarid wants," goes the argument, "then we are willing to give up on peace."

I have argued the same point with Yasser Abed Rabbo,[3] a devout Palestinian secularist. He has always fought for secularization, but most of his people say that if peace means secularization, then you will find us on the front line against peace.

Another critical factor that affects the process aimed at solving the conflict has to do with how we in Israel define the problem itself. During the 1970s and 1980s, there was a tremendously important debate between the Israeli right and center-left about the implications of the peace process on the very nature of Israel. At the heart of the debate was a triangle of three values that are all important for us as Israeli Jews. First is *Eretz Yisrael*, the land of Israel. It is vital that we have the land—a relatively small area, in fact. Second is democracy, which is crucial for the existence of our state. And the third is the Jewishness of the State of Israel—with varying definitions of what that means, but still a critical value in the triangle. Many Israelis believed that we could have all three values: we can be a Jewish state, a democracy, and can keep the land.

The great victory of the center-left in the debate in Israel of the 1990s was that it established the fact that we can't have all three. Because of simple demographics, we can't have a democracy, keep all of the land of Israel, and also maintain the Jewishness of the state. We have to give up one of the three. This was a very important cornerstone in the debate here in this country. And yet, while this demographic framing of the argument helped the center-left win the debate, it became a problematic paradigm open to misuse by those who cultivated fear and hate of the Palestinian Arab population.

The extreme Israeli right took this argument of the left and made its own policy prescriptions. The Kahanists (followers of Meir Kahane) argued that Israel should throw out all the Arabs. The followers of Rehavam "Gandhi" Ze'evi said that we should bribe the Arabs to agree to be "transferred." People like Avigdor Lieberman said that Israel could make swaps and transfer areas populated by Israeli Arab citizens to Palestine, and areas heavily populated by Israeli settlers to Israel.

This paradigm shift, in fact, led to an ideological split within the ruling Likud Party. Many of its members, especially those in its more democratic liberal wing, could no longer toe the party line of the Likud. People like Tsippi Livni and Ehud Olmert could not remain within Likud, and people like Benny Begin, Dan Meridor, and Ruby Rivlin stayed in the party but were marginalized because none was willing to give up on democracy. Keeping all of Judea and Samaria (the West Bank) and giving all its non-Jewish residents voting rights endangered the Jewishness of the state, while not giving them voting rights would be the end of democracy. The rest of Israel's political right wing, including most of the Likud and the religious right, were, ultimately, willing to sacrifice democracy rather than consider giving up on any portion of the land of Israel.

My problem with defining the issue in demographic terms is that the peace becomes one of interests rather than a peace based upon values. What kind of peace could we really have if Jewish citizens of Israel look at their fellow Arab citizens as a threat? If one sees the womb of the Arab woman as a threat, then we are basing our policies, our prescriptions for peace, on fear. This is no way to establish a real, lasting peace.

RELIGIOUS PEACE

On the other hand, a religious peace is a peace of values, where the values of the belief systems—such as that we are all created by and in the image of the same God, that crushing the other is crushing the Divine in the other—are part of the fabric of the peace. I believe that if we believe that it was God's plan for us to come back to the Holy Land and establish a Jewish state again as part of the fulfillment of our prophecies, then it was also part of God's plan that there is another people living here. It is very important to make this theological statement.

On the basis of this belief, it is clear to me we have to work it out together, not because we are doomed to be here together, but because that is part of what God expects us to do. Based on the value, "do not do unto another, that which is hateful to you," which is both a Jewish value and one shared by Christians and Muslims alike, it is incumbent upon Israelis and Palestinians to compromise and reach an accommodation together. If we expect Palestinians and Muslims to accept our right to self-determination, so too must we accept the right of the Palestinian people to self-determination, from the point of view of a basic religious and ethical value.

If we look at the other as a partner and not as an enemy, and we don't work on a "divide and conquer" attitude toward the other, then we might conclude that it would be good for all Palestinian parties to be involved in making peace with us. This would create a difference in our attitude and policies toward the Palestinians, and vice versa.

According to this viewpoint, it would not necessarily be a problem if there are Palestinians living in the State of Israel and Jews living in the State of Palestine, once peace is established. Rather than being each other's enemies, the Palestinians and Israelis would actually become partners with each other. Israeli Jews would be partners to a broader Muslim and Arab world that would also become partners to a peace process (of which they are not part today). This is another benefit of the religious peace process over the secular peace process.

My theory of a religious peace process has dominated my efforts toward peace within the Middle East for the past several decades and still guides me in all that I do in this field today.

PRACTICAL PEACEBUILDING:
THE ALEXANDRIA PROCESS

While I believe in theory, I also know that theories must be tested in practice. And this is what I have been doing for the past twenty-five years, first on a smaller scale, then on a larger scale, most of which are efforts that must remain, for now, under the public radar. We have a principle that "a blessing is hidden from the eye."

I started meeting more than two decades ago with leading Arab and Palestinian figures to confirm my belief that there are partners both on the Jewish and on the Arab side of this conflict. At every place I visited, and with so many leaders with whom I have spoken and described the idea of a peace based upon religious values, and not devoid of them, I received positive responses. I was told that if there is truly a religious peace process, then they are willing to go all the way for peace.

This led to the historic interreligious meeting in Alexandria, Egypt, in 2002. Together with my Palestinian counterpart, the late Sheikh Talal Sider, we initiated an interreligious summit, cosponsored by the Mufti of Egypt, Grand Imam of al-Azhar Mosque and Grand Sheikh of al-Azhar University Muhammad Sayyid Tantawi, the Archbishop of Canterbury George Carey, and Chief Rabbi Eliyahu Bakshi-Doron. The idea was to bring all the essential religious figures from Israel and Palestine together, under the auspices of Egypt, and the biggest religious institution in the Muslim world, al-Azhar, to adopt common principles aimed at preventing the region's religious sensibilities from being exploited during conflicts, and declaring the need to work together toward peaceful solutions of the conflicts.

At that time, I served as Deputy Minister of Foreign Affairs in the government of Israel. Sheikh Talal Sider, who was a minister in the Palestinian Government, became a close friend and excellent partner. Our work took place during the peak of the Second Intifada, which made it very complicated since bombs were going off all the time and there was much counterterrorism activity as well. Nevertheless, the process sent an important message and has had multiple effects within and outside of the region.

The Declaration of Principles we wrote and signed in Alexandria has become, in our region and in other areas of the world, the foundation for understanding how to create the religious basis for peace. The idea is that religious peace should support the secular peace, which is negotiated by the elected leaders, rather than replacing it. The religious leaders would work on Track II diplomacy to legitimize the religious perspective toward peace. Everyone involved was in agreement with these principles.[4]

Even as far away as Kaduna, Nigeria, Christians and Muslims carved the text of the Alexandria document in stone, in a place where tens of thousands of people had been killed. All the warring factions, led by courageous leaders, signed their own agreement using the same formula as the Alexandria agreement. There has not been one person killed due to religious conflict in this place since.

The major part of the text of the Alexandria Declaration reads as follows:

According to our faith traditions, killing innocents in the name of God is a desecration of his Holy Name, and defames religion in the world. The violence in the Holy Land is an evil which must be opposed by all people of good faith. We seek to live together as neighbors, respecting the integrity of each other's historical and religious inheritance. We call upon all to oppose incitement, hatred, and the misrepresentation of the other.

1. The Holy Land is holy to all three of our faiths. Therefore, followers of the divine religions must respect its sanctity, and bloodshed must not be allowed to pollute it. The sanctity and integrity of the Holy Places must be preserved, and the freedom of religious worship must be ensured for all.
2. Palestinians and Israelis must respect the divinely ordained purposes of the Creator by whose grace they live in the same land that is called Holy.
3. We call on the political leaders of both parties to work for a just, secure, and durable solution in the spirit of the words of the Almighty and the Prophets.
4. As a first step now, we call for a religiously sanctioned cease-fire, respected and observed from all sides, and for the implementation of the Mitchell and Tenet recommendations, including the lifting of restrictions and return to negotiations.

5. We seek to help create an atmosphere where present and future generations will coexist with mutual respect and trust in the other. We call on all to refrain from incitement and demonization, and to educate our future generations accordingly.
6. As religious leaders, we pledge ourselves to continue a joint quest for a just peace that leads to reconciliation in Jerusalem and the Holy Land, for the common good of all our peoples.
7. We announce the establishment of a permanent joint committee to carry out the recommendations of this declaration, and to engage with our respective political leadership accordingly.

The Alexandria document was supported by both the Israeli and Palestinian governments and many religious leaders. Many positive developments stemmed from it, but there was a major factor that kept us from progressing to the next level and creating a full religious peace. That factor was that those who participated in the Alexandria Conference were, for the most part, already believers in compromise and peace.

What I came to understand during the Alexandria process and afterward is that we need to get those who are skeptical and opposed to peace, those who are in favor of *jihad* (Holy War), those who are in strong opposition, to join our forces for a religious peace. Therefore, in the last three to four years, we have built a Jewish center called "Mosaica," and our Muslim partners have built four centers they call "Adam Centers," led by Sheikh Imad el-Falugi in Gaza, Sheikh Nimr Darwish in Kafr Qassem, Dr. Abed Abdul Rahman in East Jerusalem, and one in Ramallah. Together these centers function as hubs for our work on religious conflict transformation.

In addition, we have created a broad network of contacts throughout the Jewish, Muslim, and Christian world. Our coalition is made up of religious authorities from Egypt (from both sides in the Egyptian controversy) and leading figures from many other countries, including radical figures whom most people would be surprised to learn are willing to talk about peace. We have also gained the participation of leading figures in Israel and the Jewish world, who are joining our movement in order to create and promote religious peace under certain guidelines. In principle, the idea is to rally support from more extreme factions, from those who have been skeptical. We have reached many people in much of the Muslim world (including countries with whom Israel has no relations), who want peace with the State of Israel, not peace at the expense of the State of Israel, and who are willing to accept it, if it is done on the premise of a religious peace. These are people who distance themselves from the current secular peace process, people who have been supporting jihad, whose entire lives have become transformed when they encounter this alternative and are today willing to accept the principle of two states for two peoples. I have had remarkable encounters with Islamic figures. This is an alternative that was never presented to them before. In the past, they were only presented with secular versions of peace. Likewise, when rabbis hear the Islamists in our meetings, they are remarkably transformed. They say, "This is completely different from the concept of 'The New Middle East' from which we are totally estranged."

There is potential for a major change today in the Islamic world. We know that there were planned terrorist acts that were stopped because of this work. We know that there have been teachers in the Islamic world who are now teaching a different story because of the relationships that have been established. And on the Jewish side, we have a network of influential rabbinical figures who support our work. Therefore, I believe that this work remains essential. I think that it has all the potential to change the world. This is the test of our religions, that is, the ability to transform the world from war to peace.

One question that remains is whether the policymakers are serious in wanting to make peace. And this remains to be seen. The fact that our leaders today are theoretically working for peace while sending messages to the public totally disconnected from that effort makes me skeptical. Saying, "There is no partner for peace" and "It's not going to happen in our lifetime" and then suddenly telling Israelis, "We've given away half of Jerusalem and all of Judea and Samaria, and now we have peace" is not a recipe for success. If our leaders are serious, then the religious peace is the missing link.

The religions and religious leaders and teachers have to be part of creating an identity, a narrative, which makes Track I diplomacy possible. There has to be a change in the substance of Track I. If that happens, the religious leaders may give their support to the policymakers to legitimize the work they are doing and the path on which they are taking us. Former Prime Minister Yitzhak Rabin once said that he could never have signed the Oslo Accords without the support of Rabbi Ovadia Yosef. This is important, even though Rabin didn't necessarily think through all the implications of that statement.

When the whole issue of a religious, cultural narrative led by religious leaders and teachers comes together, there will have to be a meeting point between Track I and Track II. In this process, the religious leaders will support Track II once they feel it really benefits their communities and their societies.

Once Abu Mazen said to me at one of our meetings, "What your coalition is doing is taking the biggest stumbling block on the path to peace and pushing it aside." That was the metaphor that he used. And I think it's true. The sincere policymakers will be able to see the potential in this. I will continue to be involved in this because it is central to who we are as a religious people. It is the essence of Judaism and is an effort to help our set of values and morals survive.

As I wrote above, a peace of interests signed by political leaders alone, like that between Begin and Sadat, is not enough. If a religious peace is part of the process, then it can be a real peace between the peoples that touches on their core identities. I am not naïve. Of course security precautions will be necessary, but the issue is very different when the peoples actively support the peace. That is part of creating a whole new vision, not because we hate and fear each other, but because we are talking about a whole new way of living together, and it doesn't happen overnight. And that's why it is so important.

Unlike most people who talk about making peace, we are actually "doing it" and showing that it is possible. There is no guarantee, but I know that it is possible. It is in our hands.

Notes

1. Bishop Desmond Tutu was an Anglican bishop in South Africa who used his position to fight apartheid, long before the period of the Truth and Reconciliation Commission.

2. Yossi Sarid is a left-wing former politician who served as a member of the Israeli Knesset from 1974 to 2006. During some of those

years, he led the Meretz political party and served as a minister in the government.

3. Yasser Abed Rabbo is a leading Palestinian politician, former PLO executive committee member, minister in the Palestinian National Authority, and member of several negotiating teams with Israel.

4. On this basis, later on, the Council of Religious Leaders in the Holy Land was created.

JEWISH-
MUSLIM
RELATIONS
IN ISRAEL

Muslim Points of View

IN SEARCH OF ISLAM
The Wasatia Rainbow

MOHAMMED S. DAJANI DAOUDI

And thus We have made you a middle-ground nation.
(Holy Qur'an, Baqarat [Cow] Surah v 143)

INTRODUCTION

Moderation in the West remains, surprisingly, a neglected virtue; similarly, *wasatia* is an essential yet ignored Islamic doctrine. The purpose of this article is to shed light on this important concept particularly as adopted in Islam.

The dominant paradigm is that the prominence of extremism in the world would give rise to a strong support of moderation and moderate trends, parties, and movements. Unfortunately, such is not the case. Thus, this poses enduring questions: What is most important to us? Do we want to have moderation in our lives and politics? If so, what should we do to achieve it? Are our priorities in order? The clock is ticking. Noah did not wait until the flood came to build his ark. Focusing on radical Islamic movements is making many Western observers underestimate the glowing appeal of *wasatia* among the Muslim masses. The strength of *wasatia* flows from its secure grounding in the sacred text of the Holy Qur'an as a major source for its vision, ideology, and thinking as well as the Sunnah.

WASATIA: MEANING AND SIGNIFICANCE

Linguistically, the term *wasatia* is derived from the Arabic word *wasat* meaning "middle of the road," or "center of the circle." The top of the mountain is its center (and best location); also, the largest jewel falls in the center of a necklace. In the spring and in the fall, the sun stands at the balancing point, at the center. The word implies a balance of extremes—between rich and poor, generosity and stinginess, high and low, empty and full, rashness and cowardice.

Religiously, *wasat* in the Holy Qur'an is used to mean justice, moderation, middle ground, centrism, tolerance, temperance, and fairness. Like the word *equinox*, *wasatia* is about balance. To activate peace and justice in the current climate of escalating fear and violence, one must reclaim that balance between adulation and hate, affinity and enmity, deep despair and high expectations.

MODERATION IN ISLAM

There are two core sources of Islam: a major source—the Holy Qur'an—and a minor source—the *Sunnah*. "*I leave behind two things, the Quran and the Sunnah, and if you follow these you will never go astray*" (quoted from the Prophet's "Farewell Sermon," delivered on Mount Arafat in the year 632).

Muslims believe that the Holy Qur'an is the Word of God revealed to Prophet Muhammad by the Archangel Gabriel. "And the Word of your Lord has been fulfilled in truth and in justice. None can change His Words" (Cattle Surah v 115). "He guides whom He will to the right path" (Cow Surah v 142).) The *Sunnah* relates the life and *hadith* (sayings) of the Prophet that illuminate his thoughts and actions, accompanied by their sources.

The Surah in the Holy Qur'an that tends to capture the religious mind set of the Muslim people is this: "Thus have We made of you an Ummatan Wasatan [justly balanced, mid-ground nation]" (Cow Surah v 143), which calls upon Muslims to avoid extremism. In the Qur'anic Surah of Al-In'am, God instructs Muslims to avoid extremist religious practices. Prophet Muhammad is quoted to have said, "The best affairs are those that are centrist" (v 153).

The concept of moderation (*wasatia)* is reflected in a variety of

Qur'anic verses such as the following: "Be neither miserly nor prodigal, for then you should either earn reproach or be reduced to penury" (Israa' Surah v 27); "Do not squander (your wealth) wastefully, for the spendthrifts (wasteful) are Satan's brothers" (Israa' Surah vv 26–27); "And let not your hand be tied (like a miser) to your neck, nor stretch it forth to its utmost reach (like a spendthrift. So that you become blameworthy and in severe poverty.' (Be neither miserly nor prodigal, for then you should either be reproached or be reduced to penury.)" (Israa' Surah v 29); "Pray neither with too loud a voice nor in a low voice, but seek between these extremes a middle course" (Israa' Surah v 110); "Do not treat men with scorn, nor walk proudly on the earth: Allah does not love the arrogant and the vainglorious. Rather let your gait be modest and your voice low: the harshest of voices is the braying of the ass" (Luqman Surah v 19); "Eat and drink, but avoid excesses. He does not love the intemperate (He likes not those who waste by extravagance)" (Al-A'raf Surah v 31); "O people of the Book! Do not transgress (overstep) the bounds of your religion, nor say of God anything but the truth" (An-Nisaa Surah v 171); "As for those who are scornful and proud, He will sternly punish them" (An-Nissa Surah v 173).

Similarly, Judaism and Christianity call for moderation. Both faiths emphasize the avoidance of extremes and the rejection of fanaticism and radicalism. "The Torah may be likened to two paths, one of fire, the other of snow. Turn in one direction, and you will die of heat: turn to the other and you die of the cold. What should you do? Walk in the middle" (Talmud: *Hagigah* 2:1); "Three things are good in small quantities and bad in large: yeast, salt, and hesitation" (Talmud: *Berahkot* 34a); "There are eight things of which a little is good and much is bad: travel, mating, wealth, work, wine, sleep, spiced drinks, and medicine" (Talmud: *Gittin* 70a); "Too much sitting aggravates hemorrhoids; too much standing hurts the heart; too much walking hurts the eyes; so divide your time between the three" (Talmud: *Ketubbot* 111b); "Give me neither poverty nor riches" (Prov 30:8); "A soft answer turneth away wrath" (Prov 15:1); "He that is slow to anger appeaseth strife" (Prov 15:18); "Let your moderation be known unto all men" (Phil 4:5); "Be not righteous over much; neither make thyself over wise; why shouldst thou destroy thyself?" (Eccl 7:16); "Every man that striveth for the mastery is temperate in all things" (1 Cor 9:25); "The fruit of the spirit is...temperance" (Gal 5:22, 23); "Be not drunk with wine, wherein is excess" (Eph 5:18); "A bishop must be...sober, just, holy, temperate" (Tit 1:7, 8); "Add to your faith virtue; and to virtue knowledge; and to knowledge temperance" (2 Pet 1:5–6); "Let every man be swift to hear, slow to speak, slow to wrath" (Jas 1:19); "Too much good food is worse than too little bad food"; "Moderation is the silken string running through the pearl chain of all virtues" (Joseph Hall, Bishop of Norwich [1574–1656] in his introduction to *Christian Moderation*).

The Holy Qur'an confirms religious freedom and calls for its establishment on a foundation of conviction and free will in a number of verses: "Say: Unbelievers, I do not serve what you worship, nor do you serve what I worship....You have your own religion, and I have mine" (Unbelievers Surah vv 1, 6); "Had your Lord pleased, all the people of the earth would have believed in Him. Would you then force faith upon men?" (Jonah Surah v 99); "Say: This is the truth from your Lord. Let him who will, believe in it, and him who will, deny it" (Cave Surah v 29); "There shall be no compulsion in religion. True guidance is now distinct from error. He that renounces idol worship and puts faith in God shall grasp a firm handle that will never break. God hears all and knows all" (Cow Surah v 256); "Among His other signs are the creation of heaven and earth and the diversity of your tongues [variations in your languages] and your colors. Surely there are signs in this for all mankind" (Romans Surah v 22); "Had your Lord pleased, He would have united all mankind. But only those whom He has shown mercy will cease to differ. For this end He has created them" (Houd Surah v 118).

Islam views the world and humanity as multinational, multicultural, and multireligious. Islam reveres and respects all heavenly religions and calls the faithful to believe in God, his angels, his apostles, and his holy books: "He has revealed to you the Book with the Truth confirming the scriptures which preceded it. He has already revealed the Torah and the Ingeel [Gospel] before for the guidance of mankind, and the distinction between right and wrong" (Imran Surah v 3); "O mankind! We have indeed created you from one man and one woman, and have made you into various nations and tribes so that you may know one another; indeed the more honorable among you, in the sight of Allah, is one who is more pious among you; indeed Allah is All Knowing, All Aware" (Hujurat Surah v 13); "Had your Lord pleased, He would have made you one nation" (Table Surah v 48); "Among His other signs are the creation of heaven and earth and the diversity of your tongues and colors. Surely there are signs in this for all mankind" (Greeks Surah v 22); "Had it been Allah's will, He could have made them all of one religion" (Shura Surah v 8); "Had He pleased, He would have guided you all aright" (Bee Surah v 9); "We raised an apostle in every nation, proclaiming: 'Worship God and avoid false deities.' Amongst them were some whom Allah guided, and others destined to go astray" (Bee Surah v 36); "Oh People, We have created you from a male and a female and divided you into nations and tribes that you might get to know one another. The noblest of you in God's sight is he who fears Him most" (Chambers Surah v 13).

The Holy Qur'an recognizes the preceding Holy Scriptures: "And to you, We have revealed the Book with the truth. It confirms the Scriptures which came before it and stands as a guardian over them" (Table Surah v 48).

Jews, Christians, and Muslims all worship God, who is one, living and subsistent, merciful and almighty, the creator of heaven and earth, and await the Day of Judgment and the reward of God following the resurrection of the dead. "God is our Lord and your Lord; for us falls the responsibility for our deeds and for you for your deeds. There is no contention between us and you. Allah will bring us together, and to him is our final destination" (Consultation Surah v 15); "Say: O People of the Book! Come to that which is common between us and you; that we worship none but God, and that we ascribe divinity to nothing besides Him; and that we shall not take human beings for our lords besides God. And if they refuse, then say: 'Bear witness that it is we who have surrendered ourselves unto Him'" (Imran Surah v 64).

Islam makes the faith of the Muslim incomplete until one believes in God and his apostles without any distinction: "O believers! Believe in God and His Messenger; and the revelation which He has sent to His Messenger, and the revelations which He sent to those before him. Those who deny God, and his angels, His Books, His messengers, and the Day of Judgment, have gone far, far astray" (Women Surah v 136); "Those that deny God and His Apostles and those that draw a line between God and His apostles, saying: 'We believe in some, but deny others,'—thus seeking a middle way—these indeed are the unbelievers....As for those that believe in Allah and His apostles and discriminate against none of them, they shall be rewarded by God" (Women Surah vv 150–51); "Those that believe in God and His apostles are the truthful ones" (Hadid Surah v 19); "Say: We believe in Allah and that which is revealed to us; in what was revealed to Abraham, Ishmael, Isaac, Jacob, and the tribes; to Moses and Jesus and the other prophets by their Lord. We make no distinction amongst any of them, and to God we submit ourselves" (Baqara Surah v 136).

The Holy Qur'an cites both the Torah and the Bible, describing them as truthful, revealed for the guidance of people: "He has revealed to you the Book with the truth, confirming the scriptures which preceded it; for He has already revealed the Torah and the Gospel for the guidance of men, and the distinction between right and wrong" (Imran Surah vv 3, 4). Muslims are urged to seek council from Christians and Jews in understanding the Holy Qur'an: "If you are in doubt of what We have revealed to you, ask those who have read the scriptures before you" (Yunis Surah v 94).

There are nearly sixty verses in the Holy Qur'an that mention Jews or refer to them. At times, the Holy Qur'an uses the term *sons of Israel* to describe Jews. It also refers to Jews and Christians as "People of the Book" and "those who were delivered the Book." "And do not dispute with the People of the Book, except with means better (than mere disputation), unless it be with those of them who inflict injury; but say, 'We believe in the Revelation which was revealed to us and in that which was revealed to you; Our God and your God is One, and it is to Him We bow'" (Spider Surah v 46); "O Children of Israel, Keep in your minds the favors I bestowed on you, and fulfill your covenant with Me as I fulfill My Covenant with you" (Cow Surah v 40); "Children of Israel, remember the blessing I have bestowed on you, and that I have exalted you above the nations" (Cow Surah v 47); "And remember We took a Covenant from the Children of Israel to worship none but Allah" (Cow Surah v 83); "Children of Israel, remember that I have bestowed favors upon you, and exalted you above the nations" (Cow Surah v 122); "O you Children of Israel! We delivered you from your enemy, and We made a Covenant with you on the right side of Mount [Sinai], and We sent to you manna and the salwa [quails]" (Taha Surah v 80); "We did aforetime grant to the Children of Israel the Book, the Power of Command, and Prophethood; We gave them, for sustenance, things good and pure, and We favored them above the nations" (Bowing the Knee Surah v 16); "We delivered aforetime the Children of Israel from humiliating punishment, inflicted by Pharaoh, for he was arrogant

[even] among inordinate transgressors. And we chose them afore time above the nations, knowingly, and granted them signs in which there was a manifest trial" (Smoke Surah vv 30–33).

A persistent claim is spread by many that the Qur'an describes all Jews as "apes." In fact, this is a misinterpretation of the following verse, which says that God had punished those who transgressed on the Sabbath by turning them to apes: "And you know well those amongst you who transgressed in the matter of the Sabbath: We said to them: Be you apes, despised and rejected" (Cow Surah v 65). In Judaism, the Hebrew Bible warns, "He who works on a Sabbath should be put to death" (Exod 31:15).

God in the Holy Qur'an chides those Jews who behaved wrongfully: "There came to you Moses with clear signs, yet ye worshiped the Calf after him, and ye did behave wrongfully" (Cow Surah v 92). Also, he warns Muslims that Jews and Christians may not be pleased with the new Islamic faith: "You will please neither the Jews nor the Christians unless you follow their faith" (Cow Surah v 121).

With regard to Christians, the Holy Qur'an states, "We sent forth Noah and Abraham, and bestowed on their offspring prophethood and the scriptures....After them We sent other apostles, and after those Jesus the son of Mary. We gave him the Gospel and put compassion and mercy in the hearts of his followers" (Iron Surah v 27); "After those prophets, We sent forth Jesus, the son of Mary, confirming the Torah already revealed, and gave him the Gospel, in which there is guidance and light, corroborating that which was revealed before it in the Torah, a guide and an admonition to the righteous" (Table Surah v 46); "O believers! Be helpers of Allah. As Jesus the son of Mary said to his disciples: 'who will be my helpers in [the work of] God?' The disciples said: 'We are God's helpers!' At that time, a portion of the children of Israel believed, and some disbelieved. But We gave power against their enemies to those who believed, and they were the ones who prevailed" (Battle Array Surah v 14).

THE *WASATIA* MOVEMENT IN PALESTINE

The flames of religious radicalism continue to be fanned across the globe and in much of the Muslim world. In Palestine, Islam as a religion remains a focal point in the lives of the Palestinians and in molding and shaping the content and vision of Palestinian society. However, one of the consequences of the Israeli continued occupation of Palestinian territories has resulted in the radicalization of society. Palestinian youth are growing up believing that Palestinian Muslims, Christians, and Jews are not meant to coexist, let alone thrive together.

In the last decade, Islamic religious radicalism has been growing sharper among the religious preachers of the Palestinian community. As a result, an entire generation of Palestinians is becoming increasingly radicalized in their religious views and their hostilities to the other, creating communal discord rather than peaceful coexistence within the Palestinian community. There is deep ignorance about Islamic *wasatia* religious values and their place in Islamic thinking, even among religious Muslims.

The *Wasatia* movement in Palestine was founded in January 2007 in response to the challenges facing Palestinian society. Its founders carved for it a multifold task:

- To clarify the distortions to which Islam has been subjected at home and in the West;
- To bring a deeper and more rational understanding of Islam to Muslims as well as to non-Muslims;
- To seek answers for the deep political, social, and economic crises affecting Palestinian society;
- To strive and work for ending the Israeli military occupation through negotiations and peaceful means;
- To spread and promote Islamic concepts, values, and principles of tolerance within the Palestinian community;
- To encourage the practice of moderation among Palestinians in order to mitigate religious radicalism and bigotry and reduce political extremism;
- To bring a message of peace, moderation, justice, coexistence, tolerance, and reconciliation to the Palestinian community through vocal civic leaders;
- To teach creative and critical thinking and open-mindedness.

The *Wasatia* movement emphasizes avoidance of extremes and the rejection of radicalism. It aspires to foster a culture of justice and balance that would attract Palestinians who are centrist in their political and religious beliefs. In fostering coexistence and tolerance, the *Wasatia* movement aims to create a culture in which Palestinian children will not grow up with the literature of hate and violence, but rather will blossom in a culture of coexistence, peace, tolerance, and harmony. The main thrust of the *Wasatia* movement is to create a culture of moderation within the Palestinian community in the hope that this would contribute to healing political, social, and religious divisions within society and help build a more peaceful community. "*Wasatia* culture" in this context means tolerance, speaking out against bigotry, countering extremism and fanaticism, upholding the freedom of religion, empowering minorities and women, and coexisting peacefully with oneself as well as with the other.

The *Wasatia* movement aims to correct extremist ideas and encourage Muslims to discard extremist beliefs and ways of thinking by focusing on a moderate interpretation of the Holy Qur'an to combat the influence of radical extremists. It employs three types of education: (1) *talim*—formal education, by promoting basic knowledge and information; (2) *tarbiyyeh*—proper upbringing by focusing on ethical behavior and teaching Islamic morality; (3) *hiwar*—dialogue and discussions with radicals to hear what they have to say and to explore their point of view.

In Palestine, there is a multivaried elite, a combination of those who studied in Western Europe and the United States; those who studied in Arab universities such as Jordan, Egypt, Syria, and Iraq; and those who studied in the Soviet Union and the Eastern Bloc. Secularism bonds them together and unifies them against religious fundamentalists. While secular and liberal ideas join them together, however, these same ideas separate them from the masses that are deeply attached and committed to Islam. While the Palestinian elite reads such authors as Rousseau, Voltaire, Kant, Locke, Nietzsche, Marx, Lenin, and Guevara, the Palestinian masses read the Holy Qur'an, the *sira* (life of the Prophet), and the teachings of the Islamic caliphs and thinkers. Even the secular elites have a strong attachment to Islam.

A trend engaged in a challenging endeavor requires a capable enlightened leadership to provide *al-qiyada al-hakima, al-rashida, wa-al-adela* (just, capable, and wise leadership). The qualifications of such a leadership should combine courage in the face of adversity, scholarly abilities, and personal openness that enjoy respect in their community.

They should be connected by long-standing personal relationships, durable intellectual connections tangibly expressed by joint lectures, conferences, and public seminars, and should be known for their devotion and commitment to the Palestinian cause. They would be filling a leadership void at high risk and danger to their personal safety.

The *Wasatia* movement appeals to a constituency of individuals who have a deep commitment to Islam and to its approach to conflict resolution through moderate and peaceful means. On this foundation it aspires to build a more promising future. The goal will remain the establishment of a Palestinian state with Jerusalem as a shared capital, as stipulated by the Oslo Accords. By cherishing Islamic values of centrism, moderation, justice, balance, and tolerance, the *Wasatia* movement adopts dialogue and negotiations as the best way to resolve conflicts or differences to reach a win-win situation, that out of the ashes of agony, pain, and suffering, a mutually accepted compromise may emerge.

The *Wasatia* movement in Palestine is not about the dialogue taking place in other Islamic countries between the Islamists and the secularists on the relationship between state and religion. Palestinians are paying little attention to the call by Islamists for an exclusive Islamic Caliphate formed on the foundations of the *khilafa* since it does not provide the people with a moderate democratic state that would meet the conditions of the modern globalized world.

Islam as a civilization is inclusive and tolerant, far from the closed and rigid ideas that the notion of a religious state invokes. However, an exclusive secular state would not provide the kind of political system required by the conditions of a multireligious Palestinian community. Thus, the debate that *wasatia* stirs among Palestinians is not about the idea of a secular order versus a religious state, nor is it about the role of sharia in society, but is rather about where Islam stands vis-à-vis Jews and Christians and what type of relationship they should have.

CONCLUSIONS

From its early history, the Muslim *Ummah* (community) has been treading a mid course in its religious journey between radical fanaticism and total secularism. It is time for the *wasatia* creed to emerge and rise in the Muslim world that it may guide the Muslim *Ummah* in its search for the right path. Muslims should always be proud of their moderate Islamic traditional heritage. No one needs to be reminded that it was Islam that kept learning alive during the Dark Ages. The goal should be not to focus on problems and conflicts but to search for ways and means to solve those problems and conflicts. It is not enough to identify the disease; it is necessary to find the cure. Here, we need to remember, peace starts with moderation, peace continues with moderation, and peace is sustained by moderation.

THE DISCOURSE OF CHILDREN

GHASSAN MANASRA*

*Arise, wake up, there is not much time left for the morning prayer, come meet yourself....*My grandfather's hand caressed my arm gently and with spiritual love. I arose lazily, purified myself, and went to stand by his side with the others, my cousins, on the porch of his house in Nazareth, in the Galilee. It was after a fascinating Ramadan night spent in the company of grandfather, the Sufi sage, who would tell us and teach us his wise stories. At that time, when I was seven or eight, I first understood what it meant to "meet yourself" as you prayed.

When my grandfather passed away, I looked for a sheikh who could guide me along the path of life and show me the way of religion and spirituality. I found in Jerusalem, the holy city, a greatly respected sheikh, Sheikh Mohammad Hashem Al-Baghdadi, who in time became both my spiritual guide and my father-in-law.

The first time I came to him, I was about fifteen years old. In our first meeting I asked him many questions. He looked at me with warmth in his eyes, with a fatherly smile on his face, and replied, "My son, know yourself." I said to him, "Sheikh, what is it about you Sufis? My grandfather would say to me, 'arise and meet yourself,' and now you are telling me, 'know yourself.'" He said, "At the right time, you will understand what I mean." And then he nodded with his head, as if to indicate our meeting was over.

The years have passed. I have immersed myself in Sufism to the best of my ability, studied Sufi wisdom at every moment. At the same time, I studied Islam diligently, learning about the teachings of the

---

* Translated by Rakheli Hever.

greatest thinkers and philosophers in the world of Islam, such as Al-Ghazzali, Al-Shaf'i, Ibn-Rashad, Ibn-Arabi, Saharurdi, and others.

After I began engaging in dialogue with the Other, I was finally able to understand the sayings of these two Sufi wise men, their true essence. This deeper understanding made me realize that it is hard for me to know or to meet myself within *myself*, but that through the Other it is possible for me to meet myself as I am reflected in him or her. This added another dimension to my process of self-discovery, as one of the elements of this world.

MY FIRST ENCOUNTER

As the first ray of light touches the earth at dawn, so did I feel when I first entered an interreligious dialogue encounter. I felt internal warmth and started to come closer to parts of my religious thought that had previously been distant from me, merging fable with reality, that which is revealed and that which is hidden. I had a very strange feeling, so much so that it led me to study Jewish thought. This took me further than I had ever anticipated. I discovered the affinity between Islam and Judaism, both in terms of how religious law is structured and in terms of theoretical concepts. I found many more points of convergence that can motivate creativity in religious, spiritual, and literary thought, such as happened in medieval Spain during the Golden Age.

Several things strengthened my resolve to engage in the field of dialogue and to bring the children of Abraham closer together. These included verses in the Qur'an, traditions related to the prophet Muhammad, and the sayings and poetry of Sufi sages, especially the Greatest Master, the thirteenth-century Andalusian Sufi mystic Ibn-Arabi, who said the following in his beautiful poem:

> My heart can take on any form:
> A meadow for gazelles,
> A cloister for monks,
> For the idols, sacred ground,
> Ka'ba for the circling pilgrim,
> The tablets of the Torah,
> The scrolls of the Quran.
> My creed is Love;

Wherever its caravan turns along the way,
That is my belief,
My faith.*

This huge and diverse body of literature awakened within me the desire to delve deeply into the process of self-exploration through the Other, to get to know the Other through the human essence I carry within me. This poetry inspired my motivation to become part of the wave of group dialogue as a therapeutic process for the political, social, religious, and stereotypical problems and diseases of society.

Since the 1990s, I have engaged in interreligious and intercultural dialogue with guests that came into our home. My father, Sheikh Abdessalam Manasra, and I have had conversations at all levels, focusing in particular on the process of understanding the Other as a partner for life and creativity in this country. But to be a leader and a facilitator of interreligious dialogue groups, that is something quite different, a much greater responsibility.

That is why things changed for me when I suddenly became a facilitator. A dialogue group set up by the NGO Yesodot, comprising Jewish, Christian, Muslim, and Druze religious leaders, and facilitated by Khaled Abu Ras, Dr. Dov Maimon, and Fr. Dr. George Khouri, found itself without a Muslim facilitator when Khaled Abu Ras left his position. Without any preparation I was asked to fill in for him. I remember Dr. Maimon saying to my father, who was part of the group in his role as a religious leader, that I didn't have what it takes to be a facilitator of such a group, that I was not familiar with the tools and techniques and had no training for this. I remember my father telling him: "Take him, teach him, and train him, so that we will have Muslim facilitators who are able to promote and guide others with you toward the path of dialogue here and in the world at large."

I entered the group like a little boy afraid of walking on his own, looking toward his father for encouragement. And I found two teachers who taught me and supported me in a wonderful way, Dr. Dov Maimon and Dan Nevo. I felt safe when they were near me. They helped me with every challenge that I encountered and gave me good advice regarding how to succeed as a group facilitator.

---

* Poem 11 of the *Tarjuman Al-Ashwaq*, trans. by Michael A. Sells.

What is a facilitator, and what is a group? It is truly hard to define who is the facilitator or leader in a group of people who are themselves leaders. Many times they facilitate themselves, while the facilitators attempt to guard their ego and maintain their role as those who guide the group's discussions. The group itself is comprised of opposites sitting together in the same room, each of them a world unto himself—a thinker, leader, and facilitator in his own community. That is why the facilitator of the group must be both sharp and sensitive when forging a bond with each of the participants.

It is therefore a sensitive and complex process: bringing a number of people together and turning them into an active and vital group that plays a central part in the dialogue involving the country's leaders, members of two peoples and three religions. In a group comprising twenty-four people, it is possible to find the history, the religious-national and political-cultural heritage, that attempts to guide the group's steps according to the partisan affiliation of each individual within it. The fact that the group also contained secular people added a dimension to the group process, enriched the group's collective thought and its discussions, and led to criticism toward the self, not just toward the Other.

I still remember a crisis of political identity experienced by my cofacilitator and myself in one of the interreligious/intercultural dialogue groups that reflected the political conflict between the Israeli side and the Palestinian side. The conflict penetrated our group, and we almost reached a crisis that threatened the group's existence. Sometimes what you need isn't truth, but rather reconciliation and wisdom, so that you may be able to protect the group from challenges, whether external or internal. Reflecting on how to get the group members out of this difficult situation, I realized that we had to throw a religious challenge at them, to divert them from the political controversy threatening the group. I raised a question for discussion that posed a challenge to the secular people in the group and, wishing to defend their position, they replied rather quickly. After a while, both the Jewish and the Palestinian (Christian and Muslim) religious people in the group stood their ground together, defending religion against secularism. Thus I was able to save the group and take its internal discussions one step forward. In the end, we were able to foster understanding and mutual respect between both groups, the secular and the religious.

THE CHALLENGES INVOLVED IN DIALOGUE

Sometimes when I sit by myself, thinking about starting a new group or looking for an existing group to work with, the difficulties I have encountered with each group in the past come to mind. This is quite interesting: when I'm thinking about these things alone, I always think of the difficulties, but when I'm with others, we always talk about our successes and achievements throughout the years of engaging in dialogue. Perhaps internal dialogue is more affected by our fears and doubts, especially in light of the current political situation in the region. Being in a group makes us stronger; whether or not the people in the group share our religion or our nationality, we feel we are not alone.

I would be lying if I said I haven't paid a heavy price for my work in the field of interreligious and intercultural dialogue. But my faith in this field pushed me deeper and deeper into it. Whenever one of my family members or I was attacked, I would consider leaving this type of work, but after thinking about it for a while, I would realize I must continue and even increase my activities.

One could say that people are naturally afraid of the difficulties, conflicts, and extremism. I'm not really a hero, someone able to withstand the wave of extremism that also reflects on us as a minority within the State of Israel. Many times I also was afraid—so afraid that I didn't want to leave my house and forbade my children to go to school…because the threats are there. Several times I couldn't make it to dialogue meetings I was supposed to facilitate, because I was afraid. I didn't tell the truth at the time, but I tried not to lie. But what can you tell your employers? That you were too afraid to come to work?

I remember a trip to Spain undertaken as part of the Interreligious Coordinating Council in Israel's KEDEM project, with qadis, priests, and rabbis. When I reached Ben Gurion airport at 4 a.m., my mobile phone rang and an unfamiliar voice began threatening me, telling me that I must repent and stop engaging in dialogue, because what I'm doing is heretical. Right before he hung up, he also told me that if I didn't stop, they would kill my sons. Shaken, I approached Sheikh Kamel Riyan, a wise and worldly man who was with us on the trip, and explained to him what had happened. He said that I should ignore the call, that he knows that type of people and that we should just carry on walking in our own path.

That is the external aspect of fear and doubt. But even when I sit alone, thinking about the nature of the dialogue we're engaged in, especially the religious aspect, I encounter a sort of internal tension between my thoughts and my religious identity. Is what I'm doing allowed by the law of my religion, or isn't it? The recurrence of such thoughts isn't only a result of constantly changing human nature, but also has much to do with the institutionalized aspect of religious identity, which tries to close us in our own religious circle, and the traditional religious heritage, which stops us from looking at things more openly, including the Other—in short, the religion that sees itself as the only true one, superior to all other religions. I'm not trying to dismiss or discard the basic tenets of my religion. On the contrary, I'm very proud of my religion and my faith is strong. I don't want to be in conflict with religion. It's true that some important issues should be addressed when it comes to our religious thought, especially in light of changing realities and modernism taking over the world, but we should also maintain the basic guidelines of our religious essence.

All the above, and all the dilemmas running through my head, always lead me to doubt, causing me to wonder whether I'm betraying my religion by doing what I do. But I always kept going without hesitation, because I always felt, intuitively, that this is what I have to do. I felt that I have the responsibility as a human being to do something that, through creating relationships based on understanding and dialogue, can save not only individual people but also the religious and social way of thought. Politics will follow.

A journalist asked me once why I work in the field of dialogue. I said to him that many work at creating conflicts and wars, but I decided to work in the field of reconciliation and mediation. But he should have asked me a different question: What do you get out of this work, personally? I told him that I have a personal stake in this. In every partnership there's a personal stake. If we lose the personal stake in this work, our process might fail, because everyone is looking for their personal gain. My personal stake in this has to do with advancing Arab society, raising its level of education, providing education for tolerance, and making it a more active and open partner for the other nations of the world, able to take part in the current global culture, at all levels. My work in the field of dialogue can promote the realization of these ambitions.

While initiating a dialogue group is something beautiful and important, we cannot expect things to go quite how we'd like them to go. At the beginning of working with one group, my cofacilitators and I had a very positive impression, thinking we had everything under control. But when push came to shove, we realized we were dealing with a very complicated and multifaceted reality in terms of language and political identity. The participants had a strong desire to take part in a dialogue group, but there were many pressures involved from each and every one of them. Slowly, we began to understand each individual and each side's psychology.

During the first encounter, we felt that we were facing a great test. We were afraid of failure. The participants were artificially polite, shying away from expressing themselves verbally, but tension was at a peak. We were just hoping to make it through the first encounter in peace, without crisis. Indeed, all group members seemed pleased and expressed their wish to continue the encounters.

Typically, things would run quite smoothly during dialogue group encounters, especially in religious groups, when the participants discussed topics such as the basic tenets of religion, human dignity, and religion facing changing realities. But when such sensitive topics as bombings or holy places (especially the Al-Aqsa mosque) were discussed, things could heat up to a critical point quite quickly and threaten the cohesiveness of the group. In such cases, we had to save the group from falling apart, and our motto was, "You do not have to agree with the Other, but you do have to respect the Other and his or her faith."

Another issue we had to deal with was challenges to the authority of the facilitators, especially with one group of intellectuals that we worked with, who took it upon themselves to do the facilitation. Facilitators must beware of this, and must be wise, gentle, and sensitive to every undercurrent in the group.

When I worked at Mosaica as a facilitator, we once traveled to Seville for an end-of-the-year conference for a group of school principals and teachers from Jerusalem. In one of the final days of the conference, some members of the group challenged the authority of the facilitators and assumed a leadership role. I remember that we allowed them to lead the discussion throughout that workshop, and after that we went on a break. After the break, we returned to our places gently, with a slight change of the plan.

Sometimes there is the risk of the facilitators themselves losing control. During a KEDEM conference at the Mt. Zion Hotel in Jerusalem, one of the discussions revolved around the Holocaust. One of the Muslim participants protested the quoted number of Jews murdered by the Nazis. At that moment, my Jewish cofacilitator lost his impartiality as a facilitator and brutally intervened in the group discussion. I immediately took the reins to return my partner to the point of balance. Something similar happened to me as well. In one of the encounters I facilitated I almost yelled during a discussion about the character of the prophet Mohammad, but my wise partner helped me regain my balance.

Some say that interreligious/intercultural dialogue groups should only discuss commonalities. There is a lot in common, I agree, but in my opinion, we do not have to focus only on that. We shouldn't fear our differences; I would go as far as saying that we *must* talk about them. We have to touch the core issues of the conflict, because as long as we embellish reality, we cannot be honest with ourselves or with the Other, and we cannot have true dialogue based on transparency and honest intentions.

We kept holding dialogue meetings for religious leaders, social activists, educators, and a few politicians. For the most part, we didn't try to engage entire families. For that purpose, we at the NPO Lights of Peace established the Families Forum. The encounters of this forum involve the family as a whole, parents and children together. It was not enough to just have intellectual discussions, we thought; we also needed the warm and touching personal encounter between all parts of the family, parents and children.

Once a former cofacilitator, Dr. Dov Maimon, invited me to his son's *brit* (circumcision) ceremony. As is my custom whenever I'm invited to a religious or cultural event of a member of another religious group, I took with me one of my children, so that they would be exposed to different cultures and practices. This time it was my daughter Zainab, who was then ten years old. I thought I would be able to keep her with me during the event, but because this ceremony took place within the orthodox Jewish community, she was not allowed to stay with me and had to go to the women's area. I spent my time in the men's area worried that she would not be able to understand the Jewish women: she only speaks Arabic, and they only speak Hebrew. When the ceremony ended and we were driving home together, I asked her how it was for her. I expected a negative reply, but she surprised me by saying that she understood many things. She also had a conversation with Dov's daughter, who explained many things to her. In return, Zainab told her about Muslim traditions. Amazed, I asked Zainab whether Dov's daughter spoke Arabic, and she replied no, and neither does she, Zainab, understand Hebrew. Yet they spoke with each other. I understood that sometimes we don't need to have a shared language in order to connect with someone; all we have to do is be willing, ready, and pure in our desire to create a true bond.

Generally speaking, I do not regret the path my life took on the road of dialogue. I feel that I have grown in wisdom, developing my religious and philosophical thought through intercultural discourse. I was able to get to know myself and my environment in a deeper, more complex way. Dialogue strengthened my universal identity and gave me many tools to communicate with the rest of the world, especially with myself. I started "meeting myself" more, even criticizing myself more. Criticism about one's own self is important, listening to what the Other says, especially when he or she is being honest and just. I don't want to think of myself as being one who is absolutely right; rather, I see myself as an inseparable part of the universe in which we all live.

WAHAT AL-SALAM/ NEVE SHALOM
Community Responses to Conflict

ABDESSALAM NAJJAR,
EDITED BY HOWARD SHIPPIN¹

Dispute resolution methodologies traditionally appeal to shared values and norms that are universally accepted within a given culture. A different type of challenge is involved when it comes to approaching conflict in a multicultural society or between two separate groups that do not share a common belief system, background, or values.

Given that human society is fraught with competition and conflict, one of humanity's responses has been to group together in communities for mutual protection. Each community is founded on bonds based on nation, ethnicity, faith, ideology, and so on. Every one of us belongs to multiple communities with broader or narrower definitions, some imposed upon us by birth or circumstance, others adopted by choice. Each community creates a means of governing various aspects of the life of the individual, sets up an integral system of norms, values, and restraints, and provides the individual with a moral compass.

In traditional societies, the interwoven levels of community to which individuals belonged were usually mutually supportive and non-contradictory. The values of a family would not contradict the values of the community church, mosque, or temple, and the laws of the state would not be out of line with the sermons of its religious leaders.

Today's societies are diverse, multiethnic, and multireligious. Their foundations are less secure, and even long-standing units such as the nuclear family have begun to erode. Within the same state, one can find groups that live in social isolation from one another, lacking the means to communicate or build relationships for mutual benefit.

In our own region of Israel and Palestine, the reality is one of conflict. The divisions are national, ethnic, and religious. Two peoples, each with historical and other claims in the region, are locked in a struggle for land and resources.

WAHAT AL-SALAM/NEVE SHALOM

Within this reality, a small group of Jewish and Palestinian Arab citizens of Israel took the unusual decision to establish a joint community. Coming together at the initiative of a Dominican priest, Bruno Hussar, we settled a twenty-hectare tract of land (almost fifty acres). Our motivation was to see if we could build, within our conflictive reality, a community based on equality and shared responsibility. Further, we hoped to influence the broader society by conducting educational work, dialogue, and joint projects.[2]

As of 2014, we are a village of about sixty families and have established three main educational institutions: first, a bilingual, binational primary school and early childhood center that serves children from the village and from towns in its vicinity; second, the School for Peace, which conducts outreach educational projects throughout Israel and Palestine; and third, the Pluralistic Spiritual Center, which conducts a range of projects, including work with religious institutions, community mediation projects in mixed Jewish-Arab cities, and a crosscultural program for young persons.

From its inception until today, Wahat al-Salam/Neve Shalom has been a living experiment in establishing a heterogeneous community based on the ideal of finding new ways to deal with the reality of conflict, which affects each individual member. To be clear: this is not a utopian experiment based on establishing a common identity. The bonds established between people within the community do not erase the ethnic, religious, national, and linguistic divisions among the residents, and they all continue to feel primary allegiance to the group into which they were born.

Given that the residents of the community of Wahat al-Salam/Neve Shalom are not exceptional people with special qualities (other than the desire to attempt to live together and develop a community together), it is natural that the same challenges to a shared, equal coexistence (within a reality of conflict) that exist in the broader society remain for the residents. Each person who arrives in the community comes with his or her own "baggage," conditioning, prejudices, stereotypes of other people, and so on. Liberal values, tolerance, and acceptance of the other are often severely tested within the web of relationships that is inherent in any small self-governing community.

Communities have traditionally been based on a common nationality, ethnicity, faith, ideology, and so on, and here the challenge is to create a heterogeneous community within a reality of conflict. Obviously, then, the development and sustenance of such a community depend upon vision, learning from shared experience, agreements, and deployment of methodologies and tools found to be useful.

Notwithstanding the desirability of reaching a consensus upon such factors, a community, especially one like ours, does not function like an organization that can commit its members to rules and provisions. In such a community, agreements must, to some extent, be voluntary. The shared framework should be broad enough to facilitate integration of new members and families, who must each go through a personal process of acclimatization to the unusual reality (in Israel) of a small, binational, multifaith community.

Wahat al-Salam/Neve Shalom's vision of itself has grown in parallel to its educational work. The first members were involved in dialogue projects between Jews and Palestinians before taking up residence in the nascent community. They went on to develop the educational institutions of the community, and these have remained central to the life of the community. The ideas and methodologies of their work have evolved as the work continued, and they continue to affect and inform the community. For example, prospective members take part in encounter workshops run by the School for Peace. Parents are closely involved in the work of the primary school and are themselves educated by their children as they experience the festivals and traditions of the other people together in the school. Lectures arranged for facilitators of the School for Peace are open to villagers. Many community members are involved in teaching at the school or have taken facilitator training courses offered by the School for Peace. At various times, the community has engaged in community-building initiatives led by expert consultants. Cultural programs are arranged, and the shared experience of the community is imparted to newcomers or second-generation members through presentations, memorial days for the community's founders, and so on.

THE PLURALISTIC SPIRITUAL COMMUNITY CENTER

In recent years, one of the most significant influences upon the community has been the Pluralistic Spiritual Center (PSC). The PSC is based on and takes its inspiration from its other name, Doumia/Sakinah. *Doumia* is a word appearing in the Hebrew Bible: "To thou Lord, silence [*doumia*] shall be as praise" (Ps 65:2). *Sakinah* is derived from a line in the Qur'an: "He sends tranquility [*sakinah*] into the hearts of the believers, that they may add faith to their faith" (Surah 48.4). The first building in the PSC was a dome-shaped structure intended for meditation, known as the House of Silence.

Like the other educational institutions of the community, however, this center is outward looking: its programs are intended for the benefit of people beyond the community. Yet the community has requested that the center also conduct many of its programs for the residents themselves. Thus it came to be that this rather secular community made the decision that its community center, that is, the heart of its community life, be the *spiritual* center. Part of the reason that the community was willing to give the PSC such a role lies in the definition of spirituality here adopted.

The PSC differentiates itself from religious definitions. Echoing Abdul Aziz Said, Nathan C. Funk, and Lynn M. Kunkle in their article "The Role of Faith in Cross-Cultural Conflict Resolution,"[3] the center declares,

> We believe that it is important to make a distinction between spirituality and religion, because both refer to matters of faith. The term religion refers to an institutional framework within which a specific theology is pursued, usually among a community of like-minded believers. Spirituality, on the other hand, transcends the boundaries of religion, suggesting broader human involvement that comes from the inner essence of a person.

In a heterogeneous and divergent society that lacks uniformity with regard to matters of faith (and where some persons define themselves as atheists or agnostics), a spirituality based on each person's "inner essence" can have an important role in managing or resolving conflict.

The PSC does not present the community members with an escape route from the conflict. Instead, its activities are aimed to provide a safe space in which the conflict, and the role each person plays in it, can be explored. It does so by creating community events and activities that touch upon various aspects of the conflict and stimulate honest and heartfelt discussion. Activities sometimes employ art, music, or drama. Young community members are also invited to attend. For example, at a recent year-end celebration of Christmas, Hijra, and Hanukah, the young people were invited to light candles while expressing their New Year's wishes for social justice, equality, and peace.

Wahat al-Salam/Neve Shalom bases all of its educational work upon the experience of living in a binational community. In the same way, the PSC exists because of the small community but defines its goals in terms of the broader regional context. It lists its aims as

- supporting dialogue among the followers of religions and cultures;
- enhancing dialogue, respect, and cooperation between nations;
- encouraging peace, justice, and reconciliation;
- countering the justification for violence and conflict under any cover.

The PSC provides a framework for encounter activities, study, and reflection based on values of equality, justice, and reconciliation. Its activities draw inspiration from the resources and spiritual traditions of the Middle East and the world at large. It conducts interfaith and cultural dialogue programs and conflict management/resolution projects that focus on open, interreligious, and intercultural dialogue for the advancement of peace and peaceful coexistence between Palestinians and Jews in our region. Many of these are conducted in partnership with other organizations and institutions.

A NEW MULTICULTURAL COMMUNITY CONFLICT RESOLUTION/MEDIATION PROGRAM

Among these activities is a multicultural community conflict resolution and mediation program. We will discuss the underlying ideas of this program more fully because they are relevant to the main theme of this chapter. Dispute resolution methodologies traditionally appeal to shared values and norms that are universally accepted within a given culture. A different type of challenge is involved when it comes to approaching conflict in a multicultural society or between two separate groups who do not share a common belief system, background, or values. To a large extent, this is true of the conflict between Jews and Arabs.

In order to investigate this subject, we conducted a study aimed at developing a new perception of nonviolent conflict resolution in a multicultural context—a concept that would suit our reality. To do this, we wanted to learn first

- how cultural differences affect our behavior,
- whether the power relations between the two groups affect the dynamics of conflict resolution between the two groups,
- whether the imbalance in power relations issues from the cultural differences between the sides, and if so, in what way.

Our main aim was to arrive at a conflict resolution methodology that could be useful in our multicultural context. The resources available to us were the lessons from our experiences as a community, the knowledge derived from our educational work, and theoretical material available in the field.

When two or more groups with different cultures exist together in the same space, there may take place a conflict over resources, status, and so on (the social psychologist Muzafer Sherif's realistic conflict theory). A strong justification given for this rivalry may be cultural differences between the groups.

The social psychologist Henri Tajfel, in his social identity theory, says that we shape our behavior and our identity according to various sets of values and beliefs. Usually, we attribute positive values to these.

Conversely, we assign negative values to modes of behavior seen as inappropriate in our culture. This is true even though these same modes of behavior may be viewed as positive in other cultures. Thus, in evaluating other cultures, we assign the same significance to modes of behavior as we would if these were manifested in our own culture. For example, in Western culture, individual freedom is a supreme value and rises above the needs of the group. On the other hand, in Muslim Arab culture, the needs of the group (society), hegemony, cohesion, and warm relationships often outweigh the needs of the individual.

The concept of culture contains more than a set of values and beliefs that produce norms and certain forms of behavior. The culture into which we are born programs our analysis of a particular event and our reaction to it. This programming becomes the basis for intuition and common sense. To all of those born to the same culture, there is a similar line of reasoning and joint rationale that determines how events and the motivation behind them are analyzed.

Conflict resolution models developed within one culture prove deficient when applied to another, despite attempts to modify or adapt these programs in order to adjust to cultural differences. The theorist J. P. Lederach describes this very well. He suggests that models for conflict resolution must emerge from the culture experiencing conflict. This is based on a belief that every society contains the knowledge to produce solutions to conflictive situations arising within that society.[4]

In our reality, the Jewish-Palestinian conflict is not contained within a single culture or society. It is waged between interest groups from different cultures. The conflict is difficult and ongoing and is characterized by inequality of power relations, the dynamics of majority-minority relations, relationships of dominance and subjugation, and dehumanization of the other. What is viewed as justice by one side will be seen as a burden by the other. Similarly, concepts of justice and mercy are often seen in an opposite light.

Justice, it is often assumed, requires determining the truth and punishing the guilty party. Does mercy, on the other hand, imply forgiveness? Thus, if one prosecutes and punishes the guilty, can mercy at best involve leniency in the sentence? Punishment, however, seldom results in either reconciliation or restitution. Thus, the resulting justice is illusory. The challenge, according to Lederach, is "to pursue justice in ways that respect people, and [at the same time] to achieve restoration of relationships based on recognizing and amending injustices."[5] Thus, Lederach argues that reconciliation involves the identification and acknowledgment of what happened (that is, truth), an effort to right the wrongs that occurred (that is, justice), and forgiveness for the perpetrators (mercy). The end result is not only reconciliation but peace.

Aided by this literature from the field and our experience from conducting mediator training projects, and enriched by contacts with organizations such as Mediators Beyond Borders (United States), we have begun to conduct multicultural mediation projects. A thirteen-week program was concluded in 2011 in the mixed (and tension-fraught) Arab-Jewish city of Acre. Afterward, the group asked to continue. The PSC also provides consultation for other mixed groups.

This engagement with the regional conflict as a whole was the original vision of Wahat al-Salam/Neve Shalom's founder, Father Bruno Hussar, as he describes it in his autobiography:

> People would come here from all over the country to meet those from whom they were estranged, wanting to break down the barriers of fear, mistrust, ignorance, misunderstanding, preconceived ideas—all things that separate us—and to build bridges of trust, respect, mutual understanding, and, if possible, friendship.[6]

Notes

1. This article was originally published in *Dharma World* (July–Sept. 2012) and is reprinted with permission. Abdessalam Najjar passed away in 2012, before finishing this article, and it was completed by his neighbor and friend Howard Shippin, who was also his colleague on Neve Shalom's public relations team.

2. In 1993, Father Bruno Hussar accepted the Niwano Peace Prize on the community's behalf.

3. Abdul Aziz Said, Nathan C. Funk, and Lynn M. Kunkle, "The Role of Faith in Cross-Cultural Conflict Resolution," http://www.amer ican.edu/sis/islamicpeacechair/upload/Role-of-Faith-in-Cross-Cultural-Conflict-Resolution-Said-Funk-Kunkle-Sept01.pdf.

4. J. P. Lederach, *Preparing for Peace: Conflict Transformation across Cultures* (Syracuse, NY: Syracuse University Press, 1995).

5. Ibid., 20.

6. Father Bruno Hussar, *When the Cloud Lifted* (San Francisco: Ignatius Press, 1989).

IS ARAB-JEWISH COEXISTENCE IN ISRAEL STILL POSSIBLE?

ISSA JABER

I am pleased to have been invited to write this essay on the subject of Arab-Jewish coexistence in Israel, since I have been working in this field for the past thirty years. This is a good opportunity for me to share some of the central challenges that we, as Palestinian Arabs of the Muslim religion, face in Israel and the ways we are trying to overcome them.

The subject of coexistence is not only of central interest to me as an educator, but is close to my heart as a human being and as a religious Muslim who believes that the culture of Islam has been, and should continue to be, an open-minded and tolerant one.

PERSONAL HISTORY

I grew up in the village of Abu Ghosh, just west of Jerusalem. If you have been to Israel, you will probably know about many of our Arab restaurants on the main road that are visited by secular Jews from Jerusalem and Tel Aviv, mainly on Saturday.

I have been an educator for most of my adult life, first as a teacher of civics and sociology, then as the principal of the high school in my town, and then as the Director of the Education Department for the municipality. I now serve as mayor of my town. In addition, I have worked as an educator in the Knesset, where I facilitated discussions among Arab and Jewish youth and teachers as part of the Ministry of Education's Unit for Democracy and Coexistence, which operated during the 1990s but has unfortunately since been closed.

In addition, I am one of the founders of the Association for the Promotion of Tolerance and Coexistence in the Judean Hills, which includes kibbutzim, moshavim, and Israeli Arab towns and villages in the area. I have also been proud to serve as the cochairperson of the Interreligious Coordinating Council in Israel (ICCI) for many years and have participated in many of its programs and projects. As such, I have traveled and spoken, with the director of ICCI, in many communities in North America, where we have explained to a wide variety of audiences the importance and the impact of our common educational work for coexistence in Israel.

I am including this background because it is important to understand that I tend to see the world as an educator, not as a politician, even though I have lately entered into politics and was elected mayor of my town (in October 2013). Therefore, this chapter focuses on education, not on politics, because I believe that education is the most important method for ensuring our long-term future as Arabs and Jews living in the same state, and as Palestinians and Israelis living in the same region. Based on my personal experience as a professional educator and as a citizen of the State of Israel, I believe sincerely that coexistence between Jews and Arabs in Israel is possible. Contrary to the many naysayers in our country and abroad, I am confident that we can make it happen and that this is the best option for Jews and Arabs alike. It is the best option for us. The other option—of ongoing war, violence, and hatred—is much less desirable.

THE ISSUES

Nevertheless, this will not be easy. There are some problems and issues concerning our status as members of a minority in a Jewish state that need to be explained in order to understand the situation. The central questions are these: How does the Arab minority in Israel (about 20 percent) live alongside the Jewish majority? What are some of the key issues that we face together as Arabs and Jews? I will discuss four issues: ignorance, identity, education, and problems of community life.

Ignorance

The first problem we face is ignorance. This is a major problem and it has been with us for a long time.

There is almost a total lack of knowledge about each other's religion, history, and culture in Israeli society, among Arabs with regard to Jews and Judaism, and among Jews with regard to Islam and Muslims as well as Christianity and Christians. Speaking personally, I feel that most of my Jewish neighbors and fellow citizens in Israel don't really know me and my community very well, and therefore they continue to live with many dangerous stereotypes, such as that all Arabs are terrorists, or that all Arabs in Israel are a "fifth column" and therefore cannot be trusted.

I would like Jews in Israel and abroad to know and understand the real me and the real us (Israeli Arabs), not just in negative terms but also in positive terms. They should know that we have our own aspirations and dreams—to be normal people, to live a good life—and that we have our own educated and professional class—doctors, lawyers, academics—and that we are not all day laborers.

We Arabs in Israel also don't know very much about our Jewish neighbors—about their culture, history, and religion. We teach a little bit about this in our schools, but most of our children study it in order to pass the exams and don't really like it very much. Too much of what we think we know is superficial and not very deep, because we haven't had enough serious and in-depth educational encounters with our Jewish neighbors.

This ignorance, which can be found on both sides, is the cause of so much mistrust and misunderstanding. It must and can be overcome. We must change the way we teach and the way we learn about each other. Fortunately, this has begun to change in recent years, in the formal educational system and in the informal systems, but much more needs to be done.

Identity

I believe that it is essential for people in Israel and abroad to come to know more about my identity as a Palestinian Muslim Arab, living as a citizen in the State of Israel. Let me explain.

I am a citizen of the State of Israel. I have an Israeli identity card and carry an Israeli passport. I vote in Israel's elections and participate fully in the democratic process. I speak the Hebrew language, even though it is my second language. And I share in the State of Israel's achievements and problems as an equal citizen before the law in this state. This is one part of my identity.

I am also an Arab, which means that my language and my culture are based on Arabic. My native tongue is Arabic; my holy books, especially the Qur'an, are written in Arabic; the poetry and literature that I read are in Arabic; and I educate my children in this language. In this sense, I identify with Arabs around the world, wherever they may live, and share in their culture as it has developed throughout the ages.

I am also a Palestinian. My nationality is Palestinian. I identify with and share in the aspirations of the Palestinian people, even though I will continue to live in Israel, where my home and the homes of the members of my extended family have been for generations, and where I enjoy full citizenship by law and participate fully in the Israeli democracy.

In addition, I am a Muslim, a traditional Muslim. I celebrate the major Muslim festivals with my family and my community. I pray in the mosque in my village. I educate my children about the religion of Islam, a religion that I believe preaches the values of tolerance and peace. I share the basic humanistic values of Islam, which are shared by most Muslims in the world, and I feel a sense of religious kinship with Muslims everywhere.

All of these factors, in various combinations, make up the identity of Muslim Palestinian Arabs living in the State of Israel. It is a complex identity, not a simple one, one that needs to be learned about and understood in its own terms. Through interreligious dialogue and coexistence education, we can do much more in the years ahead to encounter each other and to learn much more about our diverse identities.

Education

As a minority group, we have problems within the Arab sector in Israel that are similar to the problems faced by other minorities in many Western democracies. As I understand it, even minorities in the United States have similar problems. As an educator, I am particularly concerned about the inequities in infrastructure, budgets, and curriculum in our educational system. But more important than all of these day-to-day problems, which we have lived with for too long, is the issue of our culture and identity as expressed (or not) within the educational system.

The key question we ask ourselves is the following: How do we, as Arab educators, develop an educational system that educates our children about the basic civic values and democratic norms of the State of Israel and that at the same time develops and fosters our own national/cultural identity, based upon our own religious and cultural heritage, values, and customs?

For example, for many decades our students have been learning Bible, Jewish history, and even modern Zionist history and Hebrew literature, but only in recent years has the Israeli Ministry of Education enabled us to introduce courses on the religions of Islam and Christianity—the religions of Israeli Arabs—into our curriculum. And only when Yossi Sarid (of the Meretz party) was the Minister of Education was the study of some of our most important Palestinian national poets introduced into our schools—not without controversy in Israeli society.

As the State of Israel matures, and as we continue to grow as a national minority within the Jewish majority, I believe that there will be a continuing need to address these issues of identity within our educational and cultural institutions.

Community Life

Our community institutions have also lagged behind the development of similar institutions within the Jewish sector. For example, only in 1993 did we finally get a modern building for our local council, and only a few years later did we finally succeed in building a modern comprehensive high school in our town of Abu Ghosh, just fifteen minutes west of Jerusalem. More recently, our new modern community center was completed for the benefit not only of the residents but hopefully also for our Jewish neighbors in the surrounding communities with whom we have lived in peaceful coexistence for decades.

As we continue to make progress in the areas of education and community life, it is important to keep in mind that the gaps between the Arab minority in Israel and the Jewish majority are still very wide.

Much will need to be done in the years ahead to empower the Israeli Arab sector to develop its educational and cultural institutions in much more significant and systematic ways than has been done up to now.

ADDRESSING THE PROBLEMS

Ignorance

Combating ignorance of Arabs by Jews, and of Jews by Arabs, is our number one problem. This cannot be done in the schools alone. That is why about twenty years ago I was one of the founders of a non-profit organization called the Association for the Promotion of Tolerance and Coexistence in the Judean Hills. During these twenty years, we have provided courses for Jewish and Arab youth to learn together about art, archaeology, and music. We have worked with the schools and other groups in our communities to arrange for encounters between young people and adults in order for them to get to know one another. In addition, on our holidays and those of our Jewish neighbors, we have had a tradition of *Bayit Patuach* (Open House), in which Jews from nearby kibbutzim and moshavim visit us on our holidays, and we visit them on theirs. This kind of warm and gracious hospitality goes a long way toward strengthening good ties among us, and it helps us forge coalitions of cooperation in many areas.

Over the years, I have found these personal encounters to be very important, not only for our youth but for me personally as well. Not only have many stereotypes been broken down, but we have begun to work together on many issues of common concern, such as educating for coexistence and protecting our environment.

Identity and Education

Several years ago, I was fortunate to have been one of the participants in a Jewish-Muslim Dialogue group organized by the ICCI. Twenty people, ten Israeli Muslims and ten Israeli Jews, met six times over a period of ten months in order to learn about critical issues and themes in each other's religions, cultures, and customs. We learned about the value of human life; the role of women and customs concerning death, dying, and bereavement; and other subjects. In addition, we often discussed contemporary issues informally, usually over a meal together, which helped us understand each other's concerns and fears, especially since the outbreak of violence in Israel in October 2000. In fact, one of our most important meetings took place in November, six weeks after the outbreak of the crisis, and we found that we were able to have a meaningful and beneficial give-and-take. We resolved at that session to continue to meet for another year and to focus on issues of identity in our discussions and to address other issues of mutual concern.

We are also finding that issues of identity are very much on the minds of the teachers in our schools, as well as on the minds of their students. Accordingly, we have developed new materials and new teacher-training programs, in cooperation with the Interreligious Coordinating Council in Israel, to strengthen the Arab cultural identity of our children, while at the same time reinforcing their links to Israeli society through the teaching of civics.

The Community

Like the rest of Israeli society, the Israeli Arab sector is developing modern communal institutions. For example, our new community center in Abu Ghosh was dedicated several years ago. In addition, a new Islamic Cultural Center and mosque—which will serve our community and the wider Arab and Jewish communities in the area—was dedicated in October 2013.

One of the positive outcomes of the Jewish-Muslim dialogue group in which I participated was the development of a new program in community outreach in the community center with the cooperation of ICCI and the National Association of Community Centers in Israel. This was a pilot project in which we helped the local community develop its own professional and lay leadership, not only for the benefit of our town, but for the entire region. In addition to learning together, we engage in social activist projects, such as the betterment of the environment, and we hope these kinds of projects can be expanded throughout Israel.

CONCLUSION

In conclusion, I want to emphasize my main point. Despite the political and security-related problems that we face within the State of Israel, I believe that it is in our power to find ways and means to continue to live in peaceful coexistence and to resolve our differences through peaceful means, via sincere efforts at mutual understanding and not by violence and terror, God forbid. In addition, I believe that a Palestinian state will soon be established next to Israel, with full mutual recognition and normalization between the two states. When this happens, the principles and practice of coexistence that we have developed within Israel can be adapted and taught in the region as well.

As a Muslim Palestinian Arab of Israeli citizenship, I not only believe that coexistence is possible but also that it is imperative. It is the correct moral thing to do, from the point of view of my religion, which promotes tolerance and mutual understanding as part of our religious and cultural way of life; and it is in everyone's self-interest—Muslims as well as Jews—to learn to live together in the same society and the same region. We will all benefit from this—religiously, educationally, culturally, and even politically.

DEVELOPMENT OF ISLAMIC JURISPRUDENCE IN ISRAEL

IYAD ZAHALKA

Islam was introduced into the area known today as Israel-Palestine during the years 634–38 CE, when the Muslim army defeated the Byzantine army. From that time on the majority of the inhabitants and rulers of Palestine were Muslim, except for limited periods when the region was controlled by the Crusaders or the Mongols. During World War I the Ottoman Empire withdrew from Palestine, ending Islamic rule there. The British gained control of Palestine and obtained a mandate from the League of Nations to administer it; however, the majority of the region's inhabitants at the time were Muslim, and this demographic dominance lasted until the founding of the State of Israel in 1948.[1]

In late 1947 the Palestinian Arab population (within the historical borders, under the British Mandate) numbered 1,300,000. Seven hundred thousand inhabited areas that now lie within the State of Israel. Subsequent to Israel's establishment and the 1948 war, many of the region's Arab residents left. According to a Pew Research Center study, over the past few decades, Israel's Muslim population has more than doubled. It grew from 0.6 million in 1990 to 1.3 million in 2010, for an increase of 103 percent. The next twenty years are likely to witness a 66 percent increase in the Israeli Muslim population, from 1.3 million in 2010 to 2.1 million in 2030 (these figures include the Muslims of East Jerusalem).[2]

The 1948 war left a sparse Arab minority that, due to the nearly total disappearance of its leadership, remained without a social, religious, economic, or political elite. Many of these minority residents had lost their livelihoods and, often, their homes. They were therefore preoccupied with the struggle to ensure their immediate survival, and with anxious efforts to decipher the new reality in which they found themselves.[3]

Most Israeli Muslims, who are Sunni, tend toward the Shafi'i school of Islamic jurisprudence, with the exception of cities in which the Hanafi school holds sway. The Hanafi school is that which is embraced by the Israeli sharia courts, in consequence of a sultan's order that became enshrined in Ottoman law and was later incorporated into Mandatory and Israeli law. Israeli Muslims did not, in fact, develop a uniform Muslim religious consciousness or code of practice based in a conscious and consistent way on a specific Islamic legal school, despite their ostensible affiliation with the Shafi'i or Hanafi schools. This is because their religious outlook was passed down as tradition from generation to generation in accordance with each generation's religious-educational background, in the absence, due to the events of 1948, of an educated religious leadership or institutions of higher religious education.

A religious awakening among the Israeli Muslim minority began during the period following the State of Israel's establishment, and became a significant force only in the late 1980s, with the Islamic Movement's strong showing in the municipal elections. It was precisely the fact that up to then there had been no uniform, clearly formulated religious outlook that enabled the Muslim public to display religious flexibility and accommodate the differing approaches and attitudes of the various parties active within it, such as the sharia courts' commitment to rule in accordance with the Hanafi school. The Muslim public was therefore able to accept innovations in religious jurisprudence and sharia law without reservation, especially with regard to the rulings handed down by the sharia courts.

The early 1990s witnessed a major turning point in Israeli Muslim religious activity and consciousness. The parties responsible for this turning point were the religious forces active in the community, particularly the sharia courts. Another force active in the religious sphere is the two-branched Islamic Movement, which founded religious study institutions and centers for Islamic jurisprudence. Moreover, the center established by the Sufi *masdar* (spiritual order) Al-Tariqa al-Khalwati al-Qasemiya al-Jemaa in the city of Baqa al-Gharbiyye is an entity operated via the Al-Qasemi Academic College of Education.[4] These entities set in motion a process of innovation in Islamic jurisprudence as practiced in Israel. The new interpretations embodied in sharia rulings in Israel focused on issues of personal status—matters that fall under the jurisdiction of the sharia courts.

In this chapter I will discuss the work of each of the Islamic entities involved in Islamic jurisprudence in Israel: the sharia courts, the southern and northern branches of the Islamic Movement, and the al-Khalwati al-Qasemi Sufi *masdar*. I will look at each entity's contribution to the development of Islamic jurisprudence in Israel and at its specific legal methodology, in order to delineate the contours of identity, religious consciousness, and Islamic jurisprudence as they are emerging within Israel's Muslim minority. This article will also elucidate the linkage between *fiqh al-aqalliyyat* (jurisprudence for the sake of Muslim minorities in non-Muslim states) as shaped by al-Qaradawi and al-Alawani and the development of Islamic jurisprudence within Israel's Muslim-Arab minority from the 1990s onward. The background to my analysis will be the unique characteristics of Israel's Muslim minority, as noted in the previous section.

THE SHARIA COURTS

In the early 1990s a process of reform and innovation got underway with respect to sharia law as practiced in the Israeli sharia courts, in those spheres that are within the courts' jurisdiction. This process sprang out of a desire to address the challenges facing the country's Muslim public. The reform and the legal innovations encompassed all of the areas on which the sharia courts are authorized to rule, with special emphasis on personal-status issues and on Islamic religious endowments or *waqf*. Legal innovation is effected by means of selective imitative *ijtihad*, that is, the adoption of legal rulings from other schools and other Islamic legal scholars in order to adapt sharia law as practiced in the local courts to suit the needs and conditions of Israel's Muslim community. The innovations and changes are effected in accordance with the principles and rules of Islamic jurisprudence, and without deviating from *usūl al-fiqh*—the "sources" of Islamic law.

On the practical plane, the reform was implemented via two main mechanisms:

1. the legal platforms intended to represent an Islamic juridical position on matters of public concern, which were

employed, on the approval of the Islamic judges—the *qadis* —to change the law on a specific issue;

2. the rulings of the appeals court, which were accorded the status of binding precedent that must be applied by the regional courts.

Within the framework of the legal platforms, reform has been effected in two spheres: Legal Platform 1 and Legal Platform 4 emphasize the collective rights of Muslims to their religious endowments and their distinctiveness as a cohesive minority community striving to preserve its uniqueness and the special character of the legal code by which it lives—a code that differs from the prevailing code of the surrounding political and legal environment. Such was the case with respect to the guidelines and instructions of Legal Platform 1 regarding the Islamic *waqf*, which sought to safeguard it and address in advance any action liable to undermine its continued existence or its religious-legal status. Such was also the case regarding Legal Platform 4, which called for the adjudication of routine disputes lying outside the sharia courts' jurisdiction through arbitration within the court framework.

The other sphere in which reform has taken place is that of women's and children's rights, which have been liberalized via interpretations favorable to these sectors. Legal Platforms 2 and 3 annulled the "informant" institution in the sphere of alimony/child support, leaving decisions about the amounts to be awarded in the hands of the qadi, in accordance with prevailing conditions and emerging needs. The right of a child, whose father predeceased his grandfather, to his father's portion in the grandfather's estate was recognized as well.

The other, and highly important, mechanism—employed by Qadi Achmed Natur in order to advance reform in sharia law—is the principle of binding precedent. This principle stipulates that the rulings handed down by the Court of Appeals are precedents that must be applied by the regional courts, inasmuch as the Court of Appeals is the highest judicial court for matters pertaining to Muslims in Israel and is therefore the entity entitled to set judicial policy for the regional courts. Qadi Natur made this determination, which stands in contrast to the legal rulings that are subject to *ijtihad* and are not binding on other muftis without their consent, inasmuch as each mufti has his own opinion.

The Court of Appeals ruled that, in cases featuring similar causes and circumstances, the local courts must apply the principles of sharia law delineated by the Court of Appeals. They must apply them in order to ensure that justice is served and to make known to the public the courts' position on the topic in question.[5] However, these principles are binding on the regional courts only, and not on the Court of Appeals itself.[6] In this way, rulings of the Court of Appeals became a means of exerting direct and certain influence on the first-level courts and on the sharia judicial system as a whole.

The principle of binding precedent does not exist in Islamic sharia, which simply relies on the ruling of the individual qadi, whose decision heralds the culmination of legal deliberations and terminates a given dispute. The Court of Appeals justified the use of the principle of binding precedent in terms of the need to enact a judicial policy capable of imposing legal stability, in contrast to those rulings that are open to *ijtihad*. In this way, the public would know, in advance, the applicable law and the courts' position on the topic in question.[7] The innovations enacted have encompassed all spheres of personal status and *waqf* that lie under the courts' jurisdiction.

The reform that has taken place in the sharia courts does not, in fact, constitute a deviation from classic Islamic jurisprudence; however, the innovation with regard to the sharia court rulings represents a change vis-à-vis the jurisprudence that was practiced in the Israeli sharia courts on the local level during the preceding period. The reform was based primarily on importing the rulings of Islamic legal sages from all of the schools into the sharia law practiced in Israel. This trend led to a weakening of the status of the Hanafi school, which is binding per Ottoman law. The most striking innovations in the platforms is the very fact of a legal mode of action, the first of its kind in Muslim consciousness to have been created; the initiative to issue the platforms; and implementation of the law as embodied in the platforms and its incorporation into local legal practice.

An analysis of the innovation and reform processes that have taken place in sharia law in the personal status sphere shows that the sharia courts have upheld Muslim sharia law despite their subjugation to Israeli law. The courts have deviated from Ottoman legal practice and have developed legal tools for contending with interference on the part of Israeli civil law and with changing circumstances. The foundations and guiding principles of the legal methodology developed by the sharia courts are similar in character to the *fiqh al-aqalliyyat* doctrine, despite the courts' affirmation that they are not applying this doctrine.

The courts have also displayed creativity in contending with Israeli law. They have established a defensive legal policy that disregards any legal norm contradictory to Islam, while at the same time accepting any legal norm that does not conflict with Islam and whose meaning and essence are embraced by Islam. The courts have accepted such norms and infused them with Islamic content, thereby upholding the law of the land without deviating from Muslim law.

The way in which religious law has developed since the reform has affected the courts' religious and national discourse, and the courts have come to be perceived as a force working to strengthen the Muslim community's autonomy and to advance the demand for the community's collective rights. The reform has also led to liberalization with respect to the rights of women and children, who are perceived as the weaker parties within the Muslim public—especially in the Israeli environment, which poses a challenge in this sphere. The sharia courts have thus become the religious entity that is accepted by all streams within Israeli Muslim society, and they enjoy support from across the religious and civil spectrum. The way in which the sharia courts have developed Islamic jurisprudence has had ramifications for the other Islamic entities and has had a methodological impact on their legal positions.

Adjudication in the Southern Islamic Movement

In 1996 the Islamic Movement split, due to internal disagreements that intensified over the issue of participation in the Knesset elections. One branch, headed by Abdullah Nimar Darwish, based in Kafr Qasim, and referred to as the Southern Islamic Movement, supports participation in the Knesset elections; the other branch, headed by Raed Salah, based in Umm al-Fahm, and referred to as the Northern Islamic Movement, calls for boycotting the elections.

Following the split, most of the movement's original founders continued to head the Southern Islamic Movement.[8] They influenced its activity, which focused on *da'wa* or Islamic outreach and proselytizing, in addition to preaching and social, public, and parliamentary activity. The Southern Movement did not concern itself intensively with matters of religious law and did not invest resources or effort in this sphere. In 2001 it founded the Al-Hoar College for Islamic Studies in Tira (the college's activity is not yet broad-based) as well as a legal ruling committee that meets on an ad hoc basis, as needed, and has no permanent, active membership.[9]

At the fundamental level, the Southern Islamic Movement is not bound to a specific school of jurisprudence; it embraces the legal heritage of all four schools and prefers one religious law to another based on its compatibility with the conditions in which Israeli Muslims live—with an emphasis on the principle of *al-taysir* or "leniency," due to the special circumstances of minority status in Israel. The Southern Movement embraces the doctrine of *wasat*—the "middle way." It regards Israeli Muslims as an indigenous minority that underwent harrowing experiences, resulting in great suffering and the community's transformation from a majority group to a minority in its homeland. This situation entitles the community to a special adjudicatory approach that strikes a balance between all aspects of its existence. The *fiqh al-aqalliyyat* doctrine closely corresponds to the situation of the Israeli Muslim minority; it is not foreign to the Muslim public. Its methodology employs mechanisms that take into account the unique conditions of time and place in which every Muslim minority finds itself, including those of the Israeli Muslim minority.[10]

Adjudication in the Northern Islamic Movement

The Northern Islamic Movement has concentrated on internal activity relating to the *waqf* and the religious endowments, support for prisoners, aid to the needy, establishing medical institutions, and ensuring the exercise of the Arab public's individual and collective rights. On the Islamic legal studies plane, the Northern Movement founded Al-Da'wa al-Uloom al-Islamiya (the "Islamic Studies") College in Umm el-Fahm, which has been recognized as an academic institution by academic organizations in the Arab and Muslim world, though not by the Council for Higher Education in Israel. The movement established the Islamic Council for Adjudication, Al-Majlis al-Islami al-Iftaa.

Al-Da'wa College was founded in 1989 by the Al-Nour organization operated by the Islamic Movement. The college's mission is to train imams, preachers and exegetes, and teachers of Islam for the school system; to prepare students for higher learning in Islamic studies and potential scholars of Islam; and to disseminate the Islamic religious heritage.[11]

A look at the college's offerings indicates that the Al-Da'wa student studies Muslim history and the history of Islamic jurisprudence, Qur'an and hadith studies, the biography of the Prophet, theology, Islamic legal theory (*usol al-fiqh*), ritual law, the laws pertaining to financial transactions (*fiqh al-muamalat*), personal status law, Islamic criminal law, comparative law, the foundations of *da'wa*, Arabic language, English language, computer science, teaching methods, and research methods.

Since its founding, the college has educated many young people, and its graduates have gone on to become imams, preachers in mosques, and teachers. Al-Da'wa graduates' thorough grounding and expertise in Islamic studies have enabled them to exert an impact on the Muslim public, and by their means, the Northern Islamic Movement has attained leadership status in the sphere of religious knowledge and has become the entity to which the public turns for assistance in this area.

In 1996 the Northern Islamic Movement began to operate an adjudication committee affiliated with the movement. The committee responded to inquiries posed to it directly or via the movement's *Sawt al-Khak wal-Khuriya* (Voice of Justice and Freedom) journal. In 2002 the movement conferred official status on the Islamic adjudication sphere and established the Islamic Council on Jurisprudence.

The movement's rationale for this council's establishment was the need to fulfill the religious requirement that every Muslim community have legal scholars capable of adjudicating for it, so as to thwart those who would make a mockery of Islamic law. Another reason for the council's establishment was the need to provide urgent legal rulings in emergency situations, as in the decision to abort a fetus. In this context, the movement maintains that there is no framework of trust between the Israeli Muslim community and the legal scholars of the Islamic world, and that a great distance divides the two. According to the movement, adjudication via satellite is not enough: the scholars of the Islamic world lack sufficient knowledge of the special conditions of Muslim life in Israel; what is required is expertise based on observation of the community's actual status, an understanding of its vital needs, and an examination of issues that fall into the category of "matters of necessity" (*dharura*) or matters of conflict-related turmoil (*harj*).[12]

Another justification offered by the movement for establishing the Islamic Council on Jurisprudence was the need for a consensus among Israeli Muslims on issues of Islamic law, in light of the fact that many of the issues are complicated (such as the laws of financial transactions) and unique. There was also a need for an entity to determine dates of religious significance, such as the start of the month of Ramadan and the Muslim holidays, and to set the sums of money paid for the expiation of sins, such as taking a false oath or violating the Ramadan fast. Sums to be paid in compensation for killing (*diyya*) must be determined as well. The movement maintains that the council was also founded in order to create a legal entity to address questions that come up before the local committees and institutions, including those of the Islamic Movement, so as to ensure that the activity of these institutions is fully compatible with sharia law.

To sum up, the Northern Islamic Movement's activity in the sphere of Islamic jurisprudence reflects a conservative approach regarding innovation in religious law. Its rulings are, however, in line with its contention that Israeli Muslims live under unique circumstances and conditions that differ from those of Muslims in the Islamic world, and that legal rulings for this community must therefore address the special challenges faced by Israeli Muslims. At the same time, the movement's rulings demonstrate a deep commitment to the heritage of Islamic jurisprudence and a constant deference to the global Islamic organizations' rulings on new and modern issues, alongside a small degree of legal innovation.

ISLAMIC JURISPRUDENCE IN THE SUFI AL-QASEMI AL-KHALWATIYA AL-JEMAA ORDER

The Sufi order Tariqat al-Qasemi al-Khalwatiya al-Jemaa was disseminated in Israel by Sheikh Abd al-Rahman al-Sharif al-Khalili (d. 1887). In the early twentieth century, leadership of the order passed to Sheikh Husni al-Qasemi (d. 1944), for whom (and for whose family) the order is named; it was al-Qasemi who disseminated the order's doctrine to northern Israel in general and, in particular, to the Baqa al-Gharbiyye area, where he worked to institutionalize the order and build its religious institutions.[13] The order flourished up until the 1970s; most of those residing in the areas in which it was active belonged to it, and the order's leadership was regarded as the religious authority to which all questions and issues must be referred. From the 1970s onward, however, and subsequent to the strengthening of the other political streams, both national and Islamic, the order declined in status and its Israeli adherents and supporters dwindled in number.[14]

In 1990 the adherents of Baqa al-Gharbiyye established the *College for Sharia and Islamic Studies*, the name of which was later changed to Al-Qasemi Academic College. In 1993 the college was recognized by the Council for Higher Education in Israel and authorized to grant academic degrees in education.[15]

DEVELOPMENT OF LOCAL ISLAMIC JURISPRUDENCE IN ISRAEL

An analysis of the innovation and reform processes that have taken place in sharia law in the personal status sphere shows that the sharia courts have upheld Muslim sharia law despite their subjugation to Israeli law. The courts have deviated from Ottoman legal practice and have developed legal tools for contending with interference on the part of Israeli civil law and with changing circumstances. The foundations and guiding principles of the legal methodology developed by the sharia courts are similar in character to the *fiqh al-aqalliyyat* doctrine, although the courts do not affirm that they are applying this doctrine.

The Southern Islamic Movement essentially adopted the legal methodology of *fiqh al-aqalliyyat*. This is reflected in statements by the movement's leadership and, particularly, in its decision regarding participation in Israeli elections. On this issue the Southern Islamic movement set a precedent that it is permitted, and even obligatory, to take part in elections—for the same reasons that justify electoral participation on the part of Muslim minorities living in Western countries.

By contrast, the Northern Islamic Movement took a conservative stand and ruled in accordance with the classical legal heritage, or with the rulings of institutions of Islamic jurisprudence elsewhere in the world. The movement's adjudicators do not relate directly to the *fiqh al-aqalliyyat* doctrine; however, the rulings of the European Council for Fatwa and Research are one of the sources to which they refer in their rulings on new issues.

The Sufi Al-Qasemi order devotes effort to instruction and education within the framework of Al-Qasemi Academic College, and it guides the order's adherents and supporters by means of unwritten rulings, based on a methodology similar to that of the sharia courts. They do not regard the *fiqh al-aqalliyyat* doctrine as a binding source for their adjudication activity, although their methodology is, in essence, close to that of the doctrine.

The sharia courts have, in effect, become the religious entity that is accepted by all streams within Israeli Muslim society. They enjoy support from across the religious and civil spectrum. Their legal methodology would therefore appear to exert a profound impact on the development of Islamic jurisprudence within Israel's Muslim community.

When one compares the Islamic jurisprudence that has developed in Israel with *fiqh al-aqalliyyat*, one finds that, despite the great difference between the two in terms of their basic characteristics, there is nevertheless considerable similarity in their legal methodologies and in the rulings that they have issued. This similarity does not exist in all areas or with regard to all of the Islamic entities in Israel, because they differ in character and in religious outlook. The similarity can, however, be found with regard to some of the entities and certain specific topics.

This activity in the sphere of Islamic jurisprudence has, therefore, resulted in the development of a local judicial code of practice in Israel, one that derives from general Islamic jurisprudence and constitutes a direct continuation of it—although it differs in its details from the jurisprudence practiced in the Islamic countries, including those closest to Israel. This development of a local Islamic jurisprudence is not a phenomenon peculiar to Israel; it has parallels in the Islamic jurisprudence that developed in the West in the framework of *fiqh al-aqalliyyat* —each instance in accordance with its respective conditions and circumstances.

Notes

1. Ori Stendel, *The Arabs in Israel: Between Hammer and Anvil* (Jerusalem: Academon, 1992 [Hebrew]), 36–44.

2. Pew Research Center Study, 2011.

3. Ra'anan Cohen, *Strangers in Their Own Home: Arabs, Jews and State* (Tel Aviv: Diyonon, 2006 [Hebrew]), 42–46; see also Stendel, *The Arabs in Israel*, 1–5.

4. Each of the aforementioned entities has contributed significantly to the emergence and shaping of a religious consciousness. The specific contribution of each will be examined below.

5. Appeal 93/97 of the Sharia Court of Appeals.

6. Appeal 88//01 of the Sharia Court of Appeals.

7. See Appeal 97/39 of the Sharia Court of Appeals.

8. The ruling on participation in the Knesset elections was issued by Al-Fatawa and Al-Bahut al-Islamiya—al Kharakeh al-Islamiya.

9. This information was obtained during an unpublished correspondence, and contains responses garnered from questions I posed to Sheikh Ibrahim Sarsur, former head of the Islamic Movement and present leader of the Southern Islamic Movement's United Arab List party (since July 29, 2012).

10. Ibid.

11. See Dalil al-Talib, *Student Guidebook*, Al-Da'wa al-Uloom al-Islamiya College, Umm el-Fahm, 2nd edition.

12. *Fatawa al-Majlis al-Islami l]al-Iftaa*, Preface, vol. 1 (unpublished document, 2005).

13. On the Sufi Al-Qasemi order, see, Daphna Efrat, *Spiritual Wayfarers, Leaders in Piety: Sufis and the Dissemination of Islam in Medieval Palestine* (Cambridge, MA: Harvard University Press, 2008).

14. Explanatory remarks by Dr. Khalid Mahmud, Vice President of Al-Qasemi Academic College and Deputy Sheikh of the Sufi Al-Qasemi order, in an interview that I conducted with him on 23 July 2012.

15. See Al-Dalil al-Adademi, the academic guidebook of Al-Qasemi College, 2009–10.

TRIALOGUE WITH JEWS, CHRISTIANS, AND MUSLIMS

INTERRELIGIOUS DIALOGUE IN ISRAEL
Lessons Learned

RONALD KRONISH

INTRODUCTION

For more than twenty years, I have been actively engaged in the grass-roots work of interreligious dialogue and education.[1] While this work has had its share of ups and downs, successes and obstacles, challenges and setbacks, I can say that without a doubt, I have learned a great deal about the role of dialogue in peacebuilding in our part of the world by trial and error and by persistence and partnership with key organizations.[2]

This chapter will be divided into three parts:

1. A theoretical section on the importance of peacebuilding programs as a supplemental and parallel track to peace-making political processes
2. A description of some of the most important peacebuilding programs that we have implemented with some success in Israel and Palestine in recent years, with a special focus on programs for youth and young adults
3. A new model, which is an outgrowth of *best practices* in this field as seen through the work of the Interreligious Coordinating Council in Israel (ICCI) in recent years.

THE IMPORTANCE OF
PEACEBUILDING PROGRAMS

We are often asked, sometimes cynically, whether our interreligious dialogue and action programs will solve the Middle East conflict. All too often people feel that all dialogue must be political or diplomatic and that only such processes will actually solve our core problems in Israel and Palestine.

Accordingly, it is important to state at the outset what the purpose of interreligious dialogue is and should be in our political context. In order to do this, I want to draw an important distinction between *peacemaking* activities and *peacebuilding* programs.

In my view, *peacemaking* is the work of the politicians and diplomats. The goal of those who engage in such work is to create peace treaties between governments. While acknowledging the importance of these political and diplomatic processes, we need to be mindful of their limitations. Once these documents are prepared and agreements are reached, then public ceremonies take place with lots of fanfare, publicity, and photo opportunities. They are considered *historic* and offer new frameworks and possibilities for the peoples who have suffered through an intractable conflict for many years, even many decades. After the agreements are signed, sealed, and delivered, however, both sides spend the next several years blaming the other side for not living up to its part in the agreement (in the case of the Oslo Accords signed on September 13, 1993, on the White House lawn, this has been the case for the past twenty years). This is the work of diplomats and politicians, who constantly remind each side of the supposedly legally binding nature of the agreement and the obligations of *the other side* to live up to the agreement.

Peacebuilding,[3] on the other hand, is not the work of diplomats or politicians. Rather, it is the work of rabbis, imams, priests, educators, social workers, and psychologists, who bring people together to enter into dialogical and educational processes that are aimed at helping people figure out how to live in peace with each other. This process— which is sometimes called *Track Two Diplomacy* or simply *People-to-People Programs*—supplements the political processes but is somewhat different in nature and substance. This involves psychological, educational, and spiritual transformations, which take place over many years.[4]

There is, of course, a close connection between peacemaking and peacebuilding processes. When there is a momentum in the political realm—as there was in the 1990s with the Oslo Accords (1993), followed by the Fundamental Agreement between Israel and the Holy See (1993), the peace treaty between Israel and Jordan (1994), and the Wye River Agreement (1998)—then the existential and immediate need for people-to-people programs is more obvious and clear. Conversely, when there is a total freeze in political progress, as has been the case in Israel/Palestine from 2000 until now, then the existential need for peacebuilding programs is perceived to be more distant and difficult.

Nevertheless, I believe strongly in the importance of peacebuilding programs, even when the political peace processes are hardly functioning. These programs keep a flicker of hope alive in an ongoing conflict. They point the way to the future. They remind us that the goal of peace is normalization, not separation. They train the people for the possibilities of peaceful coexistence among people and peoples for the future, even if this is not the reality of the present moment.

One more theoretical note is in order here. My organization's programs are part of a growing field in the world known as *religions and conflict resolution*. The idea is that religions, that is, their leaders and followers, are especially capable of taking a role in helping to resolve conflicts in various parts of the world, or at least to mitigate, manage, and transform conflicts, if they can't solve them!

Yet in recent years, there has been much less focus on *resolution* (in fact, the word is hardly used any longer) and much more focus on conflict mitigation, management, or transformation. Indeed the government of the United States began a program a few years ago under USAID that it calls *Conflict Mitigation and Management (CMM)*.[5] In other words, those who engage in peacebuilding programs are no longer expected to solve the macro political conflict. But, if they can reduce hatred and violence, then they will be accomplishing something important, at least in the short term.

Moreover, conflicts can be *transformed* from a violent phase to an educational and social phase, as in the cases of Northern Ireland and South Africa, where the bloodshed has ended and now what needs to be done is to overcome hundreds of years of hatred and separation. We in Israel/Palestine will be happy to arrive (the sooner the better) at this stage, in which the war will have ended and we will be able to focus all of our societal energies on educational, spiritual, and psychological transformation. But even though we are not there yet, we need to begin wherever possible to bring people together to experience and learn about the possibilities and benefits of living together in the same country or same region. This is precisely what we try to do through our dialogue and action groups.

DIALOGUE AND ACTION GROUPS FOR YOUTHS AND YOUNG ADULTS

Dialogue and action groups can be a powerful method for transforming people into change agents for peace in their communities in both Israel and Palestine. Through the implementation of programs for teens and college students, we at the Interreligious Coordinating Council in Israel have learned firsthand the importance of a model that includes dialogue, intensive experiences together, volunteerism, and action projects.

In cooperation with Auburn Theological Seminary of New York, we offered for many years an annual program for high school youth called Face to Face/Faith to Faith. The program included twelve months of dialogue and an intensive summer experience abroad. As a result of a comprehensive evaluation process of the program that was implemented a few years ago,[6] we discovered that there are ten transformative ways in which participants were affected by such programs:

1. Seeing that the conflict has two legitimate sides, and being able to accept people who have different opinions
2. Becoming better listeners
3. Realizing that not everything is solvable
4. Looking at the conflict in a more complex and realistic way
5. Realizing that people are similar in many ways yet still have strong differences
6. Allowing them to grow up and become more confident in their own abilities
7. Influencing them to become more active in society
8. Becoming stronger in their own opinions while simultaneously becoming more tolerant and accepting
9. Having more knowledge about other religions
10. Realizing that *the others* are also human beings

In addition, for four years we conducted an innovative program for college students from both East and West Jerusalem that sought to engage in interreligious dialogue and action in order to change the tenor of public discourse and improve relations between Christian, Muslim, and Jewish students at their universities and in the city of Jerusalem as a whole. Jerusalem is divided by both physical and psychological barriers in such a way that young people growing up in the same city almost never visit the *other* side. Participants in this program attended different universities or colleges, spoke different languages, and belonged to nations of opposing political objectives. They lived in different realities.

During the course of the full-year program, the participants discussed various topics dealing with the different holiday traditions, and they visited one another's homes and celebrated one another's holidays together in fulfillment of one of our central goals—to eliminate the psychological barriers that divide Jerusalem and expose the participants to the life of the *other*. In order to get to know one another better, one group engaged in a photography project wherein they divided up into pairs—one Israeli Jew with one Palestinian Christian or Muslim—and took photos of themselves in places they love in Jerusalem. Even the simple task of visiting different neighborhoods in East and West Jerusalem was a challenging and eye-opening experience for the participants; many had to overcome fears about visiting the other side of the city.

In 2008–9, all of our dialogue groups experienced difficulties during the war in Gaza. The college student group met twice during this period, once during Hanukah, on the first day of the war, at the home of one of the Jewish participants. During this meeting, participants decided that despite the war, and the difficulties of the time, it was important for them to continue meeting. During the height of the war, they met again, and the participants had a difficult discussion about how they felt about the war and what it meant for them to engage in interreligious dialogue at such a time of conflict, demonstrating their commitment to dialogue even when the going gets rough.

As a result of this program, a number of our graduates went on to attend peace camps or work as counselors in interreligious camps during the summers. One participated in a "Building an Interfaith Community" seminar in Bossey, Switzerland, through the World

Council of Churches, where she was given a wonderful opportunity to meet new people, encounter new points of view, and learn new perspectives on religions, peace, and community-building. A number of our graduates have served as counselors in the Face To Face/Faith to Faith Summer Intensive Experience, hosted by Auburn Theological Seminary; and a third traveled to Walberberg, Germany, and participated in "Breaking Barriers," an Israeli-Palestinian Solidarity Project founded in 2002, an initiative by Israelis and Palestinians with aims to end the vicious cycle of violence in Israel/Palestine by building mutual interest, solidarity, and trust between the people.

The fact that many of our youth and young adults go on to be involved in other peace and interreligious seminars and camps is the true success of our informal educational programs for peace.

In recent years, we have made a strategic decision to focus more on young adults than on high school students. In 2011, we established our Jewish and Palestinian Young Adult Community for Peaceful Coexistence, which draws upon a database of hundreds of young adults who have been participants in our Dialogue and Action programs over ten to twelve years. At the end of August in 2013, we sent sixteen of these alumni—eight Jewish and eight Palestinian—to a special seminar in Northern Ireland, at the residential center of the Corrymeela Community in Ballycastle, where they spent an intensive week in deep dialogue with Protestant and Catholic young adults from Northern Ireland. Following this, they returned with energy and ideas to engage in action projects in Israel and Palestine, for the betterment of both communities.

This Alumni Community became branded with Face to Face/Faith to Faith, which also decided strategically to focus on young adults, beginning in 2013. These young adults are to become leaders in their field since they hold the powerful potential for effecting meaningful social change in the years ahead.

KEDEM—Voices for Religious Reconciliation

The Interreligious Coordinating Council in Israel's most ambitious and most important program was entitled KEDEM, a Hebrew acronym for "Voices for Religious Reconciliation." This project offered a new model for interreligious reconciliation and peacebuilding that could have a long-range impact in Israeli society. KEDEM was the longest lasting systematic and substantive effort ever undertaken in Israeli society to bring grassroots religious leaders of Israel's Jewish, Christian, and Muslim communities together to get to know one another and to learn to work together. Influential religious leaders searched together for new and innovative ways of bringing about interreligious and inter-communal reconciliation. Over six years, the main programs of the KEDEM process were the following:

- *Ongoing monthly encounters* that brought religious leaders together from communities within Israel to meet one another, build mutual understanding and trust, and plan action projects that catalyze Jews and Arabs to work together to constructively address societal issues of mutual concern. Each dialogue session included study of each other's sacred texts on themes of common interest, as well as discussions of core issues of the conflict that were of mutual concern to the participants.
- *Historical narrative curriculum.* In 2006, the KEDEM group published a booklet for the classroom entitled *I'm from...Stories from Biram Village and Kfar Etzion from 1948*, which is based on two incidents from Israeli/ Palestinian history: the uprooting of Palestinian Christians from Biram in the northern Galilee and the massacre of Jews at Kfar Etzion. In addition to preparing additional classroom aids, ICCI began to recruit teachers and offer training workshops based on this innovative and inspiring new curriculum.
- *Expanding the impact of KEDEM via outreach to the media.* In order to increase the impact of the religious message of coexistence and reconciliation, members of KEDEM were involved in reaching out to the Israeli public via radio and television interviews and op-eds in the Hebrew, Arabic, and English media.
- *Educating about the other in Israeli high schools.* Many of these religious leaders have given lectures in a high school in the community of one of his colleagues of another religion, on subjects such as "Relating to the

189

Other," "Basic Concepts in Judaism/Christianity/Islam," and "Common Values—Different Sources."

- *Summer seminar.* Each summer for four years, KEDEM participants spent five to six days in an intensive summer seminar abroad, in which they learned about how other countries dealt with their intergroup conflicts. In addition, they continued their learning, coalesced more tightly as a group, and planned their joint action projects. During these summers, KEDEM members traveled together to Ireland, Bosnia, Cyprus, and Spain to engage one another in dialogue and learning, which led to some very powerful personal transformational experiences.

The Story of Personal Transformation during One Summer Seminar

The first KEDEM summer seminar was particularly dramatic and groundbreaking. In July 2003, ICCI took fourteen Israeli grassroots religious leaders to Ireland—Northern Ireland and also the Republic of Ireland in the south—for an intensive week-long seminar on the theme of reconciliation. The group was comprised of seven orthodox rabbis and seven Arab religious leaders—five Muslim and two Christian (representing the percentages within Israeli society).[7]

The fourteen local religious leaders were all carefully chosen for their participation in this unique, groundbreaking dialogue process. Never before within Israeli society had Muslim and Jewish grassroots religious leaders met over a sustained period of time to learn about one another and one another's history, tradition, and contemporary concerns, and also to see what could be done together in the area of reconciliation between Palestinian Arabs and Israeli Jews within Israeli society. Each person was selected because of their openness to the process of sustained dialogue on this theme and because they represented a local community in Israel, where the lessons of this dialogue process could be applied in a practical, concrete way in the years ahead. In other words, the participants came to this process willing to undergo both personal as well as communal transformation and eventually to become voices for religious reconciliation within Israeli society.

The first stage of the project, which included two full study days in a conference center outside of Tel Aviv in the spring of 2003, as well as the week together in Ireland (Northern Ireland and the Republic of Ireland) in July of that same year, focused systematically on getting to know one another on a personal basis and building relationships of trust and respect. Through active listening to one another's personal stories—which were all particularly poignant and meaningful—these fourteen religious leaders came to know one another as persons rather than as media stereotypes.

More than this was achieved during the week in Ireland. In addition to getting to know one another well on a personal basis—a process that took place over coffee breaks and meals and on the field trips near the sea, as well as in the formal group discussions—some rather special moments occurred.

After focusing both on personal stories and on the conflict in Northern Ireland during the first two days of the seminar, the group decided on the third day to focus more on itself and less on the Irish experience of reconciliation. By the third night of the trip, a group decision was reached to cancel all discussions with outside experts on the Irish problem, and to focus the discussion on internal issues among the rabbis and the Arab religious leaders. This was the turning point that led to some rather remarkable results in the days ahead.

By the end of the third morning of dialogue—in which each person in the group had had a chance to share his personal story with the others in the group—it was clear that the group was beginning to be a cohesive entity. Two remarkable and surprising developments occurred on that day. The first episode occurred when one of the imams told his story about the massacre of Palestinian Arabs in Kafr Qassem in 1956 (a well-known tragic episode that has been well documented in Israeli history). He told the story of the massacre as he had heard it in his family from his aunt. It was a very gripping telling of the story. Very personal. Very sincere. Very human. Not in any way to masquerade as the one true version of history, but simply his story. There was very active listening going on in the room—you could hear a pin drop.

When he was finished, one of the Arab religious leaders told the group that each year a memorial service is held in Kafr Qassem to commemorate this massacre, and he invited one of the rabbis to come this year on a specific date at the end of October. The rabbi thought about it for a moment and then said that he would come if the event was solely an event to commemorate their pain and suffering and to express solidarity on the religious and human level and if the Arab religious leader could guarantee that the event would not be manipulated for political purposes. The sheikh fully understood what his friend the rabbi was saying, and therefore he responded sincerely by saying that he would invite all of the rabbis to attend a special memorial ceremony on the day after the communal one, so as to guarantee that there would be no misunderstandings and no manipulation of religion at the event. The response was immediate, sincere, and to the point: "If that is the case, we'll be there," the rabbis said. This was the clearest indication so far that the religious leaders were carefully listening to one another and at the same time seeking genuine opportunities for religious reconciliation and active peacebuilding.

Later that day, a second opportunity manifested itself in a surprising way.

The plan was to go to Dublin for the weekend, where the group would be hosted by the local religious leaders for a meal, for study, and to attend worship services together in a mosque on Friday, in a synagogue on Friday night and Saturday morning, and then in a church on Sunday morning. It had all been worked out carefully in advance, with the help of a good contact who was deeply involved in interreligious dialogue in the Republic of Ireland. However, that Thursday morning, I received a fax at our hotel that indicated that there was going to be a problem with our visit to the mosque in Dublin the next day: the rabbis would be required to remove their kippot (head coverings), and the Christian religious leaders would need to remove their crosses before entering the mosque. This was a sensitive matter that I felt that I needed to discuss with the group. Therefore, I brought the matter up over lunch. At first, one rabbi suggested that the rabbis could wear hats but not kippot and asked if this might solve the problem; but another rabbi said that he was not prepared to do this, that the kippah was too central to his identity.

And then, all of a sudden, something very dramatic and unexpected happened: two of the Palestinian Muslim religious leaders rose to their feet and said, "We will not go to the mosque. If our brothers and friends, the rabbis, will not be welcome as they are, we are not going. Our solidarity is with them. They are our partners in this dialogue— our destiny is with them in Israel, more than with the Muslims in

Dublin or in other places in the world." This was a moving and genuine response to a real dilemma, and it left its mark on the group in a profound and lasting way. Indeed, one of the rabbis, who had to leave to go back to Israel after lunch, said to the Arab religious leaders, "You have given me a wonderful gift to take home to Israel for Shabbat."

After this occurred, one of the other Muslims in the group pointed out the difficulty that would arise since they would need to attend Friday prayers in Dublin. During the brief discussion that followed, it was quickly decided that the group as a whole would not go to the mosque for Friday meal and hospitality as originally planned, but the Muslim members of the group would go as individuals to attend prayers.

On Friday, another crisis arose when the synagogue leadership requested that the Muslim and Christian leaders wear head coverings in the synagogue. This led to a Muslim boycott of the worship service and the Shabbat dinner on Friday night (the Christians, however, did join the rabbis for the Shabbat dinner at the synagogue, and one of them even joined for the worship service and donned a kippah for the occasion!). On Friday night, and for the worship services on Saturday morning at the synagogue, the Muslims stayed away.

Finally, a group decision was reached for the Arabs to join the rabbis for the Shabbat lunch following the Shabbat morning worship service. And at noon on that Saturday, the Muslim and Christian religious leaders joined the rabbis and the members of the Jewish community of Dublin for kiddush and lunch, where they were warmly welcomed by the Chief Rabbi of Ireland. It was a moment of great reconciliation and it reminded me a bit, with all the differences involved, of the reconciliation between Joseph and his brothers in the Bible. It was apparent from the way the group came together again that some real bonding and some genuine relationships had developed over the past several days.

The group then enjoyed its first and only Sabbath meal together. It was a moving, spiritual occasion, not only because the religious leaders were able to break bread together and share a religious meal together, but also because of the act of coming together in religious fellowship. Moreover, one of the Muslim religious leaders spoke eloquently on behalf of the group to the Chief Rabbi of Ireland and indicated how much he and his colleagues appreciated this rare opportunity to share these special moments in the synagogue in Dublin. He also spoke positively about KEDEM's dialogue process, with the hope that this would lead to more dialogue and genuine acts of reconciliation in the future. This coming together over a simple Shabbat meal was unquestionably one of the highlights of this journey on the path toward reconciliation.

At the concluding summary and feedback session on Sunday morning, all participants spoke about the need to continue the process of dialogue, reconciliation, and peacebuilding that had begun in a very deep and meaningful fashion in the intensive week together in Ireland. While some crises, large and small, were encountered during the week as part of the process, the high motivation by most of the members of the group to continue the process was very definitive. This intensive encounter apparently was important to them.[8] Following the seminar in Ireland in July 2003, plans were developed to continue the process in Israel. The group continued to meet at one another's homes. The October meeting took place at the home of one of the rabbis in his family sukkah (booth) during the holiday of Sukkot (this was the first time that the Arabs in the group had ever been invited to sit in a sukkah). And in November, the group shared a Ramadan dinner (perhaps the first kosher Ramadan dinner in Israeli history) in the home of one of the Muslim leaders. Moreover, in December the rabbis visited the village of Kafr Qassem as a follow-up to the discussion that had taken place in July in Ireland, and they stood at the memorial to the massacre in the center of the town, in solidarity with their brothers in dialogue in a poignant gesture of reconciliation that was deeply appreciated by the Arab members of the group.

The KEDEM project continued for six years and ended in 2009, but many of the religious leaders who were involved in it—who were transformed in major ways—continue to be involved in interreligious and intercultural dialogue in Israeli society.

A NEW MODEL FOR INTERRELIGIOUS DIALOGUE IN THE SERVICE OF PEACE

As a result of its work on the ground, ICCI has developed a model for successful interreligious dialogue. This model came about after many years of trial and error, especially during the last difficult years, since the eruption of the second intifada (uprising), which began in September 2000.

Our model is comprised of four major elements:

- Personal interaction: getting to know each other as individual human beings
- Interreligious, text-based learning
- Discussing core issues of the conflict
- Taking action, separately and together

The Personal Element

All of our dialogue groups bring together a diversity of people from various religious and national groups. Each comes to the dialogue with his or her own personal identity, which he or she shares with the group. The group learns to understand and respect the identity and narrative of each of its members, by listening carefully and genuinely seeking to come to know a lot about each participant. Through this process, people in the group come to recognize one another's human dignity and integrity.

We have come to call this process *de-demonizing the other.* In our part of the world, due to the ongoing violent conflict of many decades, Palestinians and Israelis—who have never met each other before—coming to our dialogue group usually see the other through the prisms of the conflict and the negative media stereotypes that dominate our print and electronic media. In our dialogue groups, we shatter these stereotypes by asking each person to share their identities and life stories with the other. When this is done over time—at least a year—we find that people are actually quite shocked to discover that the other, who is supposed to be *the enemy*, is actually a human being!

This first layer of our dialogue process builds an important foundation of trust that is essential for the rest of the dialogue. It often creates lasting friendships or at the very least much collegiality, which is a critical component for constructive, honest, and fruitful dialogue as the year progresses.

Interreligious Learning

We have discovered over many years, to our sorrow, that individuals often know very little about the cultural practices and theology of other religions in Israel and Palestine. Accordingly, Israeli Jews know almost nothing about Islam or Christianity. And what they do know is usually negative and was learned in courses in Jewish history in which they learned that Muslims or Christians either oppressed or massacred Jews throughout the centuries. Nor do Muslims or Christians who live in Israel or Palestine know much about Judaism. Much of what they do know is negative, as they learn it mostly from their print and electronic media and from the *street* and the family.

Therefore, a little education, properly and sensitively imparted by good teachers, can go a long way in a short time toward breaking down ingrained negative stereotypes of each other's religions. These teachers choose good texts with a positive message—from the sacred canons of each religion, such as the Bible and later commentaries (the Midrash and Talmud), the Qur'an and the Hadith, the New Testament and the church fathers—and teach them in a way that can be readily understood and appreciated by *the other side.*[9] When this is done well, another very important level of trust is developed. Participants who have gone through this process in our dialogue groups can talk about common humanistic values shared by the three major monotheistic religions, and they can sense a spirit of religious partnership, which motivates them to continue the dialogue and to seek meaningful paths of action together.

Discussing Core Issues of the Conflict

Since our dialogue process takes place in Israel and Palestine in the midst of an ongoing and often violent conflict, we cannot ignore the contemporary context in which we live and function. More accurately, we choose not to ignore the conflict (whereas other organizations actively seek to prevent *politics* or *the conflict* from entering into the discussion).

We believe that in a genuine dialogue process, the core issues of the conflict can be discussed in an open, honest, and sensitive fashion, guided by careful and consistent professional facilitation, without creating animosity or acrimony. In fact, we have found that participants in our dialogue groups continue to participate in the group all year precisely because the discussion is frank and forthright. This means that the discussions in this part of the dialogue process are often very painful and difficult. But when significant levels of trust have been developed beforehand, most people find this phase particularly meaningful and enriching as a way to genuinely get to know the other. It leads to deep mutual understanding of the other's religious, cultural, and existential reality, even if it also delineates where people fundamentally do not and often cannot agree with the other.

Taking Action, Separately and Together

Many years ago, one of my Muslim colleagues said to me when we were preparing to convene a dialogue group, *Dialogue is not enough!* It is not enough for us to learn and undergo personal transformation. As responsible members of society, we must take our learning to heart and create change. We are obligated to work for peace, to influence others, and to cause a ripple effect. As a result, we strive for our groups to experience both dialogue and action. In other words, all of our participants—religious leaders, women, youth, young adults, educators—are asked to take some action, separately or together, as a result of the personal transformational processes that they go through within this intensive experience.

Action can take many forms—personal, social, educational, or political—but it is agreed that every person who is moved by the dialogue process is obligated to share their experiences with others in whatever ways possible, even through gestures of reconciliation. From our experience, we have found that often simple human gestures of reconciliation, such as visiting the sick or the bereaved, can go a long way toward cementing personal relationships and creating genuine trust and profound relationships among friends and colleagues (former *enemies*) who are involved in long-term dialogue processes. Moreover, each person—through personal and professional networks and associations—should be committed to acting in such a way as to bring the insights and lessons of their dialogue processes to the attention of people in their own communities. In this way, each person in each dialogue group is a *multiplier*, who can spread the message of the possibilities and benefits of peaceful coexistence, and the method of dialogue and education, to many other people in his or her society.

CONCLUSION

The work of interreligious dialogue in the service of peace goes on in Israel and Palestine despite the ongoing political and military conflict, which as yet is to be resolved. In our part of the world, we continue to live in the midst of an ongoing hot conflict that makes the work of interreligious dialogue complex, complicated, and challenging. We hope that a two-state solution—an independent State of Palestine to exist side by side with an independent State of Israel—will become a reality in the near future. In the meantime, we have continued to bring religious leaders, educators, youth, young adults, and other groups in civil society together to encounter one another as human beings created in the divine image and as people who will need to take leadership roles in helping both Palestinians and Jews find the ways and means of learning to live together in peaceful coexistence, for the mutual benefit of both peoples.

Notes

1. This essay has been adapted in part from two previous articles in online journals: "Interreligious Dialogue as a Method of Peace-Building in Israel and Palestine," *Journal of Interreligious Dialogue*, December 21, 2010, available at http://irdialogue.org/journal/issue05/ %E2%80%9Cinter-religious-dialogue-as-a-method-of-peace-building-in-israel-and-palestine%E2%80%9D-by-rabbi-dr-ronald-kronish/ and "Interreligious Dialogue in the Service of Peace," *Crosscurrents*, Feb. 4, 2009, http://onlinelibrary.wiley.com/doi/10.1111/j.1939-3881.2008.000 19.x/full.

2. Over the years, the Interreligious Coordinating Council in Israel (ICCI) has partnered with the World Conference of Religions for Peace, Auburn Theological Seminary in New York, St. Ethelburga's Centre for Reconciliation and Peace in London, and Risho Kosei-kai in Japan.

3. According to Catherine Morris ("What is Peacebuilding? One Definition," 2000), "The term *peacebuilding* came into widespread use after 1992 when Boutros Boutros-Ghali, then United Nations Secretary-General, announced his *Agenda for Peace* (Boutros-Ghali, 1992). Since then, *peacebuilding* has become a broadly used but often ill-defined term connoting activities that go beyond crisis intervention such as longer-term development, and building of governance structures and institutions. It includes building the capacity of non-governmental

organizations (including religious institutions) for peacemaking and peacebuilding."

4. Peacebuilding involves long-term processes and the transformation of human relationships, according to John Paul Lederach, *Building Peace: Sustainable Reconciliation in Divided Societies* (Washington, DC: United States Institute of Peace Press, 1997), 82–83.

5. According to the USAID Guidelines: "Mitigating, managing, and responding to violent conflict are priority areas for USAID assistance. This policy defines conflict mitigation as activities that seek to reduce the threat of violent conflict by promoting peaceful resolution of differences, reducing violence if it has already broken out, or establishing a framework for peace and reconciliation in an ongoing conflict. Conflict management refers to activities explicitly geared toward addressing the causes and consequences of likely conflict."

6. Based on an evaluation report prepared by Rebecca Russo, a Dorot Fellow interning with ICCI during 2008–9.

7. The seminar was made possible by a major grant from the Embassy of the Federal Republic of Germany in Tel Aviv.

8. It was a good beginning, and even though many obstacles had to be overcome, they were indeed dealt with in a positive and constructive manner throughout the week under the leadership of Dr. Yitzhak Mendelsohn, the facilitator of the group. By engaging the group in uninational and binational group process and decision making, he had involved the participants successfully in determining how the group would proceed. In so doing, the participants felt that they were partners in a developing process of interreligious reconciliation.

9. This educational component to our dialogue process is especially important in our work with religious leaders from the three Abrahamic faiths, as in our KEDEM Program (Voices of Religious Reconciliation) from 2003 to 2008. In dialogue groups conducted by the ICCI, Muslim, Jewish, and Christian religious leaders not only brought texts with positive messages in text study sessions, but they also reinterpreted problematic texts in creative and beneficial ways in the spirit of reconciliation.

RELIGIOUS SELF-CRITIQUE IN THE TRUSTED PRESENCE OF OTHERS

PETER A. PETTIT AND MENACHEM FISCH

INTRODUCTION

Nearly a decade ago the authors of this chapter arrived in Rome for a conference marking the fortieth anniversary of the promulgation of *Nostra Aetate* by the Second Vatican Council. *Nostra Aetate* paved the way in the Roman Catholic Church for an era of dialogue in which many Jews and Christians had taken part up to that time. The rich, productive legacy of that era was well known to participants in the conference. Without rejecting that legacy, we proposed that the limitations of dialogue needed to be overcome in order to chart a productive path forward. It is the experience of the Shalom Hartman Institute's annual theology conference, underway since 1984, that both underlies and extends our conviction that this is still the case.

Dialogue, as the very term implies, is an exchange between two interlocutors. In the early *Nostra Aetate* era, those two were members, respectively, of the church and the synagogue (Christianity and Judaism). They had been estranged for so long that they needed the intense focus of a dyadic encounter to begin to overcome distrust and misunderstanding. They needed the "time out" of dialogue to learn to speak with each other and how to hear each other. "Dialogue presupposes that each side wishes to know the other, and wishes to increase and deepen its knowledge of the other. It constitutes a particularly suitable means of favoring a better mutual knowledge and, especially in the case of dialogue between Jews and Christians, of probing the riches of one's own tradition."[1] This perspective of the Roman Catholic Church has been echoed in statements by most of the Christian denominations in Western Europe and North America in the second half of the twentieth century. Collectively, they fashioned a model that has each partner in the dialogue focusing on the other, with the topics of the dialogue being determined primarily by the two partners' respective religious identities.

More specifically, the topics formed a syllabus of commonalities between the two religious communities and their beliefs. The cited *Guidelines* point, for example, to "existing links between the Christian liturgy and the Jewish liturgy." Protestant-Jewish dialogue agendas were often built around those *loci communes* that are most easily shared in the two communities—for example, Shabbat, Scripture, the Jewishness of Jesus (*not* the hypostatic union of his two natures), the prophetic role of God's people (*not* the fulfillment of prophecy), and so forth. Many benefits have accrued from this dialogue model in bridging a social and religious chasm to a degree that once seemed impossible, in listening actively and constructively to another's self-understanding, and in taking care about "translating" between one religious idiom and another.

The model is limited, though, to the degree that only a circumscribed field of topics is most amenable to the method. Adhering closely to those topics and seeking out parallels between the two communities can skew the perception of each faith tradition. The proximity of Hanukah to Christmas, for instance, has raised its value in dialogue beyond its place among Jewish holidays, just as Christian awareness of the colloquial Hebrew term *Abba* (= "Daddy") has cast the Lord's Prayer in more intimate terms than seems justified. Moreover, the dialogue model can project an underlying parallelism or correspondence between the two faiths that is not necessarily borne out in careful study. Even for two traditions, the model has these limitations.

In today's broadly pluralistic setting, the points of commonality or easy correspondence between any two religions, such as Jewish and Christian, do not automatically or frequently align with the points shared by either one with a third tradition—for example, Islam. Thus, in many "trialogue" efforts, we will see a further "flattening" of all three traditions in search of tripartite commonalities. Alternatively, we may see two parties in dialogue with a third group as interested observers for whom the topic is not nearly as significant.

Over a period of three decades, the annual theology conference of the Shalom Hartman Institute in Jerusalem has grown into an alternative model. This "shared study of sacred texts," or "doing theology in the presence of the Other," shifts the focus from understanding points of commonality across traditions to working together on challenging theological problems within each tradition. The challenges are taken up with religious others as companions, study partners, and critics. The other is invited to partake, not in interfaith, but in one's own *intra*faith dialogue, as it were. That was its original genius and remains a hallmark of the project, but other dimensions have contributed their strengths as it has developed through four phases. We will sketch those phases, each with its distinctive contribution, before profiling the model in its current form.

THE OTHER AS THEOLOGICAL PARTNER

In this land [of modern Israel], we are confronted with many others who are connected to the land in such different ways....I believe that the God of the Exodus drama, Who answered "I will be," is now calling upon us to respond in a different manner. Something new is happening when "the other," the stranger, the different one, impinges on our self-definition.... Our return was meant to provide us not only with a haven from anti-Semitism but also with a new way of integrating "the other," the different one, into our covenantal consciousness....No one person or community exhausts all spiritual possibilities. (David Hartman)[2]

Our Gentile identity [in the church] is a strange fact. A Gentile is by definition anyone who is not a Jew....We define ourselves by reference to the Jews because our Way has no starting point and no possible projection except by reference to the Way in which the Jews were walking before we started and are walking still.

What then is our final hope in this matter of the relationship and conversation between the Jewish people and the Gentile church?...It is at least imaginable...that a time will come in which we will find ourselves, the Jewish people and the church, walking along in such close proximity that each could see the other and see indeed that both were walking in the same direction, and that the conversation of each should be understandable and seem right to the other. (Paul Van Buren)[3]

The theology conference of the Shalom Hartman Institute emerged in 1984 from the encounter between these two theologians. In their words we find an essential characteristic of the conference as it still exists thirty years later. Their backgrounds could hardly have been more different. Their intellectual journeys came together out of disparate motivations. Yet the common cause they found has outlived both of them. The conference they created continues to shape thinkers who can draw from the deep wells of their religions to nourish healthy mutual existence in the pluralistic postmodern world of the present century.

Key to both Hartman and Van Buren is a profound humility about what any of us can claim to know about God. By 1984, Van Buren had penned both *Discerning the Way* and a subsequent volume, *A Christian Theology of the People Israel,* as the first two installments in his projected four-volume *Theology for the Jewish-Christian Reality.* As he neared the conclusion of the third volume, on the theme of Christology, he approached Hartman about conducting a seminar on the manuscript—in Jerusalem with both Christian and Jewish scholars. Together they would work through the sources and arguments of the book that eventually was published as *Christ in Context.* By subjecting his work to the scrutiny of both Christian and Jewish colleagues, Van Buren sought to remedy a key deficit in the history of Christian theology. He sought to shape Christian theology about the Messiah in a way that "should be understandable and seem right" to Jews, while still meeting the criteria of Christian self-expression.

Hartman recognized in the proposal an opportunity for "integrating 'the other,' the different one, into [his] covenantal consciousness." He later would say that Jews needed to "rethink the long tradition of messianic triumphalism,"[4] and in the rethinking of "Christ in context" that Van Buren proposed, there would be ample room to explore the topic in its Christian guise. But Hartman made clear that his interest in other religious communities and their "spiritual possibilities" was not narrowly instrumental. He would not have required any direct payoff in Jewish theological insights for the seminar to be counted a success.[5] The simple fact was that Christianity had continued clearly to "impinge on [his] self-definition" even after the establishment of a Jewish state with a Jewish majority. That fact gave intrinsic meaning and value to learning with Christians about their own self-definition. His institute would be a place for the necessary and promising encounter of Jews and the "religious other," with an emphasis on Jewish listening and learning.

One hallmark of these conferences was the adaptation of the *havruta* method of study, derived from the traditional Jewish study setting, the *bet midrash*. There, individuals pair off into study partnerships[6] to delve into rabbinic texts together in a lively verbal exchange that probes for deeper and deeper levels of textual meaning. There is no designated leader in a *havruta*, as each participant brings a distinctive perspective and set of insights to the shared study. The method affirms the potential contribution of different scholarly approaches. It affirms the value of the naïve question or interpretation offered by participants who may have been previously unfamiliar with the study text and the customary patterns of interpreting it.

Van Buren's original agenda, and Hartman's accommodation of it, went beyond the traditional dialogue model. The starting point was not a body of texts common to Jews and Christians, nor a shared theological theme. It was the specifically Christian issue of Christology. Van Buren wanted to construct it in a way that would transcend the *adversus Judaeos* hermeneutic that had characterized Christian theology in antiquity.[7] Bringing Jews into the Christian theological study, so to speak, was a radical innovation. Nor were they welcomed simply as "expert witnesses" on points of Hebrew philology or rabbinic thought. They were there as partners in conversation with Christians in working out one of Christianity's central theological themes, one that most directly embodied the church's traditional anti-Jewish posture. Their readings of the Gospels and Paul and the early church theologians would be just as vital as their expertise in Judaica. From the very different perspective that Jews would bring to the enterprise would emerge key critical insights to help reshape theology for a postsupersessionist Christianity.

The vital role of the religious "other" as a partner in self-critical theological reflection remains essential to the work of the conferences. In one sense, it retains ties with the dialogue work that preceded it, in that it focuses on misunderstandings and mischaracterizations of the other that need to be remedied. So the early conferences under Van Buren and

Hartman also took up questions of hermeneutics that clarified oversimplified views of each community's theological methods and standards. To the degree that the exploration went beyond rectifying mistaken impressions of the other, though, and opened each community to self-critique and amendment of its own practices based on insights drawn from the other's perspective, it moved into unmapped territory.

HOLY ENVY

In a series of partnerships with major American theological centers, the theology conference in the 1990s also embarked on topics that emphasized the exploration of difference. Faculties of the Graduate Theological Union, Harvard Divinity School, and the Divinity School of the University of Chicago were regular partners in that decade, as Rabbi Dr. Tzvi Marx, Dr. Alon Goshen-Gottstein, and Dr. Susan Neiman successively provided leadership in Jerusalem for the conferences. Jewish participants were increasingly drawn from across the Israeli academic world through an affiliation with the Hartman Institute, while Christians came from North America and Europe as well as several Jerusalem centers and institutes. Prof. Krister Stendahl of Harvard served as codirector of the Osher Jerusalem Center for Religious Pluralism, the institutional home of the conference, for much of the decade, and his quiet advocacy of "holy envy" shaped many of the agendas.

Stendahl spoke often of holy envy, which has been enshrined as the third of three "rules of engagement" for interreligious encounter attributed to him. (The first two are seeking information about a religion from its adherents, not its enemies, and comparing the best of religions to one another, rather than the best of one to the worst of another.) He meant that a proper spiritual and epistemological humility will lead us to be open to seeing in another religion a practice, doctrine, or posture that is appealing to us, that enriches us, and that is unavailable in any comparable form in our own religious tradition. While the example of his enchantment with Mormon baptism of the dead is widely cited, he was open to many elements of Judaism and Islam and other religions as candidates to enhance his spiritual engagement with the world.

One key aspect of holy envy is the emphasis it places on the difference between religions. In examining those differences and learning the worldviews that both support and grow from them, one gains two benefits. First, the world is revealed to us in ways that our habits of thought and belief do not afford. This is a radical extension of the basic humanist value of critical thinking, taken into the realm of religious truth and epistemological self-critique. Second, in the encounter that seeks to make differences accessible to others, we often must examine aspects of our own religion that typically go unchallenged and even unexpressed. Thereby one gains the "envy" of another's different insight into our own tradition that cannot be our own insight, because we do not see ourselves as another sees us. In both senses, it is the acknowledgment and acceptance of valuable difference as a hermeneutical principle that makes possible the encounter and the resulting holy envy.

This perspective helped to shape the continuing agenda of the theology conference in the 1990s. Topics under study in that decade included monotheisms, the holiness of places and times, the discourse of the psalms, and the ethical significance of Scripture interpretation. In each case, Jewish and Christian texts (and, beginning in 2000, Muslim texts as well) were studied in *havruta* with a subsequent plenary discussion led by the conference member who had selected the texts for study. The emphasis lay on allowing each religious tradition to emerge in its individuality and particularity, to the mutual enrichment of all the participants.

ESCHEWING EXTREMISM

In its first two decades the Hartman Institute included on its academic staff a Muslim scholar, Dr. Mohammad Hourani, who also regularly participated in the theology conference. With the 2000 conference, however, and taking the topic of "Sacred Space" in the city of Jerusalem, a larger group of Muslim participants was recruited locally and from abroad, with one-third of the study time devoted to Muslim texts. That pattern has continued to the present. In the seeming idyll of that year, the mixed company of the conference traveled together to the symbolic center of sacred space in the heart of Jerusalem's Old City, the Haram al-Sharif or Temple Mount, where we toured Al-Aqsa masjid and stood in the Gold Dome. Stops at the Western Wall and the Church of the Holy Sepulchre brought together in lived experience the very different dimensions of holy space that are held by the three religious communities in Jerusalem, and at each, the differences within those communities were noted, as well.

James Carroll wrote of his experience in the *Boston Globe* on February 23, 2000 (p. A19), "I was witness to an extraordinary effort by Jews, Muslims, and Christians to transcend religious traditions that have become both garrisons and prisons....Implicitly disputing the conventional wisdom that religion is only a stumbling block to recon-ciliation in the Holy Land, [David] Hartman said, 'Holiness is not related to possession.'" Of the discussion following the holy site visit, Carroll recalled a question about the caution a Jew had been given by the Israeli police not to pray while in the Sacred Precinct (Haram al-Sharif). A Muslim participant responded that the current political cli-mate, without a final status agreement, could render the prayer a political act of aggression. Apart from that climate, "the clear implica-tion was that Jewish and Muslim prayers were not mutually exclusive on that contested ground." He went on to report David Hartman's reflection: "It won't change the *Realpolitik*, but it offers this land the witness of a new possibility."

By the next year, the Oslo Treaty was collapsing and the Second Intifada had begun, a violent Palestinian revolt provoked in part by the Israeli prime minister's "visit" to the Temple Mount. Within another year the attacks of September 11, 2001, were dominating the headlines and the world's awareness. Maintaining its commitment to hold the theology conference as a place where difference could be explored, even celebrated, and where a shared religious sensibility could tran-scend politicized rhetoric, the Hartman Institute continued to invite Muslim scholars and religious leaders to participate in the conference and to lead its learning. The topics of the next six years reflect a stud-ied insistence on addressing theological topics that held relevance for the political tensions, without attempting to address or propose solu-tions to those tensions directly.

Each of the topics lies behind some aspect of the intense conflict between Jews and Palestinians over the land they both see as home: the challenge of relating to the "patently sinful," the aspiration to live in a more just and peaceful world, the challenges of sovereignty in a plural-istic context, and fundamentalism. Yet each could be examined as dynamics with which all three communities must wrestle. The shared study of texts in mutual respect allowed a deeper probing into the dynamics of conflict from the respective religious worldviews than more direct address to the political situation would likely have afforded. The most immediate context could not be ignored, but the deeper implications for situations not so far removed had to be acknowledged as well.

GROWING INWARD AND OUTWARD

Rabbi Dr. Donniel Hartman has taken the reins of the Hartman Institute in the last years of his father's life, and the current authors have worked together for fifteen years in leading the planning team. We are joined by Kimberley Patton of Harvard Divinity School, Adam Afterman of Tel Aviv University, Karla Suomala of Luther College, Nargis Virani of the New School for Social Research, and Shiraz Hajiani of the University of Chicago.

The work of developing a Muslim cohort of participants has continued since 2000 with growing success. Despite the obstacles both within the Muslim world and within the Israeli security system, a strong contingent of Muslim scholars of Islam has been gathered in nearly equal numbers to the Christians and Jews. With that parity, the greatest advantage of the *havruta* study method can be maximized, as study groups can be smaller and still include participants from each of the three cohorts.

The *havruta* method has been accorded an even more central place in the conference as well, with two one-hundred-minute study sessions devoted to the texts of each tradition, followed by a single ninety-minute plenary discussion on those texts. In the four-day conference, this pattern is iterated three times. A leader from each of the three communities prepares a set of study texts—usually including Scripture, but also traditional commentary and more systematic theology and philosophy—that frame a particular problem. After a very brief introduction by the leader offering literary and historical orientation to the texts along with suggestions of the particular points to be explored, participants from all three communities work in small mixed groups of three to five persons to study the texts. This familiarizes them with the "raw materials" of the theological project that the leader will then develop in a plenary session.

Those who are within the leader's religious tradition, of course, become key resources to the small groups as well as collaborators with the leader in the theological task undertaken during the plenary. Those from the other traditions are important partners in the process, with their engagement serving two functions. It holds the theological work to an immediate, distinctive accountability regarding the place and picture of their communities in its formulations. It also presses those doing the theological work to articulate and clarify assumptions and connections that may be taken for granted by their home communities and therefore glossed over among colleagues who share them. The point is not for those outside the tradition to find analogous patterns or comparable ideas within their own religion (though often enough such an analogy or comparison can prove helpful). Rather, the point is from their different perspectives to enter as fully as possible into understanding the dynamics of the other's theology in itself.

Consistently, the highest evaluations by participants go to the *havruta* study. Its informal character, its democratic model, its culture of questioning, exploration, and collective learning all contribute to its power for building a strong community of scholarship and discourse. Its strongly textual focus lessens the tendency of participants to embark on didactic excursions that stray from the text at hand. The fact that participants are neither asked nor expected to offer prepared papers for the conference or for publication sustains a spirit of shared inquiry. It allows for all the creativity of tentative thoughts, serendipitous encounters, and spontaneous insights being shared before the scholarly cautions circumscribe their possibilities. Many participants have carried the *havruta* method back into their teaching practice, and many of the ideas that emerged from casual comments have later been refined for publication.

The topical range in recent years has also grown, representing a broader sweep of religious experience, including family, mortality, embodiment, morality, democracy, forgiveness, and environmental ethics. As the topics have broadened, one of the early characteristics of the conference has resurfaced. In the plenary discussions that follow *havruta* study, the leader who has chosen the texts leads off with an interpretation and application of the texts to the presenting problem. A moderated discussion follows among only those within that religious community, a so-called "inner-circle discussion." This emphasizes a dimension of self-critical, internally pluralistic awareness that is instructive to those outside the tradition and that also counteracts any tendency to frame differences along strictly interreligious lines. Typically, the range of perspectives and interpretations within any one tradition finds multiple points of connection within the ranges represented in the other two traditions.

Recognizing that few if any participants will be expert in the topic of a given conference, the continuing emphasis for the conference is on the dynamic of self-critical reflection with the partnership of trusted colleagues from other religious communities. The conference aims less at developing a theory of pluralistic theology or reaching conclusions on each successive topic than at practicing and honing a method of doing theology in a consciously pluralistic community. The impact of the conference is ultimately on the communities in which participants teach and work, as the experience of the shared study reshapes their method and sensibilities and translates into new working habits in the classroom, seminars, academic projects, and religious leadership.

This value of the theology conference was captured well in another conference in Rome, with the remarkably groundbreaking title, "The First Roman Consultation on Jewish and Canon Law." It was devoted to the dynamics of "Norm Making and Norm Changing" in the two legal systems, and Menachem Fisch spoke about the powerful promise of such shared study:

> Participating in this conference acquires, from my orthodox Jewish perspective, a special religious significance. For there is an important sense in which, by engaging in serious open and critical interfaith dialogue…with as significant and important an other as the Catholic Church,…the name of God is sanctified. It is sanctified not because we purport to bring to Rome [God's] one true word, but because there is a very good chance that we shall be returning home from Rome better equipped for the ongoing task of working it out for ourselves.

Notes

1. Commission for Religious Relations with the Jews, "Guidelines and Suggestions for Implementing the Conciliar Declaration *Nostra Aetate*, No. 4," December 1, 1974, http://www.ccjr.us/dialogika-resources

/documents-and-statements/roman-catholic/vatican-curia/277-guide-lines.

2. *A Heart of Many Rooms: Celebrating the Many Voices within Judaism* (Woodstock, VT: Jewish Lights, 1999), 143, 151.

3. *Discerning the Way* (New York: Seabury Press, 1980), 25, 33, 35, 44, 66.

4. *A Heart of Many Rooms*, 143.

5. Hartman explicitly embraced "an alternative religious sensibility" to "Maimonides' explanation of the instrumental relationship between Judaism and its main monotheistic rivals" in the same book quoted at the outset. He associates this sensibility with the Talmudic report of a divine voice that defused a potentially disastrous division of the Torah between the respective adherents of Rabbis Hillel and Shammai, in which it was declared, "These and these are the words of the living God" (*b. Eruvin* 13b; *A Heart of Many Rooms*, 148–49).

6. The word *havruta* is Aramaic for "friend" or "colleague," and its application in this context relates to the Mishnaic injunction to "acquire yourself a fellow disciple" (*Avot* 1:6, in the name of Joshua b. Perahia). Moreover, as the commentary on the Mishna *Avot De-Rabbi Nathan* (Text A, chap. 8) perceptively points out, the purpose of acquiring a close friend is to enrich one's learning by facilitating self-criticism "so that if one of them errs regarding a matter of halakha, the other will be there to put him right." In its seminar adaptation, the method more typically sets three or four people together to study. Where more than Judaism and Christianity are represented, the number may grow to a half-dozen or more, in order to ensure participation by all the groups represented and, if possible, to include multiple voices from each group.

7. See Rosemary Radford Ruether, "The *Adversus Judaeos* Tradition in the Church Fathers: The Exegesis of Christian Anti-Judaism," in *Essential Papers on Judaism and Christianity in Conflict: From Late Antiquity to the Reformation*, ed. Jeremy Cohen (New York: New York University Press 1991), 174–89; and A. Lukyn Williams, *Adversus Ioudaeos* (Cambridge, UK: Cambridge University Press, 1935).

EDUCATING FOR PEACEFUL COEXISTENCE: METHODOLOGIES AND TARGET POPULATIONS

CIRCUS IN A FRAYED TENT

MARC ROSENSTEIN

THE LARGER HISTORICAL CONTEXT

At the end of the nineteenth century, the convergence of the ancient Jewish messianic hope for restored sovereignty, secular humanism, and romantic nationalism gave rise to a new movement, Zionism, which actively sought the reestablishment of a Jewish sovereign state in the area in which one had existed during the first millennium BCE. In 1948 this movement ultimately attained its goal. Along the way it revolutionized Jewish identity, raising a question that has yet to find a definitive answer: Is Judaism a religion, a nationality, or something else?

Since the sovereign State of Israel contains, like just about every other state in the world, a population that is mixed religiously and ethnically, and since it defines itself as both a democracy and a Jewish state, this unresolved question regarding the definition of *Jewish* vexes any attempt to explain and contain—not to mention resolve—issues that are ongoing sources of uncertainty, tension, and even open conflict in the region, issues regarding individual rights, religious freedom, minority rights, cultural autonomy, and borders. "Who is a Jew?" and "What is a Jewish state?" are questions that have occupied the Israeli parliament, courts, and popular discourse since the state was formed.

This dilemma is, of course, not limited to the Jewish sphere: "Who is an Arab?" is also not obvious; is "Arab" a political, cultural, linguistic, or religious category? Are Egyptians Arabs just because they speak Arabic? There are Christian and Muslim Arabs—why not Jewish Arabs? There are Egyptian Jews and Syrian Jews; why not Palestinian Jews? For ethnographers, these are interesting academic questions; for the inhabitants of the region, they are questions that matter, a lot.

Seen in a wider context, this question of how to define identity and

215

how identity should correlate to political divisions and structures is *the dilemma* that has driven much of the history of the world in the past century. In the First World War, the pluralistic multinational empires of Europe and the Middle East exploded into dozens of ethnic nation states. The resulting division, in which these states were not and could not be homogeneous, was not stable. After Versailles, the status quo crashed and burned with World War II; after that war, the status quo began to disintegrate with the collapse of communism; and so the number of ethnic national entities has continued to grow as particular identity groups seek to attain sovereignty over their own little plots of territory (always, it seems, at the expense of others). And it seems there is no end in sight to this process. It has now spread to the Middle East with violent upheavals across the region, whose outcomes are not at all clear as yet. And then there's Africa...

THE IMMEDIATE CONTEXT

Despite the uncertainty and tension described above, surrounded by a world driven to extreme bloodshed by similar conflicts, through wars and severe internal ideological divisions, Israel has succeeded in surviving as a functioning democracy for over six decades, with orderly elections, separation of powers, a strong court system, a quasi-constitutional body of basic laws preserving individual freedoms, and relatively free and vibrant public discourse on every topic. Until 2000, one might have thought that the glass was more than half full, and that economic growth, democratic processes, and middle-class aspirations would unite the population and overcome the historical baggage and centrifugal forces. Then, in the fall of 2000, in a sudden development that shocked many, riots in the territories occupied by Israel in 1967 spread to the Arab communities within the 1949 borders, leading to violent confrontations with the police and resulting in thirteen fatalities. Now, looking again at the glass, it suddenly looked emptier than we had imagined. It became clear to many that the sustainability of the Israeli status quo was not obvious.

The population of the state is about 75 percent Jewish and 20 percent Arab, (and 5 percent "other") with the Arabs about 82 percent Muslim, 10 percent Christian, and 8 percent Druze. All are citizens of the State of Israel, with the same ID cards, passports, drivers' licenses, income tax, social security, health care, and civil and political rights. While there are some mixed neighborhoods in some cities, most Israelis live in ethnically homogeneous communities and attend separate, parallel school systems operated by the Ministry of Education—the Jews in schools where the primary language is Hebrew, the Arabs studying in Arabic.

Some areas of life are fully integrated, such as the health care system and some commercial and industrial establishments; however, for the most part, the two populations lead separate social and cultural lives, in separate residential communities. Jews, as the majority, generally don't speak Arabic and rarely enter Arab communities. Arabs, as the minority, generally speak Hebrew and often work and shop and obtain various services (notably higher education) in Jewish towns and institutions. Most Jews serve in the Israeli army, which nominally has universal conscription. Most Arabs are exempt by virtue of their identity (here religion enters and complicates the picture, as Druze Arab men and non-Arab Muslim men are drafted, while Muslim and Christian Arabs are not).

What became starkly clear in 2000, with the unparalleled rioting by Arab citizens, was that the perception that the above description represented a modus vivendi, a stable status quo, was an illusion, and we were sitting on top of a volcano. Separate but equal was painfully unequal. What looked like calm coexistence to the Jewish majority looked, from the underside, like institutionalized injustice in many spheres. When the top blew off, at least some observers realized that without change, deep change, the sustainability of the state might be in question. Is it possible to maintain a functioning democracy in which 20 percent of the population perceives itself as marginalized—philosophically (this is a "Jewish state"), economically, educationally, and culturally? If there is no common set of values, institutions, and symbols to which the vast majority of the citizens feel a sense of belonging and loyalty, what centripetal forces will hold against the centrifugal ones? Do we have the wisdom and the will to move toward creating such a shared core, toward creating a national identity that transcends ethnic or religious identity? Do we have the luxury to continue to refrain from trying?

WHY A CIRCUS?

The wake-up call of the riots of 2000 gave rise to hand wringing and soul searching and many discussions of "what should be done."

One direction that was and remains crucial is the application of the tools of democracy (public pressure, lobbying, legal action) to bring about a fairer distribution of power and resources. Another direction that has drawn less attention has been the educational and cultural effort to build a cultural common denominator and shared sense of citizenship.

Out of discussions of this challenge arose the idea of a circus. Circus is a multicultural and international tradition, language independent, noncompetitive, based on trust and cooperation, transcending divisions of class and age. Perhaps, it was suggested, circus could serve as a mechanism for creating a shared cultural experience that favored neither majority nor minority and that could have wide circles of influence since it is a performance art aimed at a mass audience.

The circus arts—juggling, clowning, acrobatics, and so forth—have been around since time immemorial and are part of cultures around the world, appearing in religious and secular contexts, from China to Rome to the Temple of Jerusalem. "Traditional" circus—the nomadic community of performers—is a fairly recent tradition, originating with equestrian ring shows in eighteenth-century England and experiencing its greatest flowering with the traveling tent shows of early twentieth-century North America and Europe.

A motif that seems common to the individual circus arts and to the tradition of the traveling ring show is the pushing of boundaries. Circus performers test the limits of physical strength, of the laws of physics, of social convention. They play with these boundaries, teasing them and the onlookers, often taking real risks themselves—and on behalf of the crowd, which identifies with them. In this sense, circus is subversive, and binds audience and performers together in a conspiracy to push the limits of what is acceptable and consensual and safe.

The traveling circus, perhaps because it was here today and gone tomorrow, not part of the established social order, gave off a whiff of the exotic and even the illicit. If one wanted to reject middle-class norms and expectations, one "ran away to the circus." The circus blurred barriers of identity and class, mixing performers and audiences from widely different backgrounds for moments of great excitement and happiness. And then it moved on and life returned to normal. Circus in this sense is part of the same phenomenon of temporary casting off of norms that is found in Carnival, Mardi Gras, and Purim.

As economics and technology and cultural shifts took their toll on the tent-show tradition, in the mid-twentieth century, a new manifestation of the circus tradition arose: social circus. Circus artists and educators around the world began to realize that there are aspects of the circus arts in general, and the circus show tradition in particular, that can serve as tools for education and social change. Adolescence, after all, is all about pushing boundaries and taking risks. Youth at risk are at risk because they feel the need to take risks.

What if adolescents could be given the opportunity to take real risks, but in a context that accepted and even glorified them, while controlling the danger involved? What if persons whose lives are constricted by boundaries of class and religion and ethnicity could experience an environment where such boundaries are at least temporarily erased? In the past half century, social circus, in particular youth circus, has grown to a worldwide movement; there are dozens if not hundreds of circuses throughout the developed and the developing world, large and small, some highly sophisticated professional institutions, some local and home grown. There are national and international networks and associations, and a growing body of academic research[1] and attempts to create standards of training and safety. There is a variety of styles and emphases, reflecting different professional approaches and different cultural environments.

THE GALILEE CIRCUS

The founders of the Galilee Circus were only vaguely aware of the history and current status of youth circus in the world. They were drawn to the idea of circus out of an intuitive sense that an activity that was not dependent on language, that required a high degree of cooperation and trust among the participants, and that represented a multicultural tradition, might be appropriate as a means of breaking down barriers of fear and alienation between Jewish and Arab youth in the Galilee, who live completely separate lives but within a compact geographical area.

In the fall of 2003, the Galilee Circus began operation one afternoon a week in a rented school gymnasium in the Jewish city of Karmiel, with nine Jewish children and sixteen Arabs. The focus was on juggling, unicycle, stilt walking, and basic tumbling. There was a performance for the families and invited community members at the end of the year. Ten years later, the circus comprises over sixty children aged six to twenty-one, holds practice four times per week, and features juggling, unicycle, tight rope, trapeze, aerial silks, acro-balance, and more. It performs frequently (for a fee) for a variety of audiences, local, national, and international.

As a result of a chance encounter in 2006, a partnership developed between the Galilee Circus and Circus Harmony in St. Louis. At that point the Galilee Circus was still a small and not particularly intensive program, with practices once or twice a week and occasional performances. Circus Harmony was already a well-established circus school with a very professional youth performance troupe. Thus, when a delegation of performers and staff from Circus Harmony spent two weeks with the Galilee Circus in Israel in 2007 and hosted a delegation from the Galilee for two weeks in St. Louis in 2008, the impact on the nature of the Galilee Circus program was powerful. In a relatively short time, the expectations, the tone, and the degree of commitment and responsibility that characterized the Israeli program underwent a massive upgrade. The exposure to a world-class youth circus raised aspirations and skill levels and instilled new habits and a new self-image. From an after-school club the Galilee Circus advanced to being a true youth circus in which performance was central. Five years (and another cycle of reciprocal exchanges) later, the Galilee Circus is unrecognizable compared to how it appeared before entering this partnership.

Other less intensive encounters with youth circuses abroad have also had an impact, notably a training exchange with Circus Poehaa in the Netherlands (funded by the Anna Lindh Foundation), which exposed the coaches and performers to European circus traditions, influenced by the Commedia del Arte. The Galilee Circus has also benefitted from professional support by volunteers for varying periods of time, bringing experience from youth circuses in Europe and the United States.

These encounters with the world of youth circuses have a significant value beyond their contribution to the level of skills and showmanship of the Galilee Circus. They link the participants into a worldwide network of "circus people," a network that, in the tradition of circus, transcends local, ethnic, religious, and national identity. In the first meeting with the St. Louis troupe, one of the American performers asked upon arrival, "How am I supposed to know who is a Jew and who is an Arab?" Which was, of course, exactly the point: the goal was to create a place where he was not supposed to know, because, at least for a few hours or days or weeks, it really didn't matter. The circus, as the place where boundaries and limits are pushed or blurred or overcome, is the place where participants can leave their hyphenated identities outside the tent and be just "circus people," sharing a language and a set of formative experiences with fellow performers around the world—the place where they are judged by what they can do (together with others) and not by their group affiliation.

CHALLENGES

Consistently, through the years, a central challenge has been the recruitment of Jewish participants. A few reasons can be suggested for this:

- There is generally a larger array of after-school activities offered in the Jewish communities of the region than in the Arab towns and villages.
- Jews are more likely to be afraid of or uncomfortable with participating in a mixed activity, feeling no particular motivation to integrate with the minority, whereas Arabs are more likely to seek out such programs as a means of integration and advancement.
- Jews tend to be unfamiliar with Arabs and Arab culture, whereas Arabs are familiar and comfortable with the majority culture.

Over the years, with the visible success of the circus and the spread of its reputation, this challenge has diminished somewhat; however, maintaining the current equal proportion requires a serious marketing effort each fall.

On the other hand, while for seven years the circus met in a school gymnasium in the Jewish town of Karmiel, in 2010 the program was moved to a community center in the Arab village of Ba'aneh, when no suitable facility could be found in Karmiel, and the proportion of Jewish participants held constant. We take this as an indication that the reluctance of Jews to participate has diminished over the years, and that the modeling by the veteran Jewish performers of willingness to travel to practice in an Arab village has served to encourage younger participants to see this aspect of the program as acceptable.

Another important challenge has, of course, been funding. Keeping the doors open and the balls in the air has required a constant effort to obtain foundation grants and individual contributions. Participants pay an annual tuition fee comparable to the cost of other after-school activities that covers about 20 percent of the cost of operation. In recent years, fees for performances, paid by groups and institutions sponsoring shows for their members, have provided another 10 percent of operating costs.

A third challenge, which has diminished over the years but is still a source of frustration, is that of visibility. The circus exists, of course, not just for its participants, but for its audience. While the improvement in quality and the growing focus on performance have led to increased audiences, the total number of people in Israel who have seen a show or who are even aware of the existence of the project remains very small. It seems that public relations and marketing must be an integral part of operating such a program, requiring serious investment of thought and resources in order to maximize the impact of the circus on Israeli society.

ACHIEVEMENTS

It was not obvious, when the project began, how great its potential was. As the years have gone by, evidence has accumulated that the implementation of social circus in the Jewish-Arab reality in the Galilee was indeed an appropriate action and has had significant impact.

One piece of evidence is the simple fact that the circus has not only survived a decade but has grown, both retaining children for years and attracting new participants every year. At the same time, it has evolved from a minor weekly informal interest group to a highly skilled performing troupe with a graded series of preparatory levels and a growing paying audience. It has taken its place as one among many youth circuses around the world and maintains active connections with several other circuses. It is interesting to note that most school- or sports-based Arab-Jewish encounter programs are quite short-term—usually a limited number of sessions scattered across a year. In the circus there are children who have worked intensively together for as long as ten years, essentially growing up together.

One very gratifying development has been the existence, from the early years, of an active parents' committee that meets periodically to discuss ways of supporting and advancing the circus and planning social and cultural events for the circus participants' families, creating a community of families around the circus and spreading the impact of the project by bringing together Jewish and Arab parents and siblings of the participants around a shared interest. Such joint informal activity by Jewish and Arab adults is not a widespread phenomenon, to say the least.

We have noted the impact of the circus on the participants' own identities and values through informal observation and, occasionally, more formal evaluation interviews. A typical example of their responses can be found in this excerpt from a feature by Kristin Holmes in the *Philadelphia Inquirer*, July 21, 2012:

> "It was weird at the beginning, to be so together with Arabs. It didn't feel normal," said Einat Opalin, 17, who specializes in performing aerial stunts while wrapped in strips of silk. "But I changed my mind. I saw that a person is still a person."
>
> Opalin and fellow performer Roi Shaffran, 15, live in Karmiel, a Jewish city near Deir al-Asad, an Arab town where fellow performer Hala Assadi lives with her family.
>
> "I've learned to trust them and believe in my friends, and not be shy," said Assadi, 14, known for her contortionist-like flexibility.
>
> Many of the troupe members' friends outside the circus question or deride their association with people who don't share their background.
>
> "I don't care," Assadi said. "I know I'm doing the right thing."
>
> Shaffran has learned not to talk about the circus with friends because of what he describes as their negative point of view.
>
> "I used to say things to them, but I found that if you talk to friends about politics and religion, nothing comes out of it," he said.[2]

DEFINING SUCCESS

There is an ongoing debate among "peace educators" in Israel as to the relevance of programs like the Galilee Circus. There is one school of thought (probably the dominant one) that argues that cultural interactions like this one merely plaster over the difficult reality, creating an illusion of "coexistence" that is just a cover-up of a deep and painful conflict. According to this view, such projects are even dangerous, for they create a false sense of security and reconciliation that will ultimately lead to bitter disillusionment when the underlying conflict erupts through the superficial sugar-coating of personal friendship. We are juggling in a burning tent, distracting the crowd from the hard truth. What we need to do is to confront the conflict, to talk about it, to process it, to hold it up to the light. Only then do we have a chance of overcoming it. There are many programs that follow this approach, in which participants go through an often painful process of trying to listen (or trying not to listen) to the historical grievances and personal fears of the other, and through this to reach some kind of common ground.

Another perspective is this: before we can have a serious and effective discussion of the historical and ideological conflicts that divide us, we have to have a common language, some kind of cultural common denominator, a joint loyalty, an awareness of the humanity of the other—otherwise, the other remains other to us, and his or her claims are the claims of a group, or a caricature, not of a person toward whom we feel any affection, responsibility, or commitment. If we really share nothing but the conflict itself, if we and our relationship are defined by the conflict, then maybe we almost have a perverse interest in its perpetuation.

Circus will not bring peace to the Middle East. But it can help to make dialogue possible by reducing fears, lowering barriers, and building trust. It can provide a model, unattainable perhaps on the large scale, of a shared loyalty that transcends ethnic identities. It can teach the art of taking risks for the common good. It can demonstrate to a wide audience that what appears to be impossible is indeed possible. None of these may be sufficient to bring about the requisite social change, but without them, no change is possible.

Notes

1. For a partial bibliography, see http://community.simplycircus.com/research/thesis_papers.htm.

2. Kristin E. Holmes, "Youthful Circus Troupe Bridges Arab-Israeli Divide," *Philadelphia Inquirer*, July 21, 2012, http://articles.philly.com/2012-07-21/news/32765060_1_arab-teens-arab-town-jewish-federation.

LIVING TOGETHER IN THE SAME LAND

The Use of Film as Text in Understanding the Other

AMY KRONISH

INTRODUCTION

Film can be used as a unique tool in providing a window into understanding the other in a society in which people live mostly separate lives. The use of film can enrich the learning process that is already going on in dozens of educational settings in both Arab and Jewish sectors of Israeli society. Although there is an artistic value in showing a film in its entirety, there is also a legitimacy in using film clips for specific purposes. The screening and analysis of a film clip, similar to the analysis of a written text, can provide insight that is between the lines or behind the scenes. In addition, it is possible to gain a better understanding of each other's cultures and historical narratives through the careful textual study of a piece of film. This article will discuss a number of films that provide insight into the controversial issues and trends in contemporary Palestinian and Israeli society. Moreover, it will help us understand some of the key obstacles and major challenges that face Israeli Jews and Palestinian Arabs who share the same land.

THE ISRAELI JEWISH VOICE

One of the major challenges facing Israeli society is the coming to grips with the Holocaust in the second and third generations. Israeli Jews, who used to be silent on this subject (similar to other Jews around the world), are now struggling to deal with their feelings and perceptions of this watershed in modern Jewish history. Like a prism, film reflects trends and issues of the society at large. At the same time, it is a therapeutic device that helps us grapple with this complicated cognitive and emotional issue.

Of all of the Israeli films produced during the early years of the State of Israel, there is one particularly interesting portrayal dealing with the aftermath of the Holocaust, the classic film *Hill 24 Doesn't Answer* (1954), directed by Thorold Dickinson. The film tells three parallel stories about the period of the War of Independence in 1948. One of the three stories is the story of an Israeli who fought in the battle for the northern Negev, where he encounters a Nazi mercenary fighting for the Egyptians. The scene that we will analyze opens with the Israeli soldier dragging the wounded Nazi mercenary into a cave, so that he can treat his enemy's wounds. Then he sees the Nazi insignia tattooed on his enemy's chest. Although he is considerably surprised, the Israeli soldier continues to bandage him anyway, highlighting the humanity of the Israeli soldier in battle.

The Nazi begins to explain his actions during the war and moves from begging for understanding to fear and then to hatred. First he explains, "We couldn't help ourselves," and he says, "We did some terrible things—but those were our orders." So he uses two excuses here: the first is that everybody was doing it and the second is about following orders, an issue that was debated so heavily in Israeli society, especially during the period of the Eichmann trial (1960–62). It is important to note that this film was made a number of years before the Eichmann trial. Then the Nazi becomes suddenly afraid of his captor and he demands forgiveness. He says, "We are soldiers. You must forgive me. It is your law."

Only when he realizes that forgiveness is not readily forthcoming does he suddenly change gears entirely and begin to rant, shouting anti-Semitic remarks, calling the Israeli a coward. This is when the camera swings around, and we see the Israeli soldier as a helpless ultra-Orthodox

Jew with payes (sidecurls). A similar technique is used years later in *Annie Hall*,[1] when the neurotic Woody Allen saw himself as a pitiful Jew at the dinner table of the highbrow family of his girlfriend. As a result of his embarrassment with his heritage, Woody Allen was showing the audience how he imagined that a WASP American family would see the Jew. Similarly, the filmmaker of *Hill 24 Doesn't Answer* was illustrating how a Nazi would see a Jew—as a Diaspora Jew, exactly that image that the Israeli "new" Jew[2] was trying to negate, an ultra-Orthodox Jew dressed in black garb who was weak and helpless. Or perhaps, this is not only the way the Nazi sees the Israeli but also the way the Israeli fears that he will be perceived—Israelis are afraid of being perceived as weak and helpless.

Then finally the Nazi begs the Israeli to kill him. But the Israeli only laughs. This is when the viewer really understands the reaction of the Israeli soldier: he's not about to do any favors for this Nazi, not even kill him. Finally, the Nazi salutes and dies from the effort.

Why has the filmmaker portrayed the Arab enemy as a Nazi? Was he a figment of the imagination of the Israeli who sees Nazis in all of his enemies? When the Israeli Jew feels his life threatened and his entire nation endangered, he imagines another time and place and sees the danger as a potential Shoah. Thus we can understand that this Israeli soldier sees every Arab as if he were the embodiment of the forces of evil, the Nazis.

And so it is with contemporary Israeli society—Israeli Jews see every embodiment of evil or danger as a potential Nazi, wanting to wipe them off the face of the earth. And whatever their politics, right or left, Israelis worry that if they let down their defenses even for a moment, the entire nation might be "pushed into the sea." This is a heavy burden for all Israelis to carry. On the one hand, they are afraid of being seen as weak and helpless, like the Diaspora Jews from the ghettos of Europe, and on the other hand, they are terribly afraid that their Arab enemies, seen as Nazis, will succeed in wiping them and their entire nation from the face of the earth.

YOU WERE A PERSECUTED MINORITY

Any possibility of achieving understanding and coexistence between Israeli Jews and Palestinian Arabs is complicated by the fact that Israel has been in a continuous state of war with its Arab neighbors since its existence. For the first nineteen years (from the establishment of the State of Israel in 1948 until 1967), the Arabs in the region comprised the major power bloc, both militarily and politically. Following the Six Day War of 1967, the tables were turned and suddenly they found themselves as the losers in battle. At that time the Jews, who had been the underdog for thousands of years, found themselves in a position of strength. *Avanti Popolo* (Rafi Bukai, 1986) explores this reversal of roles.

During the final hours of the Six Day War, two Egyptian soldiers retreating from battle are desperately trying to find their way back to the Suez Canal on their way home. The film comprises a series of surreal episodes and encounters along the journey. Stumbling across the bleak desert landscape, the two Egyptian soldiers come across an Israeli patrol. Immediately, they catch sight of a jerry can of water. One of the two Egyptians, an actor on the Cairo stage, uses the language of the theater to beg for water—and for understanding. Reciting the famous monologue of Shylock, the Jew from Shakespeare's *The Merchant of Venice*, he intones (in English), "I am a Jew. Hath not a Jew eyes? Hath not a Jew hands, organs, emotions, senses, affections? If you prick us do we not bleed? If you tickle us do we not laugh? If you poison us do we not die?"

This powerful scene is a metaphor for the great role reversal that took place as a result of the war. Previously, Israel was a besieged country, encircled by millions of Arabs, who held all of the power in the Middle East. With the stunning results of the Six Day War in 1967, Israel, as the victor, suddenly became a major power in the Middle East. Things have changed in this part of the world and Jew and Arab have exchanged roles. The Jew is no longer the victim, and the Arab is no longer in a position of strength. The Arab soldier, having suddenly found himself in the position of the loser in battle, now better understands the Jew/victim, and he requests the same understanding in return.

By including such a scene in the film, filmmaker and scriptwriter Rafi Bukai was taking a risk with the Israeli filmgoing public. It is a scene that would make average Jewish viewers squirm, bringing to mind a terrible period of anti-Semitism in Europe, not only in Shakespearean literature but also during thousands of years of Diaspora. At the time of the production of the film, the use of the Shylock monologue infuriated many people and the film was not very well received.[3] However, Bukai had an important message to offer. In making a plea for mutual self-expression and understanding, and by including a scene from *The Merchant of Venice*, he was trying to tell his public, "Once, you were a persecuted people, and now it is time to understand the persecuted Arab people within your midst."[4]

The tragic ending has the two Egyptian soldiers symbolically caught between bullets from both sides in the conflict—mistakenly hunted by Israeli troops and simultaneously shot at by their own troops as they attempt to cross the Suez Canal. During the mid-1980s, when the film was released, Israelis were not very sophisticated in their thinking about Arabs or Palestinians. There were no political nuances vis-à-vis understanding the Arabs of the area and their differing backgrounds. In fact, all Arabs—enemy soldiers from the surrounding Arab nations, Palestinian Arabs of the occupied territories, and Arab citizens of the State of Israel—were lumped together into one group.

Although the narrative construct of the film clearly refers to enemy soldiers from Egypt, the casting of Israeli Arab actors in the roles of the Egyptian soldiers provides an Israeli Arab framework or point of view.[5] The Arabs of Israel, who represent about 20 percent of the population, are symbolically caught between fire from both sides. They are discriminated against from within Israeli society, largely because of fear and suspicion based on security concerns, and also due to ideological reasons, since they are not part of the Zionist enterprise, which sees the State of Israel primarily, if not completely, as the home of the Jewish people. In addition, they are looked down upon by their own people, the Arabs of neighboring lands—especially Palestinian Arabs living in the West Bank and Gaza—as if they are collaborators with the Israeli enemy. Due to circumstances of history, they are citizens of the State of Israel, they pay taxes and speak Hebrew, and therefore appear to be traitors in the eyes of their Arab brethren.

A prize winner at the Locarno Film Festival,[6] *Avanti Popolo* is a film of humor, pathos, and insight and explores the fine line between the real and the surreal in wartime. In this film, Rafi Bukai[7] has created a metaphor for the need to perceive the human being behind the face of the enemy. According to Bukai, the film was the antithesis of those documentaries produced following the war that portrayed the Egyptian soldiers who fled barefoot in the hot sands of the Sinai Peninsula, leaving behind their shoes. In contrast to these documentaries, Bukai's fiction film is an honest attempt at looking behind the uniform and understanding the Arab enemy as an individual—his background, his plea for understanding, and his humanity. In a sense, Bukai has tried to let his viewers stand in the shoes of the Egyptians.

THE PALESTINIAN VOICE

Born in Israel, living in Holland, defining himself as Palestinian, Hany Abu-Assad is a well-known filmmaker.[8] His faux documentary, *Ford Transit* (2002), deals with issues of the occupation, portraying the daily hardships of living with the many checkpoints that dot the West Bank. The transit refers to the van that is used for public transportation around the West Bank. The film follows the driver of one van, Rajai, and his passengers, as they travel between Ramallah and Jerusalem, detouring around roadblocks and bouncing over dirt roads. The passengers in Rajai's van include both ordinary people and celebrities, including Hannan Ashrawi, articulate Palestinian spokeswoman, and B. Z. Goldberg, director of the film *Promises*.

Ford Transit[9] addresses the limitations of movement. There is hardly a moment when we are not on the move. Rajai, the driver, gets behind the wheel, sets off, stops, switches the motor on, breaks, slows down, opens a door, and closes it. The spectator is bundled along with him in the car, breathing the smell of distress, the dust, smog, and heat. The camera focuses almost entirely on characters inside the transit, which comes to function as a kind of frame within a frame, a cinematographic element emphasizing the sense of enclosure. The inside of the car encloses the characters, while the car itself moves within the claustrophobic landscape of the occupation—walls, fences, demolished homes, building debris, garbage—a constant backdrop of ugliness with precious few comforting moments of greenery.

The fierce sun, blinding white and parched urban landscape elevate the sense of congestion to a level that is truly distressing, growing with the endless noise of horns, shouting, and screeching brakes. The spectator begins to sense that he is gradually being drawn into the merciless congestion that emanates from the screen.

Everything on the screen moves in jolts. The car travels endlessly from place to place. As the film progresses, it increasingly seems as though the car is never really progressing, but simply traveling in circles, from checkpoint to checkpoint, from one makeshift bypass to the next, and round again. The car brings people to and from a given point, from which they must continue on foot through fences, over mounds of earth, in front of soldiers, through road blocks, checkpoints, and watchtowers. A man in a wheelchair must be lifted over concrete blocks along a dirt road. Yet as they move forward, it is quite possible that they will soon be obliged to return, if they have no permit, or their permit is out of date, or the road is blocked, or the soldiers are shooting, or there is a curfew, or the car has a flat tire.

The space within which the van moves is restricted. We hear the driver explain that "I have to keep on the move all the time. I can't stand working in one place. It would kill me if I had to work every day from morning to noon, eat lunch, continue until two o'clock and so on. I'd go crazy." By the end of the film, his comment seems highly ironic. It is true that he is on the move all the time, but he is not traveling anywhere. The routine of monotonous work in time and space that he seeks to avoid is precisely the reality of his life. Movement creates an illusion of traveling.

The subject of the film is this complex and stifling sequence of minute details, each of which does not seem particularly problematic on its own, but which combine to make life intolerable. The viewer spends time inside the car, senses the jolts, noise, and heat, and experiences the tension that comes with the possibility that after the enormous effort to overcome obstacles, circumvent road blocks, and travel along dirt roads, they may encounter an army jeep, waiting for no apparent purpose, that will order them to go back again.

Rajai drives along a bumpy side road between hills. A small truck full of chickens follows behind. It seems as though the crates of chickens may fall off at any time. "There are soldiers there, watch out! They're inclined to shoot." They exchange vital information. Two old women are loading crates. "What's in there?" he asks. "Cucumbers. I just hope they don't catch me." The observer realizes that even the trivial and mundane act of moving two crates of cucumbers can be dangerous. It is not entirely clear why, but the impression is that people are constantly trying to avoid being *caught* by the occupation. The observer begins to realize that routine, daily functions are virtually impossible. The sense of uncertainty and tension mounts.

There are a few moments of petty, almost childish comfort. Rajai tires of waiting in an endless line of cars at one of the road blocks and decides to use the other side of the road, driving the wrong way. The soldier stops him, but for some reason lets him go through—perhaps his audacity paid off. Rajai will receive a fine: "OK, I'll get a fine—so what? The main thing is I got through." Rajai smiles to himself with the satisfaction of someone who has managed to trick the invincible Israeli soldiers. The interviewer comments, "But now people will see the film and learn the trick." The driver boasts, "So what! They'll find out, and we'll invent loads more tricks. Everything's under control. I could get a tank through there if I wanted to."

The camera angle is from below as the van speeds along a high road, apparently strong, fast and determined, controlling the frame—as though the success in tricking the soldiers at the road block has given it a new lease on life. In the background we hear cheerful music. The sequence concludes with children inside the van dressed as clowns, singing and clapping their hands—a surrealistic scene.

This is a film about the exhausting daily struggle of life under the Israeli occupation of the West Bank, where people are trapped within small spaces and movement is limited due to checkpoints that dot the entire area.

A MODERN TRAGI-COMEDY

Actor and director Elia Suleiman[10] portrays a Jerusalem man who is trying to smuggle his West Bank girlfriend through a checkpoint in his film *Divine Intervention* (2002). He is a Buster Keaton character— stony-faced, determined and silent, trying desperately and with much humor and charm to achieve his goals. The narrative construct of the film is fragmented, making our work of analyzing scenes much easier.

In one provocative scene, a good-looking and well-dressed woman strides confidently through a checkpoint. Without hesitation, removing her sunglasses to create eye contact with the soldiers, and with total determination, she walks comfortably by while the soldiers are pointing their rifles at her. As she passes by, they lower their rifles, mesmerized by her confidence and her take-charge attitude. After she has walked by, the tower of the checkpoint begins to wobble and then falls over. Can dressing elegantly, walking tall, and having the right attitude help to bring down the checkpoints? Like Abigail in the Bible, who is described as "clever and beautiful" (1 Sam 25:3) and tries to find a way other than violence, this woman in the film, through her determination and self-confidence, finds another way.

In another scene, the main character decides to sneak his girlfriend through a checkpoint near Jerusalem. He blows up a big red helium balloon with Arafat's face painted on it, and he sends it out into the air. As it floats over the checkpoint, free as a bird, the soldiers are all watching it. The diversion works and our character can drive through with his girlfriend, while the balloon continues on its way over Jerusalem, landing on the Dome of the Rock.

The metaphor of the balloon represents freedom from checkpoints—an illusion that so easily can be burst! In quirky and metaphorical vignettes, this film provides a window into understanding some of the issues facing Palestinians today.

CONCLUSION

The films discussed above can provide important texts for those wishing to understand the complexities of the relations between Arabs and Jews, and for those dialogue groups that wish to discuss sensitive issues of Arab-Jewish relations in the Middle East. The issues raised in these films include the ongoing security fears of the Israelis, how the Arab minority is treated by the Israeli majority, and the difficulties of living under occupation. One cannot adequately educate about the Middle East abroad—whether in Jewish educational settings or in interreligious frameworks—without addressing these issues in a substantive manner.

Notes

1. *Annie Hall,* directed by Woody Allen, was made in 1977.

2. The "new" Jew was the creation of the Jews of the pioneering period who ploughed the land with one hand and defended it with the other. It was a negation of the weak and religious Diaspora Jew.

3. Meir Shnitzer, "Filmmaker from Birth," *Ma'ariv Weekend Magazine,* December 2003 (in Hebrew).

4. According to the author's notes of a lecture given by Rafi Bukai at the Jerusalem Cinematheque on May 31, 1990 (in Hebrew).

5. Ella Shohat, *Israeli Cinema—East/West and the Politics of Representation* (Austin: University of Texas Press, 1989), 249.

6. *Golden Eye of the Leopard*, Locarno Film Festival, 1986.

7. Rafi Bukai was born in Tel Aviv in 1957 and died in 2003 from cancer at the age of 47. He studied filmmaking at the University of Tel Aviv and completed his studies in 1981. Bukai directed only one other feature film, *Marco Polo—The Missing Chapter* (1996, also producer and scriptwriter), and a TV drama, *Fear of the Jews* (1991). He also worked as the producer of feature films. The student film that won Bukai his degree at the University of Tel Aviv served as the basis for the low-budget *Avanti Popolo*.

8. Born in Nazareth in 1961, Hany Abu-Assad is a Dutch-Palestinian filmmaker, well-known for his films *Paradise Now* (2006) and *Omar* (2013).

9. The analysis of the film *Ford Transit* is based on the discussion of a 2003 Focus Group, as published in a booklet entitled *Understanding Relations between Arabs and Jews in Israel—The Use of Film for Coexistence Education*, published by the Interreligious Coordinating Council in Israel (2004), written by Michal Levin, Fachira Haloun, and Amy Kronish.

10. Born in Nazareth in 1960, Elia Suleiman is known for his award-winning films *Divine Intervention* (2002), *Chronicle of a Disappearance* (1996), and *The Time That Remains* (2009). He established the Film and Media Department at Bir Zeit University.

TEACHING ABOUT THE OTHER IN RELIGIOUS ZIONIST EDUCATION
A Pilot Program

SHLOMO BRINN

KEDEM (*Kol Dati Mefayes* or Religious Voices for Reconciliation) was a unique interreligious program run by the Interreligious Coordinating Council in Israel (ICCI) between 2003 and 2008 that fostered long-term dialogue between Jewish, Christian, and Muslim religious leaders. The program's goals were to enable the participating religious leaders to get to know one another; to learn about the history, tenets, and traditions of each faith; and to discuss the possibility of working together to promote reconciliation between Jews and Arabs in Israel. The program included monthly dialogue sessions in different locations around Israel and annual seminars held in conflict regions elsewhere in the world, such as Northern Ireland, Cyprus, and Bosnia-Herzegovina. The encounters featured interreligious textual study as well as a candid and forthright look at the religious and national narratives of each side.

The dialogues held in the framework of these encounters touched on core issues of the Israeli-Arab conflict, on the character of Jewish-Arab/Palestinian relations in Israel, and on the hope of reconciliation between the groups. Program participants also visited each other occasionally in their homes and communities—including at such special times as Sukkot and Ramadan—in order to learn about each other's religious heritage and way of life. At the end of the program's first year, it numbered fourteen participants; during its second year, the participant group grew to twenty-eight. I was privileged to be among the program's earliest participants; my fascinating and deeply affecting KEDEM experience left a lasting mark on me, whose traces can be discerned even today.

I came to KEDEM via Rabbi Yehuda Gilad, a Rosh Yeshiva at Yeshivat Maale Gilboa, who approached me with news of a unique group of rabbis and Muslim and Christian clerics who were organizing, on the initiative of the ICCI (headed by Dr. Ron Kronish), for dialogue on issues related to the interreligious nature of the Palestinian-Israeli conflict. My curiosity was piqued. Although I had met in the past with Muslim Arabs in the context of neighborly interaction with residents of the villages near my place of residence (Alon Shvut in Gush Etzion), this kind of encounter was something new to me. After obtaining additional information and confirming that the intentions of the parties involved in organizing the group were serious, I decided to join and take part in the activity. An additional factor in my decision to join the group was the group of participating rabbis, whom I knew and esteemed—figures such as Rabbi David Stav (candidate for the position of Chief Rabbi of Israel, 2013), Rabbi Shmuel Reiner (Head of Yeshiva at Yeshivat Ma'aleh Gilboa), Rabbi Shai Piron (Minister of Education of the State of Israel in 2013–14), and Rabbi Eli Kahan, of blessed memory, of Kibbut Ein Hanatziv.

I was already acquainted with nearly all of the Jewish members of the group from other frameworks, and the encounter between my rabbinical colleagues and the Muslim and Christian religious leaders was fascinating. For me, it was the first time I was meeting in an intensive way and engaging in deep and highly charged dialogue with Muslim and Christian clerics. Beyond the intensive religious context in which the group activity took place, the Arab-Israeli conflict was conspicuously present during the dialogue sessions. The century-long bloody struggle, the wars and violence, left their mark on the discussions.

Alongside the interest and curiosity aroused by the dialogue, and the challenge that it posed, there were tensions and problems that we had to overcome. We benefited from good preparation for the sessions provided by the program. We worked closely with a psychologist who specializes in facilitating dialogue in conflict situations, Dr. Yitzhak Mendelsohn; his expertise was invaluable. However, the presession preparatory activity was devoted more to the human and practical issues of resolving conflicts and differences of opinion than to issues of religion or to the complexity of the various religious perspectives. While the tensions vis-à-vis the Muslim clerics were more national than theological, the main source of tension vis-à-vis the Christian religious leaders was actually the fraught historical-theological background to Jewish-Christian relations—a background that has colored Jewish history for many years and is etched deeply in our identity.

The first two years of KEDEM programs gave me an in-depth familiarity with perspectives, positions, and opinions, some of which differed from or were hostile to or conflicted with my own. It is relatively easy to engage in dialogue and to display understanding of the other, of those who differ from you; it is harder to do this when that other is your ultimate adversary. The constant, weighty background presence of the Jewish-Palestinian conflict gave rise to additional, multiple tensions during the discussions; cast a shadow over our interactions; hampered the effort to differentiate, insofar as possible, between opinions and people; and blurred the distinction between an atmosphere of trust and sincere dialogue and one of suspicion and distrust of the other's intentions.

Nevertheless, I was pleasantly surprised to find that the group atmosphere did foster a very open, unconstrained, and informal dialogue that differed from the large interreligious conferences abroad that I had been familiar with up to that time. A factor that contributed to this openness was the small size of the group, the length of our acquaintance with one another, and the absence of any predeclared intention of reaching a consensus or of formulating a joint document. We wanted, first of all, to get to know each other, to see what we shared and where we differed, and to try to act cooperatively wherever possible. This was what produced the atmosphere of openness and the relative candor that characterized our discussions. I will not go so far as to claim that our dialogue was unmarred by lingering suspicion; that would have been an impossibility given the protracted conflict that had positioned us at opposite poles. However, the suspicion subsided over time as a basic trust developed between us, against the background of a broad commonality. In my view, the openness that characterized these dialogue sessions greatly surpassed what normally transpires at encounters of this kind. I recall impassioned debates and harsh, bitter, and heart-rending exchanges that were possible because people felt free to say what they really thought.

One of the things that interested me from the start about participating in KEDEM was the theological-intellectual challenge that it
posed to me as a practitioner and representative of the Jewish religion
within an interreligious dialogue framework. Yet ultimately the true,
difficult, and complex challenge was not primarily theological but
rather sociological, political, and interpersonal. The main issue at the
encounters was, finally, that of building interpersonal trust, of clarify-
ing differences of opinion, and of understanding the outlooks that lay
behind the people before me.

The road was not easy. The period in which the encounters took
place was one of the most harrowing episodes in the bloody conflict
with the Palestinian Arabs. It was a period characterized by terrorism,
violence, and an oppressive sense of being surrounded by hostility.
Within my immediate community I sensed revulsion over the mere fact
of my meeting with those who, to so large a degree, were identified with
the goals of our sworn enemy. When people are afraid to walk in the
street—when they feel threatened—fear and a sense of menace dictate
opinions and thoughts. This is especially true when the threat is not a
theological but rather a national, existential one. Under such conditions, it is exceedingly difficult to differentiate the terrorist from
Palestinian society as a whole, to distinguish between the attacker, the
enemy blowing up buses, from the law-abiding Palestinian Arab.

It was especially important to us to take a strong stand against violence and terrorism. It is worth noting that all of the rabbis who took
part in the program saw and continue to see themselves as patriotic
Zionists. We served in the army, and our children and our pupils serve
in the army. Notwithstanding this fact—or perhaps because of it—it
was important to us to vehemently condemn such acts as the murder
perpetrated by IDF soldiers in the Israeli Arab village of Kafr Qassem
in 1956, and to make it clear that we deplore misdeeds and crimes of
this kind, which are contrary to our faith and to our conception of the
kind of country in which we want to live as Jews and Zionists. Against
this background we made a joint visit to Kafr Qassem in November
2003, to express shock and abhorrence at what took place there, and to
convey our position to both the Arab and the Jewish publics in Israel.

At the same time, denunciation of violence and terrorist attacks by
the Muslim and Christian religious leaders with whom we were inter-
acting was a major basis for the encounters—perhaps a precondition

for their very occurrence. In particular I remember a phone call that I received one night from an important qadi (Muslim judge). This was after a horrible terrorist attack in Jerusalem—the bombing of an Egged No. 2 bus on its way to the Western Wall. The qadi called to tell me how shocked and ashamed he was that a Muslim could cry "Allahu akbar" and, in the name of God, blow up a bus full of women and children. His condemnation did not strike me as mere lip service; it was real.

The great crisis that ultimately led to a cessation of the encounters came in the wake of the appalling terrorist attack on Yeshivat Merkaz HaRav in Jerusalem, in March 2008. This attack, which was perpetrated by a Palestinian terrorist from East Jerusalem, took the lives of eight young yeshiva students and injured nine other people. I and some of my rabbinical colleagues were deeply disappointed by the way in which some of our fellow Muslim group members reacted to the event.

Our Muslim counterparts split into two factions. One was willing to denounce the outrageous incident with no conditions. The other faction adamantly refused to condemn the attack unilaterally and unequivocally. Those belonging to this latter faction insistently demanded that the statement issued to the media also denounce IDF gunfire on the Gaza Strip. We rabbis, of course, refused. We argued that there was no basis for comparison and that a terrorist attack of this kind had to be condemned wholeheartedly, with no reservations, without trying to place the atrocity into a context that might justify it, or represent it in a "balanced" way.

We wanted to hear a clear, firm, and unambiguous condemnation of the murder of the yeshiva students in Jerusalem. Whatever there was to say about the conflict or about IDF activity in Gaza could be said separately, on some other day. When we went to Kafr Qassem, we unequivocally denounced the killing of Arab civilians, without trying to make excuses or to present the context of hostile Arab actions against Jews during that period, or the existential threat faced by the fledgling State of Israel. We wished, hoped, and expected a similar condemnation on the part of our Muslim and Christian counterparts.

Unfortunately, the emotionally charged atmosphere that prevailed in the wake of the attack, and the political agenda that had filtered into the discussions, led to a group crisis and, ultimately, to a termination of the encounters. I am sorry for this. I wanted the KEDEM encounters to continue and viewed them as a positive, useful, right, and important thing.

Despite the unpleasant atmosphere in which the KEDEM dialogue sessions ceased, they were, nevertheless, productive and have had a major and lasting impact. The KEDEM activity enabled me and my rabbinical colleagues to get to know Israel's Palestinian Arab minority—its problems, the hardships it faces, its needs—in a firsthand way that cannot be rivaled by academic articles, newspaper stories, or books. I came to realize that life is not easy for Israel's Arab minority and that it is indeed affected by mistakes, injustices, and discrimination on our part, on the part of the Jews who are the majority in the State of Israel.

These mistakes and injustices stem, unfortunately, from a legitimate and heroic existential struggle for our very survival. But we must, nevertheless, correct those moral failings that it is in our power to rectify. One example of this was an initiative that we, in the KEDEM framework, placed on the agenda—that of providing places of worship for Muslims in the hospitals; other examples included declarative and solidarity activities such as the visit to Kafr Qassem.

I also came to understand that there is an educational challenge here for the population in which I am active as a rabbi and educator. Subsequent to the KEDEM encounters and activity, I saw it as a personal mission, even a duty, to promote awareness and activity regarding such topics as the Torah's instructions with regard to minorities, strangers, and non-Jews.

I came to realize that the proper attitude toward the non-Jew in general, and to the law-abiding Arab in the State of Israel in particular, is not being presented or taught in accordance with the tenets of Judaism. I reached the conclusion that the educational infrastructure in this sphere is inadequate and, at times, distorted. I'll mention here a ruling by Rabbi Moshe Feinstein of blessed memory, one of the Torah giants of the last generation, who took a favorable view of Jews and Christians praying together under certain circumstances, each in the manner dictated by his faith. I have taught this ruling to my pupils, many of whom have expressed surprise.

One of the most meaningful things that this program enabled me to do, something that for me was a fascinating journey, was to design a special course on attitudes toward the non-Jew in Jewish sources, which I taught at two religious Israeli teachers' colleges during a three-year period. I called the course "Israel and the Nations." In addition to covering the relevant *halakhot* (religious rulings) and sources, one course session included an encounter with an Israeli Muslim Palestinian Arab from Abu Ghosh, who shared his unique perspective with the students. The encounter was tense and several young women who were enrolled in the course refused to be present at it. They argued that an encounter with an Arab who does not identify with Zionism constitutes a legitimization of the enemy. It should be emphasized that the period in question was one of heinous Palestinian terrorism, and the emotions and reactions that surfaced reflected a highly fraught situation.

A world of Jewish thought with which the students had never been acquainted was opened up to them, and it aroused both curiosity and criticism on their part (i.e., they asked why, if what they were now learning was really true, they had never heard of it before). I also found it gratifying to transmit important basic knowledge rooted in an educational approach that added yet another layer to their religious-Jewish perspective on the non-Jew. Many of the young women who attended the course emerged with a sense of responsibility toward the minorities who live in our country.

CONCLUSION

To conclude, I can say that the issues that I dealt with in the courses I taught, and the dilemmas that were addressed at the KEDEM dialogue sessions, became a meaningful part of my professional educational activity. Just recently, for instance, a student from one of those courses came to ask me about Rabbi Kook's approach to the topic of how Judaism relates to non-Jews.

There can be no doubt that my participation in KEDEM raised my awareness of the minorities who live in Israel. I gained a new understanding that has stayed with me and that is binding on me in my educational work. I would venture to say that, to some degree or other, this is true of all of my rabbinical colleagues who took part in the program.

REACHING OUT TO THE INTERNATIONAL COMMUNITY

WORKING FOR PEACE WITH RELIGIOUS ESTABLISHMENTS

DAVID ROSEN

BACKGROUND AND CONTEXT

Until recently the involvement of the official religious establishments in the Holy Land in the work of interreligious dialogue and cooperation had been minimal at most. There are a number of reasons for this. To begin with, the pioneers and activists in this field have overwhelmingly been persons from "Western" backgrounds who have immigrated here, or, especially in the case of Christians, have been temporary residents serving their coreligionists locally and/or representing their respective religious communities abroad. Thus there has often been local psychological resistance to what has often been perceived as a "foreign" preoccupation.

Moreover, the Jewish religious presence in this field has overwhelmingly come from the liberal streams of Judaism and even from those who described themselves as "secular." This in itself reinforced the disinterest if not hostility of the Orthodox Jewish establishment.

Yet arguably the main factors have been the sociodemographic and cultural realities on the ground. Aside from the fact that most communities tend to live among their own coreligionists, separated to a greater or lesser degree from the other communities (generally by choice), the local and regional cultural mindset—profoundly conditioned by historical experience (overwhelmingly negative)—is not one that lends itself to great interest in the inner religious world of the other. Most communities are willing "to live and let live," but each tends to believe that it is the possessor of "truth" and thus everyone else is, to a greater or lesser degree, on a false or at least inferior path.

This "culture of separation" is of course compounded by the political reality and consequences of ongoing conflict (Israeli-Arab at large and Israeli-Palestinian in particular.)

Moreover, the leadership of the official Israeli Jewish and Palestinian Muslim establishments is appointed by political processes and thus, to varying degrees, subject to the political authority. In addition, they tend to lack a broad general education, and so their world outlook tends to be limited and lacking in self-critique. These and other factors[1] often compromise their standing in the eyes of their respective communities at large. Nevertheless, these institutions and those that head them are the only official representatives of the religions that are so central to the identities of the communities that live in the Holy Land.

THE CHIEF RABBINATE AND INTERRELIGIOUS DIALOGUE

The most dramatic change in the Chief Rabbinate of Israel's relations with other faith communities resulted from the pilgrimage to the Holy Land of Pope John Paul II in the year 2000. While the first involvement of Israeli chief rabbis had begun a decade earlier, this had been on an individual and very sporadic basis. During his visit to Jerusalem, John Paul II met with the Council of the Chief Rabbinate of Israel and suggested—although there is an international Jewish body that is the official Jewish partner of the Holy See's Commission for Religious Relations with Jewry—the establishment of a special bilateral commission for dialogue between the Holy See and the Chief Rabbinate of Israel.

Unquestionably, this idea would never have occurred to the chief rabbis or almost all their colleagues on the Chief Rabbinate Council. However, both the papal nuncio and Israel's ambassador to the Vatican followed up diligently on John Paul II's proposal and, despite the objections of some its members, the Chief Rabbinate Council's commission for this dialogue was established under the chairmanship of Chief Rabbi She'ar Yashuv Cohen of Haifa. The Holy See's delegation was chaired by two cardinals—Jorge Mejia and Georges Cottier, John Paul II's papal theologian—thereby reflecting the importance that the

Vatican accorded to this bilateral dialogue, which in 2002 started meeting annually, alternating between Rome and Jerusalem.

The delegations included prominent rabbis of cities in Israel and the leading local Catholic clergy (as well as from the Vatican), thus enabling these religious figures from two major traditions of the Holy Land to develop friendships and understanding between them, in most cases for the first time. This initiative proved to be a great success in terms of the relationships established between the delegations as a whole, as well as the sincerity and depth of the discussion and issues addressed. It also, however, opened up the way for additional interreligious relationships.

In addition, with the great encouragement of individuals from the Ministry of Foreign Affairs who had responsibility for these areas, a similar Anglican-Jewish bilateral commission was established at the initiative of the Archbishop of Canterbury and the Chief Rabbis. It, too, meets annually, alternating between England and Israel and is just as successful as the former in terms of the personal relationships forged and the content of the deliberations. These developments also helped facilitate the involvement of delegations from the Chief Rabbinate to the Congresses of Imams and Rabbis for Peace (organized by Hommes de Parole), involving Palestinian Muslim and Israeli Jewish religious leaders, and has even led to two Hindu-Jewish leadership summits in New Delhi and Jerusalem.

MY PERSONAL ROLE

I had been involved in interfaith activity since having served in the rabbinate in South Africa (1973–79), where my motivation in bringing the different religious communities and, above all, their leadership together flowed from my Jewish commitment to social justice.

In my subsequent position as Chief Rabbi of Ireland (1979–85), interfaith dialogue was almost a sine qua non, as part of the necessary engagement of the tiny Jewish community with the then very religious society of Ireland.

On my return with my family to Israel in 1985, I naturally became involved in voluntary interfaith activity locally. Due to my profile in my previous positions, however, I was approached by leading Jewish-American advocacy agencies to work for them professionally in this field.

When, in 1991, the State of Israel and the Holy See commenced negotiations toward the establishment of full diplomatic relations between the two at the end of 1993, I was asked to be part of the negotiating team, out of recognition that this relationship was not only a diplomatic and legal one but also an interreligious one. These full relations paved the way for the aforementioned visit of Pope John Paul II in the year 2000.

Similarly, when the bilateral commission of the Chief Rabbinate and the Holy See was established, I was invited, by virtue of my past experience as well as being an Orthodox rabbi who has occupied prominent rabbinical positions, to advise and be part of the Chief Rabbinate's delegation.

THE ALEXANDRIA MEETING AND THE COUNCIL OF RELIGIOUS INSTITUTIONS OF THE HOLY LAND

The parallel major factor that eventually led to the establishment of frameworks that brought together official religious leadership was the Alexandria summit of 2002, which was convened as a response to the Second Intifada, the escalating violence, and the collapse of the peace process. This, in fact, was the first ever gathering of Israeli and Palestinian religious figures to include official leaders from the three Abrahamic faiths of the Holy Land, and the first ever to be sanctioned by both the Israeli and Palestinian political leadership.

The initiative came from the then Archbishop of Canterbury, George Carey, with Canon Andrew White doing the essential groundwork on his behalf. But it was facilitated by the support of then Foreign Minister Shimon Peres and, above all, his deputy Rabbi Michael Melchior. My own personal relationship with all of them, as well as my interfaith experience, led to my own inclusion in the preparations for this meeting and being part of the Israeli delegation.

On the Palestinian side the key figure was the late Sheikh Talal Sidr, a minister in Yasser Arafat's cabinet with a special mandate from the latter for this initiative. Providentially, however, Canterbury had previously established a bilateral relationship with Al Azhar, the fountainhead of Sunni Muslim learning in Cairo, and was able to enlist its head

Sheikh Sayyed Mohammad Tantawi to host the gathering in Alexandria. All this might not have been possible without the impact of the attacks on the United States on September 11, 2001.

As a result, all political authorities, Hosni Mubarak of Egypt as well as Ariel Sharon and Yasser Arafat, were eager to be associated with an initiative in which prominent religious figures came together to support peace and oppose violence, especially in the name of religion. The gathering in Alexandria included the Sephardic Chief Rabbi of Israel at the time, Rabbi Eliyahu Bakshi Doron; Sheikh Tayseer Tammimi, the then head of the PA Supreme Sharia Court; and the Latin Patriarch of Jerusalem at the time, Michel Sabbah.

The text of the final declaration had to be negotiated with last-minute telephone calls from Alexandria to Israeli Prime Minister Ariel Sharon as well as with Palestinian leader Yasser Arafat; but in the end a common text was agreed upon that inter alia condemned violence in the name of religion as the desecration of religion itself. President Mubarak hosted a concluding gathering of the participants at his palace in Cairo.

The strength of the Alexandria summit, however, also proved to be its weakness.

Most of us who attended this event were present in our personal capacities, which of course allowed for greater flexibility. But this meant that there was not necessarily institutional ownership of the event and of any possible developments associated with it. Indeed, with the conclusion of terms of office of some in leadership positions, there was no "buy in" on the part of their successors. Moreover, because the event was associated with particular political personalities, there was additional concern about being identified as politically partisan. Furthermore, not long thereafter, Sheikh Sidr died at a young age and no one was appointed to replace him. In addition, there was some resentment among some of the local Christian leadership that they were not equal partners to the "process" (or to be more precise, the brand name of the Alexandria event) in which the determining Christian involvement continued to be from "outside."

As a result, a follow-up initiative took place, facilitated by Canon Trond Bakkevig of the Church of Norway, one of the backers of the Alexandria summit, that established a Council of the Religious Institutions of the Holy Land,[2] the name of which indicates that it is made up of the officially recognized religious authorities within Israeli and Palestinian society. This Council was formed for three specific purposes: to keep open avenues of communication among the religious leadership; to combat defamation, misrepresentation, and incitement against any and all of the three religions; and last but not least, to provide religious support for political initiatives to bring an end to the conflict so that the two peoples and three main religions in the Holy Land may live alongside one another in peace.

As far as the first two goals are concerned, it has been moderately successful. The Council has responded to most attacks on local religious sites, issuing statements of condemnation and on occasions visiting the locations concerned in demonstrations of solidarity. The Council is also seeking to address the question of how other religions are presented in both Israeli and Palestinian textbooks and lent its sponsorship to an academic research program to gather the information to enable further steps to be taken accordingly.

In addition, the Council has agreed to work with a global initiative on the protection of Holy Sites that has already conducted a successful pilot program in Bosnia, in order to do so similarly in the Holy Land.

Arguably, most significant in terms of the relationships within the Council has been the degree to which the Chief Rabbinate in general and the Chief Rabbis in particular have made representation on behalf of their colleagues where necessary. This was especially evident in the case of the Anglican Bishop of Jerusalem, whose Jerusalem residence permit was withdrawn on the basis of unfounded allegations against him.

In order to address the Council's third goal, much effort has been put into setting up meetings with international as well as Israeli and Palestinian political leaders, including two visits of the senior representatives on the Council to Washington, DC, for meetings at the U.S. State Department, as well as with senators and congressional representatives. Nevertheless, those who have been involved in initiatives to advance Israeli/Palestinian negotiations appear thus far not to see any value in engaging the Council specifically and religious leaders generally.

Aside from any biases (which are not insignificant), religion is invariably seen by most diplomats and politicians as "part of the problem." As a result, there is a tendency to want to avoid the religious dimension. While the conflicts between Israel and her Arab neighbors are not religious in origin or in essence, they do involve peoples with strong national or ethnic identities that are overwhelmingly rooted in religious cultures. Consequently, religion is used and indeed abused to strengthen those identities and their claims and often to denigrate those of others. However, to think that the best way to deal with the terrible abuse of religion is to ignore it is not only a fallacy but totally counterproductive. Indeed, such an approach will only play into the hands of the extremists, as indeed we have seen in the past.

In fact, if one does not want religion to be "part of the problem," it must be engaged as "part of the solution." While steps must be taken to defend society against extremist violence, it will only really be subdued by the empowerment and greater visibility of the moderate voices (which I believe to be the overwhelming majority). Accordingly, notwithstanding the fact that official religious leadership in the Holy Land is to a greater or lesser degree subordinate to the political authorities, this does not mean that it is irrelevant in this regard, on the contrary. Through its engagement in support of initiatives for peace and reconciliation, it can provide not only greater legitimacy for such political developments, but also open the way for their progression and success.

As already indicated, this message does not yet appear to have been accepted or internalized among the relevant politicians and diplomats.

THE MODUS OPERANDI OF THE COUNCIL

The Council established a core group of three from the different constituent religions, to conduct the regular business of the Council (including serving as a response committee). The core group meets through the coordination of Dr. Bakkevig and two young part-time staff persons, an Israeli and a Palestinian. Full Council meetings are convened for special occasions, such as for meetings with prominent religious and civic figures and delegations from abroad.

Aside from the above-mentioned challenges in pursuing these goals, inevitably the Council has had to withstand regular crises that have threatened its continued existence. These invariably flow from the political context. The fact that the parties are all loyal members of their respective national groups and, moreover, beholden to a greater or lesser degree to the political authorities places inevitable pressure on them, especially when there is an eruption of violence. Moreover, just as Palestinian and Israelis in general see events in different political and security paradigms, the expectations of each side are dissimilar and often unrealistic.

Palestinians expect the Israeli members of the Council, especially as the Chief Rabbinate is technically under the auspices of the office of the Prime Minister, to be able to influence their government to improve conditions for the Palestinian population, claiming that only such action will reduce incitement and enable them to promote mutual acceptance, dialogue, and reconciliation. The Israelis overwhelmingly perceive such steps as feasible only if incitement and denial of Israel's legitimacy are addressed first. The fact that the principle Muslim in the Council is the Palestinian Minister of Waqf (Islamic Affairs), appointed by and close to the President of the Palestinian Authority, only reinforces these expectations.

Indeed, already at the Alexandria summit it was clear that the then head of the Palestinian Supreme Sharia Court was not prepared to condemn all Palestinian violent opposition to Israel's presence in the West Bank and Gaza (which at that time was still under Israeli control). Moreover, despite his declared commitment to the interfaith dialogue and his support for the establishment of the Council, he continued to use inflammatory rhetoric on many occasions both locally and at international gatherings.

This caused a number of hiatuses in the life of the Council, which led to the formulation of ground rules for engagement to which all parties committed themselves. However, this situation was not fully resolved until that figure was removed from his office by the Palestinian Authority and a new Minister of Religious Affairs was appointed who, in due course, joined and embraced the work of the Council.

Another result of this transition was that the organization Hommes de Parole, which had initiated the three congresses of Imams and Peace, engaged with the Council in order to focus more specifically on bringing together Israeli and Palestinian religious figures.

The Council has also taken its own initiative together with the Jerusalem office of Search for Common Ground in connecting a younger generation of religious figures from the three faiths. Through an "outward bound" program, young rabbis, qadis, imams, and priests have spent extended "wilderness hikes" abroad developing personal bonds of friendship and trust and becoming more knowledgeable about the others and their traditions in the process.

In addition, the Council has increasingly given its auspices to local and global initiatives and declarations on behalf of the three religions in the Holy Land. One such example is the initiative mentioned above to establish a global code regarding Holy Sites and the support of the Council for a local pilot project in this regard. Another example has been the interreligious declaration formulated by the Interfaith Initiative on Sustainable Development, to which the Council signed on. In addition, the Council has collaborated with the IISD on two conferences on environmental responsibility at which members of the Council spoke.

Undoubtedly, the Council has yet to live up to its highest expectations. Aside from some modest successes and not insignificant initiatives, however, the very fact that the Council has survived the political turbulence of recent years and ongoing violence in the Holy Land is surely quite remarkable. This is especially the case given the abovementioned cultural and sociological indisposition of the religious establishments of the Holy Land and the unhappy history of their communities' mutual alienation and rivalry. Moreover, the declared commitment of all the religious figures involved to the advancement of peace is notable and probably counterintuitive to their respective publics.

Arguably, the greatest challenge before the Council remains the task of persuading the secular authorities that do seek to advance peace negotiations to engage religious leadership as essential support for this goal.

Notes

1. An additional factor is the result of the fact that, in keeping with the Ottoman "status quo," the Muslim courts (both in Israel and the PA), some dozen recognized Christian denominations, and the Chief Rabbinate of Israel are granted exclusive jurisdiction for their respective communities on matters of family law and status, as well as in terms of official representation. While this does not appear to exclude any Muslims and hardly any Christians, it does disadvantage those Jews who do not want or do not qualify for an Orthodox Jewish marriage, etc., and "disenfranchises" the non-Orthodox streams of Judaism.

2. See www.crihl.org.

DIALOGUE AS A WAY OF LIFE

Tribute to a Man of Peace

DEBORAH WEISSMAN

INTRODUCTION

This article is dedicated to the blessed memory of Abdessalam Najjar, a friend and colleague in interreligious dialogue who died suddenly in March 2012, at the age of fifty-nine. He was one of the founding members of *Wahat el-Salam/Neveh Shalom* (Oasis of Peace), a village jointly established by Jewish and Palestinian Arab citizens of Israel. A devout Muslim, Najjar was, as his first name suggests, a true servant of the Lord and a man of peace.

In November 2011, the Interreligious Coordinating Council in Israel organized a meeting in Jerusalem for the U.S. Ambassador to Israel, Dan Shapiro. Attending the meeting were interfaith activists from the Greater Jerusalem area who represented the three monotheistic traditions. After describing some of the difficulties we face in our work, we were asked by the ambassador, "How do you maintain hope within this situation of conflict?" Abdessalam replied, "We are living the future that we are trying to create."

OPTIMISM AND HOPE

There is a joke about two friends in conversation, one asking the other, "Are you an optimist or a pessimist?" The second one replies, "I'm an optimist." The first one then asks, "If so, why do you always look so sad? "And the second one answers, "Do you think it's so easy to be an optimist?"

Some authors, including, for example, Harvey Cox, have distinguished between optimism and hope. He wrote, "When we honestly ask ourselves whether we can have…a life-affirming world, we must move beyond mere optimism or pessimism, for the empirical evidence is either mixed or unfavorable. But we can hope. Hope in the religious sense rests in part on nonempirical grounds."[1]

President of Israel Shimon Peres suggested, I believe, that optimism is based not so much on empirical reality as it is on an act of will, when he said, "Optimists and pessimists die the same way. They just live differently. I prefer to live as an optimist."[2]

Cox continued, "Christian hope suggests that man is destined for a City. It is not just any city, however. If we take the Gospel images as well as the symbols of the book of Revelation into consideration, it is not only a City where injustice is abolished and there is no more crying."[3] Further, "It is a city in which a delightful wedding feast is in progress, where the laughter rings out, the dance has just begun, and the best wine is still to be served."[4]

People often feel a need for concrete experience as a kind of evidence that their hope is well placed. The primary example of this, I would submit, is the Jew who hopes for redemption, while experiencing on a weekly basis the Shabbat as a foretaste of the world to come. The appealing description in Harvey Cox's statement above actually happens every Friday night in a traditional Jewish home: feasting, singing, laughter, wine, and so on. Without the weekly taste of Shabbat, it would have been difficult for Jews to sustain a messianic hope throughout two millennia of Diaspora life. Abdessalam's lived experience in the mixed community he helped to create sustained his hope for a peaceful future in our region.

Both Jews and Christians celebrate important festivals in what is, for the Northern Hemisphere, the season of spring. These two festivals, *Pesach* (Passover) and Easter, celebrate the triumph of life over death and hope over despair. We all, in a sense, are living a future, whether we call it "the kingdom of God" or "redemption" or "freedom." Through our respective rituals, we create at least a temporary reality that is a foretaste of a better world.

That is how I feel about interreligious dialogue. Sometimes, when people ask me what it's good for, what it achieves, and the like, I think that it isn't just a means to an end; interreligious dialogue is an end in itself. It's a foretaste of a better world.

THE PEACE PROCESS

A personal story: in 1993, from the time it was announced on the radio that Israel was involved in secret talks with the PLO in Oslo, to the famous handshake between Rabin and Arafat on the White House lawn, exactly fifteen days elapsed. At that point, I had a conversation with a colleague who is a professor of political science at the Hebrew University in Jerusalem. I said to him, "You know that I've been hoping, praying, and working for this moment for decades. But just fifteen days to go from being each other's worst enemies to a handshake and a signed statement at the White House? Isn't that a little quick? Don't the people on both sides need time to get over their fears and anxieties, break down their stereotypes, get to know each other as human beings? Wouldn't it have been better to declare that we were talking with each other and then have an actual process—in which Palestinians would be invited to speak in the Israeli media, schools, synagogues, community centers; Israelis would appear in Palestinian media, schools, churches, mosques; there would be grassroots dialogue, and then, after a few months, the leaders could meet and shake hands?"

To which my friend replied, "I can tell from this that you're an educator and not a politician; politicians seize the window of opportunity."

We were both right. He was right on two counts: politicians *do* seize the window of opportunity and I *am* an educator and not a politician (which at the time I thought was a put-down; now I take it as a high compliment). But I also think that I was right, that one of the problems with the Oslo process is that there really was no process on the grassroots level. One of the greatest flaws of Oslo was that it was almost exclusively secular Israeli men talking with secular Palestinian men. We have two questions here—whether something is lost by not involving women and whether something is lost by not involving religious people.

It has been my experience that women on two sides of a conflict often find it easier to dialogue than do their male counterparts. This is not necessarily due to some essential difference between men and women.[5] It probably reflects women's cultural roles as nurturers, who have much experience listening to others in a caring and compassionate way. Some of us also maintain that women should have special sensitivity to the Other, because of our own history of Otherness and oppression.

DIALOGUE WITH WOMEN

I will offer one example of women's dialogue from my own experience:

In 1988, the World Council of Churches invited about sixty women from all over the world, representing nine different religions, to a week-long conference in Toronto, on religion, politics, and feminism. The nine religions represented were Judaism, Christianity, Islam, Buddhism, Hinduism, the Sikh and Baha'i faiths, the Wiccan[6] religion, and Native American Indian spiritual traditions.[7]

As someone who grew up in a Christian environment, I had always felt that keeping kosher was strange or at least different; Christians don't have rules like these. Because of that, I thought that our dietary laws were simply *hukim*—laws we must follow without any further rationale or explanation. And then I began to meet Muslims, Hindus, Buddhists, and members of other traditions. I realized that in most of those religious cultures (except for Christianity) there are rules that limit the consumption of certain foods. Muslims don't eat pork, Hindus don't eat beef, many Hindus and Buddhists are vegetarians; Jains are total vegans who won't eat even onions or garlic, because eating them involves pulling their roots out of the ground, which the Jains perceive as an act of violence. All of these groups are expressing their religious and spiritual values through their consumption of food—or lack thereof. Thus it would appear that it is the Christians who are atypical in their lack of dietary laws.

The Toronto conference was totally vegetarian, in an attempt to accommodate the dietary requirements of the different groups.

Perhaps an even more significant commonality among the women in Toronto is that they all had narratives of suffering. Each community has its own stories of persecution, either in the distant past, the present, or sometimes, both. The Native Americans spoke about their conquest by white settlers; even the Wiccans described their history of witch hunts, trials, and burnings at the stake. Of course, an even more important question is what the groups do with these stories of collective suffering. Do they tell the story over and over again and continue to view themselves as victims, or do the stories become a springboard for positive action, being sensitive to the suffering of others, healing? Do they promote xenophobia or empathy?

Finally, each religious group was given a time slot—morning or evening—in which to share with the rest of us some prayers or ritual that typify their community. The Jews were given Friday evening. Putting together a *Kabbalat Shabbat* service and then the Shabbat table ritual, with eight Jewish women, including modern Orthodox, Conservative, Reform, and Reconstructionist, was no small feat. Despite our own intrareligious differences, we did succeed in putting together a candle-lighting ceremony and abbreviated Shabbat service. Friday morning, we went around to the other groups with a request preceded by an explanation that it is our custom to sing at the Shabbat table, so that if the groups had any songs from their traditions that they wanted to share with the rest of us, we would be happy to photocopy the words in advance.

We also asked the following question: "We know that some of you cannot drink wine. If we also had grape juice on the table, would the presence of wine disturb you?" The typical answer: "No, but thanks very much for asking."

We began the meal, of course, with blessings over the wine and juice and the *challot*. I was seated next to an Episcopalian nun. I offhandedly remarked to her that she could relate to blessings on wine and bread. Several women had prepared songs and in the middle of the dinner, we all got up to dance. We ended up doing Punjabi folk dances, the Punjab being the origin of many of the women —Hindus, Muslims, and Buddhists. When it came time for *Birkat HaMazon*, the grace after meals, we did parts in Hebrew and parts in English. One of the lines we said in English was toward the end: "*HaRachaman*, May the Merciful One make peace between the Children of Isaac and the children of Ishmael." A Muslim woman came up to me with tears in her eyes and said, "I never thought I'd hear Jews say that."

During the evaluation session of the conference, a great many participants—mostly non-Jewish women—reported that the highlight of the conference for them had been the Shabbat. The nun I had been sitting next to said the highlight of the week for her was my casual remark (which I had already forgotten), as it had made her aware of the Jewish roots of her Christianity. The whole week was for me a life-transforming experience, on a trajectory that led me to a life of dialogue.

The Interreligious Coordinating Council in Israel has also had good experiences with dialogue groups involving Palestinian and Israeli women—Muslims, Christians, and Jews. It is, therefore, unfortunate that the peace process has been almost exclusively a male-centered enterprise.

I now wish to focus our attention on the involvement of religions and religious people.

It has become customary to distinguish between *peacemaking* and *peacebuilding*. Peacemaking is what the diplomats and politicians ought to be doing, while peacebuilding is what should be done on the grass-roots level. Grassroots dialogue can develop a culture of peace that would be able to sustain a peace agreement made by the officials. In the Middle East, of all places, so much of the grassroots culture is perme-ated by religious traditions that it seems foolish to try to make peace without taking religions into account. From the example of the Toronto conference, it would appear that religious people can share many things in common while maintaining respect for one another's differences.

Among Israelis and Palestinians, who represent two nations but also three religions—Judaism, Christianity, and Islam—our experience has often been that people who identify with their respective religions and traditions can find a common language and establish rapport on that basis. We must learn to listen to one another's narratives, including narratives of our respective connections with the land.

THE CHALLENGE OF DIALOGUE

Interreligious dialogue is not always experienced as "concrete evi-dence that our hope is well-placed." Sometimes it is challenging and difficult, even painful. We must be prepared to listen to the other's nar-rative of suffering. We must be prepared for new insights that run counter to what we have previously taken as truth.

The most important function of learning about the Other lies in seeing her or him as a human being, like ourselves, which is the first step toward a more empathic relationship. When we encounter each other as people, we begin to communicate on a human level. A process of humanization, rather than demonization, can occur. Hopefully, this will, at the very least, stop us from killing one another and, at best, will provide the basis for the mutual recognition of our legitimate needs and rights, such as self-determination and security. What is essentially an educational encounter becomes the quintessential political act. As a leading American feminist theorist has put it:

> My hope emerges from those places of struggle where I witness individuals positively transforming their lives and the world around them. Educating is always a vocation rooted in hopefulness. As teachers we believe that learning is possible, that nothing can keep an open mind from seeking after knowledge and finding a way to know.[8]

Meeting the Other as a human being and learning about the Other and his or her culture or traditions can allay fears and anxieties and break down stereotypes and prejudices. At the same time that our educational efforts are going on—and education is usually considered to be a long-term investment in the future—other things must be happening simultaneously.

We must be improving what is called "the situation on the ground," people's lot in life. Working for social justice, for human rights and dignity, can at the least minimize, if not eliminate altogether, the social-cultural-political-economic context in which support for terrorism and other forms of violence grows. When people have no hope and see no possibilities for the future, they may despair and turn to desperate actions. Therefore, it is the responsibility of religious leaders and educators to encourage hope and help people cope with their despair in nonviolent ways. As my friend Bishop Mounib Younan, the Palestinian Lutheran Bishop of Jerusalem,[9] says, "As long as you believe in a living God, you must have hope."[10] When we believe in some transcendent power that promotes the Good, we have a way of coping with the despair that almost inevitably arises from our apparent lack of success.

A well-known joke says, "Just because you're paranoid, it doesn't mean that they're not out to get you." Even paranoiacs can have real enemies. The phenomena of anti-Semitism and even neo-Nazism are still very much with us. But in the Middle East, both the Israelis and the

Palestinians see themselves as the victims of the conflict. They seem to be competitors in what I call a "suffering sweepstakes."

As we saw above, in terms of the Toronto conference, it seems to be the case that all or, at least, most religious groups have a narrative of suffering. Suffering clearly is part of the human condition, and religions mandate different theological and existential responses to it. Paradoxically, perhaps, it is sometimes more comfortable to think of ourselves as victims. Victimhood gives one a sense of self-righteousness and surely encourages national unity. But it also obscures our culpability for unjust behavior. It often prevents the victim from assuming responsibility for his or her actions, including the victimization of others. In the Israeli-Palestinian conflict, I believe that both sides are victims and both sides are victimizers. I really think that the least helpful thing people can do—and regrettably, many well-meaning people do this—is to portray the situation in terms of a zero-sum game, in which, if you're pro-Palestinian, you must be anti-Israeli, and vice versa. We must be *both* pro-Palestinian *and* pro-Israeli, because we're pro-people and, therefore, pro-peace. The achievement of peace, I believe, necessitates a two-state solution based on some recognition of the two narratives. I also believe that the best fulfillment of Zionism will come when there is a Palestinian state alongside the State of Israel.

Rabbi Arthur O. Waskow is a religious and political radical who has worked closely with the politically involved Benedictine nun Sister Joan Chittister and other Christian and Muslim activists. Together with his wife, Rabbi Phyllis O. Berman, he published *Freedom Journeys: The Tale of Exodus and Wilderness across Millennia.*[11] There he offers a kind of modern Midrash on an important scene in the Book of Joshua. In Joshua 5:13–14, having crossed the Jordan River, Joshua meets a man, who has his sword drawn. Joshua asks, "Are you for us, or for our enemies?" The figure, according to Waskow's reading, first replies no. The Waskow-Berman commentary states, "We hear it to mean, 'I am not here to support either one of you in your war against each other, nor do I support the conflict itself.'"[12]

CONCLUSION

There is a Jewish festival that is celebrated a month before Pesach, called Purim, based on the Book of Esther in the Hebrew Bible.

Although joyously celebrated by Jewish children, this is a complex and controversial festival.[13] One of the major customs on Purim is dressing up in costume. On a certain level, the festival is really about identity—personal as well as group—and the relationship with the Other. One of the ways to relate to the Other is, quite literally, by getting into his shoes. Or, perhaps by confronting the Other within us.

In conjunction with intergroup dialogue, Leah Shakdiel[14] makes the following point:

> There is a Chassidic story about a rabbi who used to spend a very long time with every person who came to see him. When asked what took him so long, he said: "Every time the other person speaks, I must take off my clothes and put his on, as it is written in the Mishna, 'Do not judge your friend until you are in his place.' And then when it is my turn to speak or give advice, I must take off his clothes and put mine back on." A meaningful meeting, then, should combine the two seeming opposites—empathy with the other and assertion of one's own identity.[15]

Creating a life of dialogue certainly means establishing and asserting one's own identity. But it also entails listening to the other's narrative and showing empathy for it. It means not framing conflicts always as zero-sum games. It means having hope and opening up possibilities. It means together building trust as a basis for a shared future. Through all of these challenges, the figure of Abdessalam Najjar can serve us as a beacon of light.

Notes

1. Cox, *The Feast of Fools: A Theological Essay on Festivity and Fantasy* (New York: Harper & Row, 1969), 162.

2. "Serving 60 Years to Life," *Newsweek Europe*, 12/12/2005, accessed through Wikipedia, http://en.wikiquote.org/wiki/Shimon_Peres.

3. That would have been characteristic of "the secular city" about which Cox had written in 1965.

4. Cox, *The Feast of Fools*.

5. See Galia Golan, "Reflections on Gender in Dialogue," *Nashim: A Journal of Jewish Women's Studies & Gender Issues* 6 (2003): 13–21.

6. This neopagan faith includes witches who practice "white" magic, nature worship, fertility rites, Druid traditions, and lots of love.

7. This is the correct opportunity to acknowledge my deep gratitude to Ms. Blu Greenberg, perhaps the most prominent Orthodox Jewish feminist in the world, through whose intervention I was invited to participate in this conference. Within interreligious circles, Blu may be better known as the wife of Rabbi Dr. Irving "Yitz" Greenberg, author of *For the Sake of Heaven and Earth: The New Encounter between Judaism and Christianity* (Philadelphia: Jewish Publication Society, 2004).

8. bell hooks, *Teaching Community: A Pedagogy of Hope* (New York: Routledge, 2003), xiv.

9. Currently (2012) serving as President of the Lutheran World Federation.

10. In May of 2013, the International Council of Christians and Jews issued a statement on the Middle East conflict, using this quotation as its title. Accessible through www.iccj.org.

11. Arthur O. Waskow and Phyllis O. Berman, *Freedom Journeys: The Tale of Exodus and Wilderness across Millennia* (Woodstock, VT: Jewish Lights Publishing, 2011).

12. Ibid., 185.

13. For a very negative approach to the festival, see Elliott Horowitz, *Reckless Rites: Purim and the Legacy of Jewish Violence* (Princeton: Princeton University Press, 2006). For more positive approaches, see Irving Greenberg, *The Jewish Way: Living the Holidays* (New York: Summit Books, 1988); and Arthur Waskow, *Seasons of Our Joy: A Celebration of Modern Jewish Renewal* (New York: Bantam Books, 1982).

14. Leah, a long-time resident of the Negev "development town" of Yeruham, is an educator, feminist, and social activist. She made headlines in 1986 when, in a bid for the first women's seat on the local religious council, she fought her case all the way up to the Israeli Supreme Court.

15. Shakdiel, "Dialogue as an Opportunity for Spiritual Growth: Linking Tradition with Creativity," in *Israel/Palestine: The Quest for Dialogue*, ed. Haim Gordon and Rivca Gordon (Maryknoll, NY: Orbis Books, 1991), 44.

ABOUT THE
CONTRIBUTORS

Rabbi Shlomo Brinn is a rabbi and educator at the Har Etzion Yeshiva who teaches at the Herzog Academic Teachers' Training College, both in Gush Etzion. He studied Judaism at the Har Etzion Yeshiva and at the Mir Yeshiva in Jerusalem and in the Faculty of Humanities of the Hebrew University of Jerusalem. Rabbi Brinn served as a combat soldier in both the Yom Kippur War of 1973 and the 1982 War called "Peace for the Galilee." In addition, he participated in ICCI's KEDEM project (*Kol Dati Mefayes*—Religious Voices for Reconciliation) between 2003 and 2008.

Prof. Mohammed S. Dajani Daoudi is a Jerusalem-born scholar and peace activist with doctorates from the University of South Carolina, Columbia (1981) and the University of Texas at Austin (1984). He is founding Executive Director of *Wasatia*, a moderate Islamic movement in Palestine, and Professor of Political Science and International Relations and founding Director of the American Studies Institute at Al-Quds University. His latest publications are *Wasatia: The Spirit of Islam* (Jerusalem: Wasatia Publishing, 2009); *Jerusalem from the Lens of Wasatia* (Jerusalem: Wasatia Publishing, 2010); *Dajani Glossary of Islam* (Jerusalem: Wasatia Publishing, 2012); and *The Holocaust—Human Agony: Is There a Way Out of Violence?* (Jerusalem: Wasatia Publishing, 2012) (in Arabic, with others).

Prof. Menachem Fisch occupies the Joseph and Ceil Mazer Chair for History and Philosophy of Science at Tel Aviv University, where he chairs the board and academic committee of the Cohn Institute for the History and Philosophy of Science and Ideas, and is Director of the Center for Religious and Interreligious Studies (Project). He is also a Senior Fellow of the Kogod Center for the Renewal of Jewish Thought at the Shalom Hartman Institute, Jerusalem. Dr. Fisch is the author of *Rational Rabbis: Science and Talmudic Culture* (1997) and *The View* *from Within: Normativity and the Limits of Self-Criticism* (with Y. Benbaji, 2011).

Sr. Maureena Fritz, PhD, was professor on the Faculty of Theology at the University of Toronto, Canada (1971 to 1992). After a period of study at Hebrew University in Jerusalem, in response to the Vatican II document *Nostra Aetate,* she founded the Bat Kol Institute in Jerusalem, where she still continues to teach. She has published several books and articles on praying with and studying the Jewish Scriptures and has given workshops in South and North America, South Africa, Australia, the Philippines, India, England, and Ireland.

Yisca Harani is an expert on Christianity and Christians in the Holy Land and a consultant on the topic of religions and interreligious dialogue. Harani initiated a specialized course in Christianity for tour guides, the only one of its kind in Israel, in which 50 percent of the lecturers are Christians representing a wide variety of denominations. She holds workshops focusing on the encounter between Jewish tour guides and Christian tourists and pilgrims, and on the issue of using potentially controversial verses concerning Jews in the Scriptures.

Issa Jaber serves as cochairperson of the Interreligious Coordinating Council in Israel (ICCI) and as an officer in the Association for the Promotion of Tolerance and Coexistence in the Judean Hills. He has an MA in Political Science and Public Administration from Ankara University, Turkey (1985). He has served as Director of Education for Abu Ghosh and was elected mayor of the town in October 2013.

Fr. Jamal Khader is a Palestinian Catholic Priest from the Latin Patriarchate of Jerusalem, Chairperson of the Department of Religious Studies and Dean of the Faculty of Arts at Bethlehem University, a member for several years of the Diocesan Committee of Dialogue with Jews, and a coauthor of the Kairos Palestine document.

Amy Kronish lectures and writes widely on film and is the author of two books on Israeli film—*World Cinema: Israel* (Trowbridge, UK: Flicks Books, and Cranbury, NJ: Associated University Presses, 1996); and *Israeli Film—A Reference Guide* (coauthor; Westport, CT: Greenwood Publishing, 2003). She worked for three years as Director of Coexistence Activities of the Jerusalem International YMCA and served for fifteen years as Curator of Jewish and Israeli Film at the Jerusalem Cinematheque-Israel Film Archive. Born in the United States, she has an

MA in Communications from New York University, and has lived in Jerusalem since 1979.

Rabbi Dr. Ronald Kronish is Founding Director of the Interreligious Coordinating Council in Israel (ICCI) since 1992, and is a noted rabbi, educator, author, and speaker. The holder of a BA from Brandeis University and a doctorate in philosophy and history of education from the Harvard Graduate School of Education, he has represented ICCI at the Vatican and at many international meetings and conferences. Rabbi Kronish is the author of numerous articles and the editor of three books of essays: *Towards the Twenty-First Century: Judaism and the Jewish People in Israel and America, Toward the Third Millennium*, and *Pilgrimage in a New Millennium*. In addition, he blogs for the *Huffington Post* and *The Times of Israel*.

Sheikh Ghassan Manasra is the director of Anwar Il-Salaam, Islamic Cultural Center (Lights of Peace), an imam, and a teacher of Islam. Coauthor with Zeev Ben Arie of *Light upon Light: A Journey with the Sufis*, he was selected to serve on the steering committee at the World Congress of Imams and Rabbis for Peace held in Brussels and Seville.

Rabbi Michael Melchior is Founder and Chairman of the Mosaica Center for Religious Conflict Transformation in the Middle East. Born in Denmark, he immigrated to Israel in 1986, where, as a member of the Knesset, he served in such roles as Minister for Social Affairs and World Jewry, Deputy Minister of Education and Culture, and Deputy Minister of Foreign Affairs. Rabbi Melchior is the founder of several organizations dedicated to such causes as religious peacebuilding among leaders of all religions in the Middle East, promoting open dialogue among different strands of Israeli society, and building bridges of coexistence and justice between Israeli Jews and Israeli-Arabs.

Abdessalam Najjar lived in Wahat al-Salam/Neve Shalom (Oasis of Peace), the Arab-Jewish village in Israel, from its earliest days. Before Mr. Najjar's untimely passing in 2012 at the age of fifty-nine, he was Director of the village's Pluralistic Spiritual Center and an active member of the Board of Directors of the Interreligious Coordinating Council in Israel (ICCI).

Fr. David M. Neuhaus, SJ, is Latin Patriarchal Vicar for Hebrew Speaking Catholics in Israel and coordinator of the Church's work with migrants. An Israeli, he resides in Jerusalem and also teaches Bible and theology in Catholic and Jewish academic institutions.

Rev. Dr. Peter A. Pettit is a Lutheran minister, Associate Professor of Religion Studies, and Director of the Institute for Jewish-Christian Understanding of Muhlenberg College in Lehigh Valley, Pennsylvania. Since 1992 he has been the North American coordinator for the Osher Department of Religious Pluralism of the Shalom Hartman Institute. He also codirects the Hartman initiative, *New Paths: Christians Engaging Israel*, and continues as an advisor to the Lutheran Church and several international interreligious endeavors.

Dr. Amnon Ramon is a researcher at the Jerusalem Institute for Israel Studies specializing in the history of Jerusalem in the modern era, Christians and modern Christianity in the Holy Land, holy places, and extreme Jewish groups in Jerusalem. Dr. Ramon lectures at the Department of Comparative Religion at Hebrew University in Jerusalem. He is also the Editorial Coordinator of *Cathedra* (Journal for Holy Land Studies) at Yad Izhak Ben-Zvi.

Rabbi David Rosen, former Chief Rabbi of Ireland, is the International Director of Interreligious Affairs of the American Jewish Committee and serves as the Honorary Interfaith Advisor to the Chief Rabbinate of Israel. Prior to his appointment as Chief Rabbi of Ireland, Rabbi Rosen served as rabbi of the largest South African Jewish congregation. For his interfaith work he received a papal knighthood in 2005 and in 2010 was awarded a CBE by Queen Elizabeth II.

Rabbi Marc Rosenstein is Director of the Israel Rabbinical Program of Hebrew Union College in Jerusalem and recently retired after twenty years as the executive director of the Galilee Foundation for Value Education. The holder of a PhD in modern Jewish history from the Hebrew University and a rabbinic degree from Hebrew Union College–Jewish Institute of Religion, he immigrated to Moshav Shorashim in the Galilee in 1990.

Daniel Rossing, who passed away in 2010, founded the Jerusalem Center for Jewish-Christian Relations. Born in the United States, he worked for thirty years in Jerusalem in the field of Jewish-Christian relations, during which time he served as head of the Department of the Christian communities for the Ministry of Religious Affairs.

Faydra Shapiro specializes in contemporary Jewish-Christian relations, with a focus on evangelical Christianity. She has published and presented extensively on the topic of Christian Zionism and evangelical Christian support for Israel. Dr. Shapiro currently serves as the director of the Galilee Center for Studies in Jewish-Christian Relations at the Yezreel Valley Academic College outside of Nazareth.

Dr. Deborah Weissman was born in the United States and has lived in Israel since 1972. She served as President of the International Council of Christians and Jews between 2008 and 2014 and has also been extensively involved with the Interreligious Coordinating Council in Israel (ICCI). Dedicated to teaching Christians about Judaism, Dr. Weissman has been active both locally and internationally in the peace movement in Israel, religious feminism, and interreligious dialogue. She holds a PhD from the Hebrew University of Jerusalem.

Bishop Munib A. Younan has served as the bishop of the Evangelical Lutheran Church in Jordan and the Holy Land (ELCJHL) since January 1998. Educated in Palestine and Finland, Bishop Younan has been active in such faith organizations as the Middle East Council of Churches (MECC), the Lutheran World Federation (LWF), and the Fellowship of the Middle East Evangelical Churches (FMEEC). He was elected president of the Lutheran World Federation in July 2010.

Qadi Dr. Iyad Zahalka is the Muslim judge of the sharia courts in Jerusalem and previously served as the director of the Sharia Court System in Israel. The holder of a PhD from Hebrew University in Jerusalem, he has written two books on sharia law and the courts system and serves as Chairman of the Sharia Court Committee of the Israel Bar Association.